The World's Great
Guns

The World's Great Guns

Frederick Wilkinson

Hamlyn
London · New York · Sydney · Toronto

Published by
The Hamlyn Publishing Group Limited
London · New York · Sydney · Toronto
Astronaut House, Feltham, Middlesex,
England

© Copyright the Hamlyn Publishing Group
Limited 1977

ISBN 0 600 39364 X

Phototypeset by Tradespools Ltd,
Frome, Somerset

Printed in Great Britain by
Jarrold and Sons Limited, Norwich

Endpapers:
Peter Paul Rubens—An autumn landscape
with a view of Het Steen (detail)

Title page:
A top view of a typical double-barrelled
percussion-cap gun, showing the hammers
and nipples well placed to give fire into the
centre of the breeches. The rifle was made by
Charles Lancaster in 1863. Richard
Akehurst, Esq.

Acknowledgements

Richard Akehurst, Oxted 2–3, 81 bottom left; Barnaby's Picture Library—Parker-Hale 88 left; Bettmann Archive, New York City 100 bottom left, 100 bottom right, 140 bottom, 225 bottom, 234, 247 left; Bodleian Library, Oxford 10 left; Central Office of Information, London 201, 229 top, 249 centre; Crown Copyright—reproduced with permission of the Controller of Her Majesty's Stationery Office 8 bottom left, 20 top, 58, 61, 63 top, 67 bottom, 68 right, 69 bottom, 77 first to fifth from left, 77 right, 92 bottom, 97, 107 bottom right, 127 centre, 127 bottom, 140 top, 195 centre, 212 top, 222 top; Elliott and Snowdon, London 153; Mary Evans Picture Library, London 98 bottom, 195 top; Thomas Gilcrease Institute of American History and Art, Tulsa, Oklahoma 173 bottom; Photographie Giraudon, Paris 9 bottom; Richard Green Gallery, London 86; Hamlyn Group Picture Library 22–23, 24 bottom, 33 bottom, 34, 37 top, 39, 51 top, 84, 95 right, 99, 128 top, 156 bottom, 174 top right, 178 left, 184, 194 top, 229 bottom, 251 bottom; Hamlyn Group—Paul Forrester 11, 12 top, 14, 15 top, 15 bottom, 17 bottom, 25 top, 26 top, 26 bottom, 35, 38, 40 left, 40 right, 41, 43, 46 top, 46 bottom, 50 left, 50 right, 52, 55 top, 55 bottom, 59, 62, 63 bottom, 64, 66, 67 top, 70 top, 71, 74, 76 top, 82, 89, 91, 95 top, 107 top, 110 top, 110 bottom, 113 left, 115, 116, 118, 119, 125 top, 127 top left, 127 top right, 130 top, 133, 134 top, 136, 137 top, 137 bottom, 139 top, 141 top, 142, 143 top, 143 bottom, 146, 147, 148, 149, 151, 155, 158 top, 160, 161, 163 top, 163 bottom, 166 top, 166 bottom, 168 bottom, 170 top, 170 bottom, 172, 173 top, 175 top, 179, 182 top, 182 bottom, 183 left, 185, 186 top, 186 bottom, 187, 188, 189 top left, 190, 191, 193 top, 196 top, 196 bottom, 197, 199 top, 199 bottom, 202, 203, 206 top, 207 top left, 207 bottom, 209, 210, 211, 214, 215 top, 215 bottom, 216 top, 218 top, 218 bottom, 220, 221, 223 top, 223 bottom, 225 top right, 226 top, 226 bottom, 227 top, 227 bottom, 230, 233, 239, 242, 244, 245, 247 right, jacket front flap, jacket back, jacket back flap; Hamlyn Group—Ian Reid jacket front; Hamlyn Group—John Webb 28; Hereford City Library 16 bottom; Hermitage Museum, Leningrad 20 bottom; Holland and Holland, London 157; Imperial War Museum, London 189 bottom left, 198, 200 bottom, 206 bottom, 213, 236, 243 top, 248 top; A. J. Lang and Co., London 205 bottom; L. Le Personne and Co., London 225 top left; Mansell Collection, London 9 top, 16 top left, 16 top right, 31 top left, 31 top right, 70 bottom, 81 bottom right, 94 left, 101, 103 bottom, 132 top, 159, 171, 192 top, 193 bottom; Olin Mathieson Chemical Corporation, New Haven, Connecticut 175 left; Museo Stibbert, Florence 68 left; Museum and Art Gallery, Glasgow 51 bottom, 129; Muzeum Wojska Polskiego, Warsaw 76 bottom; National Army Museum, London 31 bottom, 32, 69 top, 72 bottom, 73 bottom, 75 top, 75 centre, 249 top; National Gallery, London endpapers; National Maritime Museum, London 138 bottom; National Portrait Gallery, London 56; New-York Historical Society, New York City 92 top right; Preussischer Kulturbesitz, Berlin 204, 216 bottom, 219; Radio Times Hulton Picture Library, London 8 top left, 8 right, 13 top, 21, 88 right, 93 bottom, 96 bottom, 104 bottom, 177, 178 right, 193 bottom, 207 top right, 212 bottom; Schweizerisches Landesmuseum, Zurich 19, 54; Sotheby Parke Bernet, London 13 bottom, 18, 24 top, 25 bottom, 36 top, 36 bottom, 37 bottom, 42 bottom, 45, 49 top, 49 bottom, 60, 72 left, 73 top, 75 bottom, 81 centre, 85, 95 centre, 95 bottom right, 96 top, 96 centre, 100 top, 105, 107 bottom left, 108 right, 109 top, 109 bottom, 111 centre, 111 bottom, 112, 113 right, 121 top, 121 bottom, 122 top, 122 centre, 122 bottom, 134 bottom, 135 top, 135 bottom, 138 top, 139 bottom, 144 top, 145 right, 152 top, 152 bottom, 158 bottom, 180, 181, 183 right, 217; Syndication International, London 17 top, 98 top; Tøjhusmuseet, Copenhagen 125 bottom, 156 top, 162, 164 top, 164 bottom; Victoria and Albert Museum, London 154; Wadsworth Atheneum, Hartford, Connecticut 128 bottom; Wallace Collection, London 33 top, 44 bottom, 48, 104 top; Weidenfeld and Nicolson, London 7, 10 top right; Weller and Dufty, Birmingham 81 top, 90; F. Wilkinson, London 10 bottom right, 12 bottom, 29, 42 top, 44 top, 44 centre, 47, 57 top, 57 bottom, 65, 77 second from right, 78 top, 78 bottom, 79, 83, 92 top left, 103 top, 108 left, 111 top, 117, 126, 130 bottom, 131, 132 bottom, 144 bottom, 145 left, 150, 165 top left, 165 top right, 165 bottom, 169 top, 169 left, 169 bottom, 174 top left, 176, 194 bottom, 195 bottom, 200 top, 205 top, 205 centre, 222 bottom, 235, 237, 238, 240, 241 top left, 241 top right, 241 bottom, 243 bottom left, 243 bottom right, 246 top, 246 bottom, 248 centre, 248 bottom, 249 bottom, 250 top, 250 bottom, 251 top, 252 top, 252 bottom, 253 left, 253 right; Winchester Gun Museum, New Haven, Connecticut 95 bottom left, 141 bottom, 167, 168 top, 189 right; Yale University Art Gallery, New Haven, Connecticut 93 top.

Contents

Introduction   6

How it all began   7

The evolution of the musket   18

The wheel-lock: the hunter's weapon   35

Brown Bess   53

The long rifles   80

Duelling pistols   102

The genius of Samuel Colt   124

The era of the Winchester   154

Enfield and the modern rifle   180

Automatic pistols   208

Maxim and the machine-gun   232

Bibliography   254

Index   255

Introduction

In almost every field of human endeavour and achievement there are names which are known to people who may well have no basic interest in that particular subject. These are the names of people, inventions or events which have had an enormous impact on history. Some have acquired a significance far out of proportion to their true importance simply because of quirks or accidents of fate.

The history of firearms is no different and certain weapons or their users are recognized and known to people who have never in their life handled a firearm. Some, like the musket, ushered in new and devastating styles of warfare. Others, like Samuel Colt, achieved a reputation far in excess of their true importance. Indeed, if the numerous Western films and novels are to be believed the only revolver which saw service in the Wild West was the Colt–a belief far from the truth. The same can be said of the famous Winchester–'The Gun that Won the West.' Despite its excellence it was only one of a number of good-quality repeating rifles.

In more recent times the Luger pistol has acquired a certain mystique, and its shape and 'toggle' action make it immediately recognizable. The Luger and the German Army have become inseparable in popular imagination. In fact, the Luger pistol was officially replaced in 1938 by the Walther P.38, an equally fine– some would say better–pistol, but lacking the mysterious quality that makes something a household word.

The history of firearms has, perhaps, more than its fair share of great names, and it was not easy to narrow the choice to a handful. Even if the selection were limited to the big manufacturers this book would have to be many times its present size. Thus, regretfully, much interesting material has been omitted that could have been included if space had allowed. Inevitably readers will ask why their particular favourite does not appear. The only reply must be that there just wasn't room.

Many people have helped in the preparation of this book and the author would like to offer his grateful thanks to the Staff of the Pattern Room at Enfield, to Hugh Newbury and Dave Jeffcoat, to Dusty Miller and many others. Special thanks go to Paul Forrester for all his work in taking many of the photographs, often under exceptionally trying circumstances.

How it all began

The very early history of firearms is obscure. The first date that can be given with certainty when recording the use in Europe of some forms of missile weapon powered by explosives appears to be 1326. This date is confirmed pictorially in an English source, the *Milemete Manuscript*, and also in the records of the city of Florence, when reference is made to cannon and iron bullets or arrows to be fired from them. Obviously the cannon must have taken time to become an accepted weapon, so that it can be stated with a reasonable degree of confidence that by the first decade or so of the fourteenth century a crude form of firearm had made its appearance in Europe.

With one or two exceptions all firearms include certain basic features. There is a breech or chamber in which an explosion takes place; there is a missile, whether it be a bullet or a more sophisticated form of projectile; there is a barrel which guides the projectile on its path; and finally there is some form of ignition to set off the explosion. The earliest form of propellant is that known today as black powder or gunpowder. It is a mixture of saltpetre (potassium nitrate), charcoal and sulphur. The proportions of the components varied but basically they were 75%, 10% and 15% respectively.

To the Chinese must go the credit for the earliest combination of these three ingredients. How they ever came to be united in the first place must remain a matter for speculation, but there is sufficient evidence to suggest that the Chinese were producing some form of explosive compound, almost certainly a weak form of gunpowder, as early as the eleventh century. The scanty evidence available suggests that this compound was used primarily as a firework, perhaps as a form of psychological adjunct to warfare, the flash, flame, smoke and noise being intended to frighten and disturb an enemy.

The earliest gun, known as the *huo ch'iang*, was apparently no more than a hollow bamboo tube with one end blocked. Into the open end was packed the crudely mixed gunpowder and finally a projectile – perhaps a clay ball. Then by some means, possibly a form of fuse, the gunpowder was ignited and the expanding gases produced by the rapid chemical burning forced out the ball.

How the knowledge of the black mixture reached Europe is not known for sure, and there is controversy among scholars about when it arrived. It is thought by some that the formula came by

Page from the *Milemete Manuscript* (1326). At the bottom is the earliest recorded illustration of a cannon. The knight fires it by means of a metal rod, possibly heated. Christ Church, Oxford.

way of the Arabs, for they, with their great trading interests, had contacts with China and most probably acquired the secret at an early date. Since the Arabs had invaded Europe and had a stronghold in Spain, it is not unreasonable to assume that the knowledge of gunpowder would spread, no doubt quite slowly, by means of the limited contact between the scholars of medieval Europe. However despite the obvious attraction of this theory, there is very little hard evidence to prove that this was indeed the case.

One name which is frequently mentioned by early writers on the subject of gunpowder is that of Roger Bacon (*c.* 1214–94), although it is not at all clear how much this Oxford scholar knew. He is usually credited with revealing the formula for gunpowder in his book *De Secretis Operibus Artis et Naturae et de Nullitate Magiae*. The supposed formula is only to be read when a certain anagram in the last chapter is rearranged. The solution gives the formula of a standard mixture for gunpowder, except that the proportions are equal quantities of charcoal and sulphur, and a slightly larger quantity of nitre. Why Bacon should have felt it necessary to compose an anagram is not clear, although various suggestions have been offered. Another problem is that this particular passage does not appear in the earliest known copy of Bacon's book! The debate among scholars continues, but for the moment the only verdict on Bacon's knowledge or discovery of gunpowder must be 'not proven.'

The emperor Maximilian I, a monarch with a keen interest in armour and weapons. The inventory of his armoury lists many early firearms. Engraving by Lucas van Leyden.

Among the armoured knights in the front rank of the infantry are a group of hand gunners. The heavy artillery is preparing to batter the town walls. Early sixteenth-century French manuscript. Musée Archéologique Thomas Dobrée, Nantes.

Another 'discoverer' of gunpowder is the mysterious monk of Freiburg—Black Berthold or Berthold Schwartz. There is a statue to this scholar in his native town and the stories of how he made the discovery are numerous. Unfortunately there is little solid evidence to establish even the existence of this shadowy figure, and so his claim is even less well founded than Bacon's.

In fact the only indisputable evidence for the use of firearms in Europe is that mentioned above—the illustration in the *Milemete Manuscript*. These were books of instructions written for King Edward III by his chaplain, Walter de Milemete. They include two small inset illustrations in the margins showing armoured knights, correctly dressed for the period, placing a hooked rod, which probably held a piece of glowing ember or smouldering moss, against a vase-shaped object lying on some flat surface. From the neck of these vase-like guns project the heads of arrows.

The very shape of the guns is quite consistent with the facts and indicates some understanding of the mechanics of firearms. The breech of any firearm is normally strengthened in order to withstand the very considerable pressures built up when the propellant explodes. The vase shape would suggest that the breech, or solid end of the barrel, has been so thickened, and the internal bore would almost certainly have been parallel-sided. The details of the ignition are unclear: gunpowder burns rather than explodes and the burning must be started by some means or other. The hook-like rod carried by the knights could have been a heated iron or a device which held a glowing piece of rag, tow, moss, charcoal, wood or even coal, although this is unlikely. Unfortunately the text of the *Milemete Manuscript* makes no reference to these particular illustrations.

en mille chose de ce monde
ne se pourroit trouuer mais
chascun de nous le cognoist
tard et apres ce que en a
uons en besoing. Toutes
fois vault encores mieulx
tard que jamais

Sensuit le commencent
des guerres qui furent entre
le duc de bourgongne et les
liegeois.

nisi se passerct
aucunes anees
durant lesqlles
le duc de bour
gongne auoit guerre chas
cun an auecques les liege
ops. Quant le roy le
veoit empesche il essayoit
a faire quelque nouueau
te contre les bretons en
faisant quelque peu de
confort aux liegeois.

9

Armoured knights use their traditional weapons of sword, bow and spear. In their midst one man aims a handgun fitted with a matchlock. The manuscript dates from 1473. British Library, London.

The invention of the wheel-lock made possible the use of small firearms and pistols became popular. Here Sir Martin Frobisher holds a dag—a small wheel-lock—probably made in England. Bodleian Library, Oxford.

French wheel-lock signed 'Jean Henequin à Metz' and dated 162(?)1. The stock is decorated with mother-of-pearl and wire inlay and the metal work is chiselled. The dog's head to hold the pyrites is carved to represent a man. Bayerisches Nationalmuseum, Munich.

Apart from those intended for military units, many weapons had some decoration. This is the silver butt cap from a late eighteenth-century pocket pistol. Private Collection.

Once these early firearms had been clearly demonstrated to be practicable, military thinkers of the period obviously experimented and improved on the basic design. The story of artillery does not fall within the scope of this volume, but much of the early history of firearms is concerned with the large gun. Cost and availability of materials tended to limit ownership of artillery to the richer nobles and in particular to kings and princes, thus placing them in a position of power, with the means of reducing any fortress should the need arise. This fact would not have escaped the notice of a rebellious lord, who might well think twice before contemplating any treasonable activity. The possession of gunpowder undoubtedly contributed to the downfall of the feudal system.

The principle of these early weapons was soon extended, and small, portable hand firearms were made. These early handguns were rather ineffective and probably highly dangerous to the user. The little evidence we have suggests that the first examples were merely miniature artillery pieces attached to some form of rod. Loading and ignition both presented problems and accuracy was no doubt abysmal, but nevertheless these early firearms possessed one important advantage over the other forms of missile weapons. They required little or no training in their use. The longbow which had dominated the long-range battle required a considerable degree of skill in its handling. It was extremely accurate and very deadly in the hands of a trained archer, but when used by an unskilled soldier it was probably even less effective than the early firearms.

As the technological capability of Europe developed these small handguns could be produced in quantity and in the hands of a large number of gunners they could lay down a barrage of shots. Even allowing for their inaccuracy the volume of fire was sufficient to ensure an acceptable percentage of hits. A hit even from these primitive weapons was serious for the bullet could almost certainly penetrate armour.

Loading was, of necessity, a slow business. A quantity of black powder was poured down the muzzle and this in itself could be a dangerous process, since any lingering sparks inside the barrel could ignite the powder with disastrous results to the loader. When the powder had been loaded the bullet, usually of lead but sometimes of stone or even iron, had to be pushed down and seated on top of the powder. Any gap between the top of the powder charge and the base of the ball into which air might penetrate could allow

Engraving of Landsknechts of the early sixteenth century, loading and firing the short, stubby matchlock of the period.

From top to bottom:
1. Sea service pistol with 12-inch (30·5-cm) barrel. The lock plate is engraved with the royal cypher and is signed 'WILLIS 1758'.
2 and 3. Pair of holster pistols, the barrels bearing London proof-marks and the lock signed 'I. SMART'. The walnut stock is fitted with brass furniture. About 1700.
4. Duelling pistol by H. W. Mortimer with gold vent and pan lining. The maker's name is set in a small gold plaque on the barrel. An early nineteenth-century weapon, it has all the latest features of the period including rollers and safety catch.

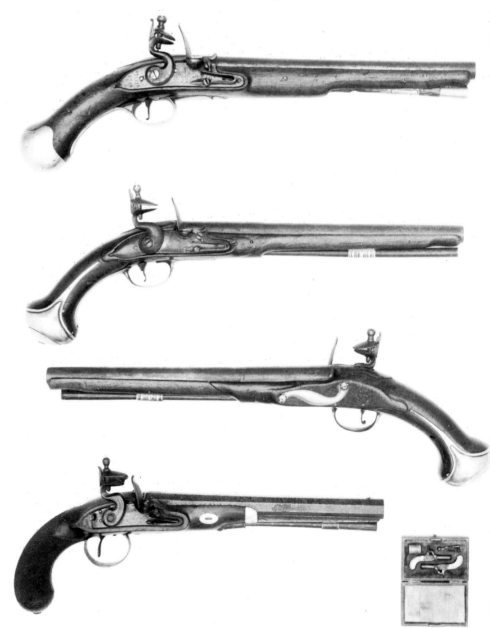

A page from one of the many hunting books of the nineteenth century giving instruction on the handling of the gun.

From top to bottom:
1. Double-barrelled half-stocked rifle marked 'Scinde Irregular Horse' (a cavalry unit). Overall length 37 inches (94 cm). Made in 1852.
2. Flintlock blunderbuss with brass barrel and spring-operated bayonet, by Simmons. Overall length 30½ inches (77·5 cm). Early nineteenth century.
3. Flintlock blunderbuss with spring bayonet by Archer. Overall length 30 inches (76·2 cm). Mid-eighteenth century.
4. Double-barrelled flintlock pistol by J. Probin, with a fitted stock. Overall length 36½ inches (92·7 cm). About 1810.

dangerous pressures to build up. These could easily split the barrel and injure the shooter. To ensure maximum efficiency the ball needed to fit tightly inside the barrel, so that little, if any, expanding gas could escape around the sides. However, if the ball was made to fit exactly inside the barrel it was difficult to push it home and, as always, there had to be a compromise – a compromise which was to continue until modern technology enabled the craftsman to work within very close limits of accuracy.

One of the earliest of the automatic pistols to use a 'blowback' system, the Browning ·32 ACP pistol, made at Liège by Fabrique Nationale, is complete with a contemporary holster. E. Kempster, Gunsmiths.

When powder and ball had been rammed home the weapon was ready for firing, but now the powder had to be set alight. Ignition in these early weapons presented considerable problems. It was no mean feat to cope with a rather unwieldy handgun, a supply of powder, a supply of bullets and some means of ignition. If, for any reason, the shooter lost his source of fire he was utterly helpless, his only hope being to rekindle the flame by means of a tinder and steel. The glowing ember or burning wood was naturally at the mercy of the elements. A sudden shower of rain and an entire army could be deprived of its firepower. A sudden gust of wind, a slip of the hand and the flame was extinguished and the gun became useless.

These early handguns had a small hole drilled through the side of the barrel at the breech end. The hole was slightly counter-sunk to provide a small depression. This access to the main charge was called the touch-hole and was filled with powder. The glowing ember was touched down into the powder which flared up and so ignited the main charge.

The hand-held ember was soon replaced by a mechanical arm known as the serpentine and a piece of chemically treated cord – the match – which smouldered slowly. This means of ignition, known as the matchlock, was to remain in military use until the early part of the eighteenth century.

Other forms of ignition were designed to overcome some of the major problems of the matchlock mentioned above. Early in the fifteenth century great thinkers such as Leonardo da Vinci were toying with the idea of providing fire by alternative means. The outcome was the wheel-lock which could produce a shower of sparks by purely mechanical means. The wheel-lock, as will be seen, was very effective but was restricted both by its complexity and cost. Consequently it was little used in warfare, although it was very popular with the wealthier sportsmen and soldiers.

Once the principle of mechanical ignition had been demonstrated there were many attempts to exploit the idea. The so-called snaphaunce and later the flintlock were to prove the simplest and most reliable methods. The snaphaunce enjoyed only limited popularity although it continued to be produced in a few places, such as Italy, until the eighteenth century. The so-called French flintlock, first manufactured early in the seventeenth century and brought to perfection during the eighteenth century, was to remain the standard means of ignition for some 200 years. It was used in every form of weapon from ships' cannon down to the tiny pocket pistol carried by a lady for her protection.

Traditionally the hand of cards, aces and eights, which the famous gunfighter Wild Bill Hickok held in the poker game before he was shot in the back on August 2, 1876. On the table is a No. 3 Colt Derringer No. 6007 – a single-shot pocket pistol introduced in 1875. The barrel pivoted sideways to admit the ·41-inch (10·4-mm) rim-fire cartridge. E. Kempster, Gunsmiths.

The business end of a Colt army percussion revolver of 1860.

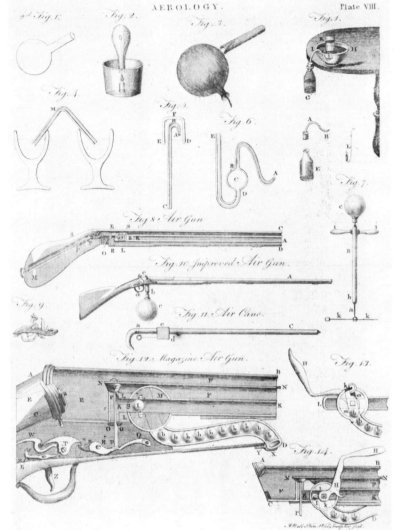

With his double-barrelled gun – either a percussion or a pin-fire – a poacher awaits his chance.

The flintlock was not without its problems and it fell to a most unlikely inventor, a Scottish clergyman, Alexander Forsyth, to devise a system of ignition which was to open the way for the development of the very latest 4·85 mm self-loading, high-velocity rifle recently produced by the British Royal Small Arms Factory.

Forsyth's percussion system replaced the mechanical method used by the flintlock and snaphaunce with a chemically controlled explosion. By the 1820s a very practical system of chemical ignition, using a compound of mercury fulminate, had been evolved, and between 1830 and 1870 the basic steps in the production of modern firearms had been mastered. With the appearance of a metal cased cartridge containing propellant, primer (the means of ignition), and projectile, it became possible to produce repeating rifles, revolvers, self-loading pistols and finally the machine gun. These advances were not solely the result of inventions in the firearms industry itself but were also complemented by technological progress in engineering. Towards the end of the nineteenth century advances in the chemical engineering industry made possible the development of smokeless powder and, for the first time in 500 years, battlefields were no longer obscured by clouds of floating grey and black smoke.

Today firearms are capable of accuracy, range and speed of fire that would have seemed impossible a century ago. New techniques are continually being developed, but the basic principles are still the same as they were 500 years ago.

The world of entertainment makes heavy demands on the firearms industry. Large stocks of modern and obsolete weapons are held for hire to cinema and television by some gunmakers such as Cogswell and Harrison.

A most successful and widely used submachine-gun is the Israeli-made UZI which fires a 9-mm cartridge at a cyclic rate of 600 rounds a minute. *Above.* Early presentation model with a wooden stock. *Below.* The standard type with a folding metal stock. Pattern Room, Royal Small Arms Factory, Enfield.

The evolution of
the musket

The earlier form of handgun had been crude but refinements in production and design had led, by the latter part of the fifteenth century, to a somewhat primitive but nevertheless manageable form of hand firearm. These handguns varied in detail but generally they were composed of a barrel of cast bronze fixed at the end of a wooden bar. Another type had the breech end extended and socketed for the insertion of a wooden pole or shaft, and there was an all-metal variety where the breech end was hammered out into a long metal arm. Some of the all-metal types were produced with the end of the bar fashioned into a ring through which a length of cord or chain could be passed. This loop was slipped over the head so that the handgun hung down on the chest of the holder, ensuring that the weapon was always conveniently within reach and also simplifying its handling. While one hand grasped the stock near the muzzle, the breech end was held against the chest supported by the cord.

The accuracy of these early handguns must have been poor and sighting and aiming were largely a matter of luck. However, the military concept of selective aimed fire did not appear until much later. If contemporary illustrations may be relied upon the usual method of holding the gun appears to have been to tuck the end of the pole under the arm, gripping it firmly with the left hand, while the right hand was used to apply the burning end of the match to the touch-hole. Other illustrations show the end of the pole being placed against the shoulder somewhat in the manner of a modern rifle, although the small surface area of the end of the pole must have delivered an extremely unpleasant and painful recoil to the shoulder.

It must have been very difficult to handle a rather cumbersome length of wood, unbalanced by the weight of a substantial barrel, a supply of powder and bullets and some means of ignition. It is, therefore, hardly surprising that one of the first modifications made was the fitting of a mechanical means of applying fire to the powder. The earliest illustrations show an S- or Z-shaped metal arm attached to one side of the wooden stock adjacent to the touch-hole. Into the top end of this arm was fastened a piece of burning match. The match consisted of a piece of cord which had been soaked in a strong solution of potassium nitrate and allowed to dry. When the match was lit it burned slowly with a glowing tip, so that a yard

length could supply a source of ignition for a reasonable length of time. The glowing end of the match was fixed to the upper end of this S-shaped arm which, in turn, was hinged at its centre. By pressing on the lower arm, which normally lay along the side or just beneath the wooden stock, the upper end was forced downwards and the arm was so positioned that the glowing end of the match would be pressed into the powder in the pan.

The next and obvious step was some form of spring action which would hold the arm clear of the touch-hole when not required. When this serpentine arm was first fitted is not known but the earliest illustrations suggest very early in the fifteenth century.

There were developments in the shape of the stock mostly designed to allow the weapon to be aimed. The first change during the fifteenth century was from a simple pole to a flattened, plank-like oblong shape. This particular style of stock was very popular with the European mercenaries known as Landsknechts. Some Landsknecht butts are shown with the end shaped to sit more comfortably against the shoulder.

Certain national characteristics in the shape of the stock became apparent by the end of the century. Sir Roger Williams, writing in 1590, specifically mentions the Spanish and French stocks. The Spanish stock was straight with just a slight droop, widening to give a fish-tail shape very similar to a modern weapon. Later, in order to afford an easier grip when pressing the trigger or lever to work the serpentine, a deep notch was cut into the upper part of the stock to accommodate the thumb. In the French stock the butt had a downward curve—slight on the earlier examples but very pronounced on later versions. The curved section was thickened

Detail from an engraving from Jacob de Gheyn's *Exercise of Arms* (1607). The details of the pan, serpentine, match, rest and loop are all clearly shown.

Opposite:
A high-grade matchlock and rest typical of the late sixteenth or early seventeenth century. The walnut stock is inlaid and the barrel is fitted with sights.

and splayed out at the rear end which was placed against the chest. It was this characteristic which gave them their name, 'petronel', a modification of *poitrine*, the French word for breast or chest. The word was later used as a generic term for all forms of light shoulder arms carried by horsemen.

During the second quarter of the sixteenth century another style of butt developed which was not unlike the French one, but with a less pronounced curve. This style in fact persisted and is to be found on Spanish weapons of the nineteenth century.

The quality of decoration on the stock varied according to the wealth of its owner. Most military muskets were of plain walnut although other woods were used. However, certain select groups such as town guards or some London Trained Bands (citizen soldiers) had matchlocks with stocks of inlaid pear wood. The inlay was usually of mother-of-pearl, stag horn or bone. Early, rather crude stocks were the work of carpenters, but already in the sixteenth century gunmaking was beginning to develop as a distinct craft. There was a division of labour, with some specializing in barrels, others in the stock and yet another group making the extra fittings.

Below:
English army matchlock muskets, all varying slightly in detail although representative of late seventeenth-century service weapons. Tower of London Armouries.

Bottom:
Fine-quality German hunting matchlock musket with a revolving cylinder carrying eight shots. The pan covers are bronze and the cylinder has to be rotated by hand. About 1600–10. Hermitage Museum, Leningrad.

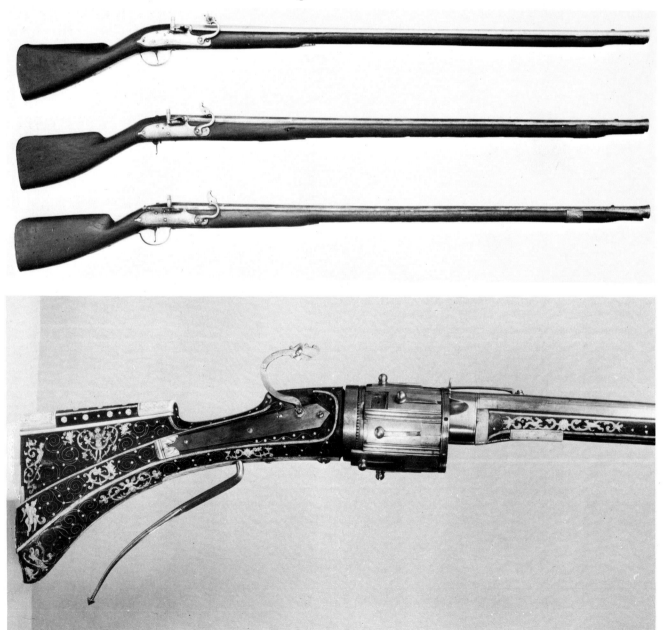

Put on yo.ʳ Bandeliers. 1

order yo.ʳ Musket ~ 5

charge with powder. 16

Draw forth yo.ʳ Match ~ 27

Blow your Cole ~ 28

Giue Fire 34

MUSKETEERS OF THE EARLY SEVENTEENTH CENTURY AT DRILL

In the beginning barrels were fashioned by blacksmiths, but, if made of brass or bronze, they were probably cast by founders. If a barrel was cast there was no great difficulty in its production, but those made of iron had to be forged as a tube and the end then blocked off. From very early in the sixteenth century the usual method was to forge a tube, the wall of which was graduated in thickness from its thinnest near the muzzle where the pressure was least, gradually thickening towards the breech where maximum strength was needed. The breech end was then threaded and a solid breech block made to be screwed in place. This was not a simple plug, but usually had a rear projection which could be used to help secure the barrel to the wooden stock.

Early handgun barrels were fastened to the stock by a series of bands but a new system was used on the matchlock. A number of small lugs were brazed beneath the barrel and a hole was then drilled through each. Corresponding slots were cut in the stock, a small pin pierced the stock and passed through the holes in the lugs, thus securing the barrel firmly in position. This method was reliable but somewhat complicated, and the Continental gun-makers later reverted to the system in which the barrel was held in place by a series of bands encircling both stock and barrel.

The length of the barrel affects the efficiency of any firearm, but basically the shorter the barrel the lower the muzzle velocity, that is, the speed at which the projectile leaves the barrel. This is not an absolute relationship and there comes a point at which lengthening the barrel will no longer increase the muzzle velocity. There are, needless to say, numerous other factors which will affect the muzzle velocity.

Illustrations of some of the sequence of commands given to the musketeer. Taken from *The Military Discipline* (1622).

21

Gustavus Adolphus, king of Sweden, leading his troops at the battle of Breitenfeld in 1631. Among his numerous military innovations was the effective use of trained musketeers. Musées de la Ville de Strasbourg.

22

Small powder horn, probably for priming powder, fashioned from a piece of antler and dated 1664.

The length and internal diameter of barrels became more or less standardized, although the names used for any particular size seem to have varied. Larger guns, primarily designed for the defence of fortified positions where they could be mounted on a rampart or castle wall, were usually described as hagbuts, hackbushes or arquebusses à croc. Smaller versions were known as half- or demi-hags although this seems to have been corrupted to 'half hawks'. The most common size of shoulder arms was the musket and although authorities are not in complete agreement the generally accepted derivation of the name is from the Italian *moschetto*, a hawk-like bird. It is possible that the flight of the ball through the air evoked this somewhat poetic nomenclature but bird names such as falcon and saker (a hawk) were applied to other sizes of weapons.

By the last quarter of the sixteenth century the English military musket had assumed a more or less standard form with a 48-inch barrel. This was to stay the basic length until well on into the eighteenth century. The musket fired a bullet approximately three-quarters of an inch in diameter, although this was by no means standard. One of the problems with these early firearms lay in forcing down a tight-fitting missile and two types, the standing and the rolling bullet, were used. The rolling bullet was slightly smaller and could be literally rolled down the barrel. The standing one was slightly larger and tighter-fitting. Ten of these bullets weighed one pound, while twelve of the rolling bullets made the same weight.

There was also a bastard musket, which was really only a musket with a shortened barrel, and the caliver, which was a scaled-down version of the musket. The caliver's barrel was some three inches shorter and the bullets were somewhat smaller – 17 to the pound. A smaller version, still with a barrel 30 inches long, was known as the arquebus and fired the same size of bullet as the caliver. For the horseman there was the carbine or petronel which had a barrel also about 30 inches in length, but fired a much smaller bullet, of which there were some 24 to the pound.

The four-foot barrel, plus the butt, brought the total length of the musket to a minimum of 62 inches. This made the weapon rather unwieldy and sufficiently heavy to render it extremely difficult, if not impossible, for the average person to hold it steady at the aiming position. Some artificial means of support was needed and by the middle of the sixteenth century most musketeers carried a stout ash wood staff, pointed at one end and fitted at the other with a U-shaped metal arm. This rest was stuck in the ground and used as a support for the very heavy barrel. The caliver, however, did not normally require the support of a rest.

At the beginning of the sixteenth century the serpentine with the S-shaped hinged lever was still the prime means of ignition. However, by the last quarter of the sixteenth century two distinct types of firing mechanism had evolved. The snap-lock, which appears to have been the earlier, was potentially a dangerous system. The match was held between the jaws of a hinged arm,

Five-shot matchlock musket. The lock is activated by the lever. About 1620–30. Musée de l'Armée, Paris.

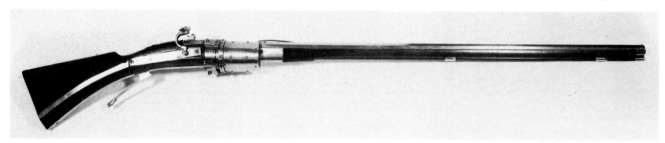

but instead of relying solely on the movement imparted by a lever, the mechanism was operated by a V-shaped spring. The arm was raised and a small bar locked it in position. When the trigger or, in some cases a button, was pressed the bar was withdrawn and the arm fell, pressing the glowing piece of match down to fire the charge. Obviously such a system was very liable to accidental discharge.

The safer and more popular form of lock operated in the reverse fashion. At rest the match holder was raised but when the trigger or lever was pressed the arm swung forward and down to fire the weapon. Early examples of both locks retained the long lower lever of the serpentine but the mechanism of the lock now made it possible to replace the arm, so susceptible to knocks, with a small trigger. This trigger could be guarded from accidental knocks by means of a shaped strip of metal fitted to the underneath of the butt. The matchlock mechanism was fastened to the inside of a metal plate which fitted over a shaped recess cut in the wooden stock.

There were further changes to the musket during the sixteenth century, all aimed at improving the ignition system. Most of the early handguns had a small-diameter hole drilled vertically down through the barrel at the breech, and this hole, the touch-hole, was filled with a pinch of fine-grained priming powder. When the soldier wished to fire he pressed his piece of glowing match or moss down into this touch-hole. It was realized that ignition could be made more certain by increasing the amount of

Jacob de Gheyn's fine engraving of a musketeer of the early seventeenth century showing all his impedimenta: spare match, powder flasks, bullet bag and glowing match.

Musketeer's powder flask, made of wood with applied decorations. Most were far less elaborate than this example. Seventeenth century.

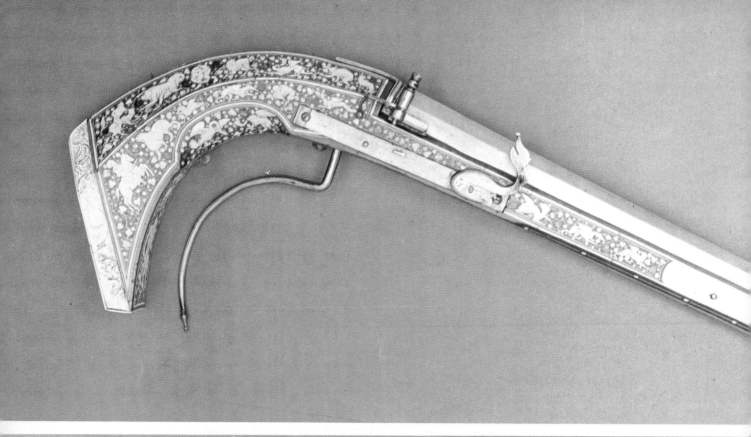

powder around the touch-hole, but since it was situated on the top of the barrel this was a little difficult to achieve.

During the sixteenth century the gunsmiths altered the design so that the touch-hole was drilled through one side, usually the right, of the barrel. Just slightly below the touch-hole and projecting horizontally they fitted a small tray or pan, suitably shaped to hold some extra powder. A cover, pivoted on the pan, was fitted so that when the priming powder was in place it could be protected from rain and wind, or simply prevented from falling out. Before firing the musketeer had to open his pan cover and in the heat of battle he might well forget, with disastrous results. Some of the later matchlocks had a linked arm which automatically pushed open the pan cover when the trigger was pressed.

It was essential that the bullet, whether of the rolling or standing variety, should sit securely on top of the charge with no dangerous gaps where high pressures could develop. Since the barrel was four feet long, some means of ramming home the bullet was essential and this led to the development of the ramrod or scouring stick. This long, thin wooden rod was obviously susceptible to breakage and loss and so had to be carried in such a way so that it was safe and readily available to the musketeer. The solution found by the gunmakers, and one which was to continue in general use until the late nineteenth century, was to cut a channel in the stock beneath the barrel. The scouring stick was then pushed into this channel where it would be held in place by friction or, on later guns, by a small spring fitted inside the stock.

Matchlock muskets were not particularly accurate, especially if loaded with the rolling ball. However, some matchlocks were fitted with sights which were usually of the peep variety, with a small tube situated above the breech, and some form of aiming mark or foresight at the muzzle.

This then was the weapon of the musketeer from the latter part of the sixteenth century until the latter part of the seventeenth century. It was heavy, cumbersome and subject to a number of limitations. The greatest danger was from the weather, since even with a pan cover in place the wind could dislodge the priming powder and rain could seep beneath the cover. All this made it extremely difficult to ensure that in bad weather the weapon was fully primed and ready for firing. When action was imminent the match had to be kept constantly smouldering, which meant that it was being continually consumed. The musketeer, therefore, had to carry reserve lengths of match dangling from his belt or tucked inside his hat to protect them from the weather.

It was common practice to light both ends of the match and, although this doubled the rate of consumption, it ensured that if one end was extinguished the other end could be used instead. The match, like the priming, was vulnerable to the elements. Various devices to give some protection against wind and rain were tried, but none was totally effective. This problem was to remain with the matchlock until it was eventually replaced by other forms of weapons.

The burning match end also acted as a very clear marker for an enemy, since it was virtually impossible for an army of musketeers to move at night without giving away their positions. The effect of large numbers of matches glowing in the darkness must have been quite picturesque, even if it rendered secrecy impossible!

Apart from these various problems the musketeer had to cope with all his extras. He carried with him a supply of priming powder, normally composed of finer grains than the main charge, in a small powder flask suspended from the belt or from a cord across the shoulder. In addition to this he may have had a much larger flask full of the charge powder. It was, of course, essential that only the correct amount of powder be loaded, and the powder flask had a metal pourer, which was a tube with a simple but nevertheless ingenious double cut-off. When it was pressed and the flask was tipped up the powder filled the nozzle with just the correct charge of powder. When the operating lever was released the cut-off sealed the body of the flask, but opened the nozzle and the powder could then be poured down inside the barrel.

Another type of powder measure adopted by many of the Continental armies, was the charger. This was normally of wood, metal or horn and was of such a size as to hold just the correct amount of powder. In fact the amount of powder held in these

Portrait of an officer by William Dobson (1610–46). It is thought to be that of Sir Charles Lucas. He wears a breastplate and carries one of the plain, wheel-lock pistols favoured by cavalry and officers. Tate Gallery, London.

chargers probably varied slightly, so rendering really consistent, accurate shooting virtually impossible. Nevertheless, an approximately correct amount was quickly available. These chargers were suspended from a belt, the bandolier, which the musketeer wore across his chest. He normally carried twelve such chargers, which were ironically known as the Twelve Apostles.

The use of chargers must have speeded up the process of loading, but they could be a hindrance. Unless the musketeer used the chargers in strict sequence it must have been easy to grab an empty one and in the heat of battle it might not be obvious that no powder had been loaded. The musketeer would then, no doubt, wonder why only his priming flashed.

Writing in 1619 Edward Davies stated that the practice of using chargers was developed in the Low Countries by the Walloons. He describes their chargers as being made of tin or copper and goes on to say that the Spanish troops had no faith in them and stuck to their powder flasks. The French used both chargers and flasks, while 'some of our English nation [use] their pocket'. Later both flask and charger were superseded by paper cartridges.

How effective then was the matchlock musket? One of its greatest advantages was that unlike the more powerful and accurate longbow it required only a minimum amount of skill to use. Certainly, as will be seen, musket drill was complicated and tedious, but it had been reduced to a number of mechanical movements which could be learned by any but the most stupid. Musketeers could lay down a barrage of bullets, any one of which was capable of killing or maiming a horse or a man even if he wore armour. It was not difficult to make armour thick enough to stop a bullet but its thickness increased its weight. The new tactics of seventeenth-century warfare called for greater mobility and heavy armour slowed down movement. As a result armour was gradually abandoned from the latter part of the seventeenth century onwards and by the early eighteenth century only a few cavalry units still retained their breast and back plates.

One physical quality that the musketeer needed was strength. He was expected to march and fight when he was encumbered with a host of items—a musket nearly six feet long and weighing up to ten pounds, a rest, a bandolier and twelve chargers, a leather bag of bullets, a large powder flask or cartridge box, priming flask, spare lengths of match, a sword and a helmet.

One great disadvantage of the musket was its slow rate of fire and there were many writers in the seventeenth century who opposed its use, claiming that six arrows could be discharged from a bow in the time it took to fire one bullet. This slowness was due to the necessity of so many separate movements in loading. Writing in 1622 Francis Markham lists some eighteen movements for charging or loading the weapon and fourteen for discharging. In battle the orders were reduced to just three—make ready, present and give fire.

The sequence of orders given by Markham (other writers varied in detail) is as follows:

Pistols were carried by officers and cavalrymen in holsters fixed to the front of the saddle. This pair are eighteenth-century and are plainer than those used in the previous century. In the nineteenth century personal belt holsters came into general use. Private Collection.

1 Open your pan.	The cover was pushed clear.
2 Clear your pan.	Any dust and unburnt powder was blown clear.
3 Prime your pan.	Powder from the small flask was shaken in.
4 Shut your pan.	
5 Cast off your loose corns.	The musket was tilted and loose powder shaken clear.
6 Blow your pan.	Loose grains of powder were blown away.
7 Cast about your musket with both your hands and trail your rest.	The musket was moved across the body so that the butt rested on the ground and the muzzle was waist high.
8 Open your charger.	The cap of the charger was pushed clear with the fingers of the right hand.
9 Charge your musket with powder.	
10 Draw out your scouring stick.	
11 Shorten your stick.	The ramrod was gripped near the centre.
12 Ram in your powder.	
13 Draw out your stick.	
14 Charge with bullet.	One was taken from the pouch or in battle spat from the mouth.
15 Ram in your bullet.	
16 Draw out your stick.	
17 Shorten your stick and put it up.	The ramrod was returned to the groove beneath the stock.
18 Bring your musket forward with your left hand.	
19 Hold it up with your right hand and re-cover your rest.	

To discharge the weapon the following sequence applied. Carry your rest in your left hand preparing to give fire. Slope your musket and let the rest sink. In the right hand poise your musket. In the left hand carry your musket with the rest. In the right hand take your match between the second finger and the thumb. Hold the match fast and blow it. Cock your match (this meant placing the patch between the jaws of the cock). Try your match. Guard the pan (close the cover) and blow your match. Open your pan. Present your musket. Give fire! Dismount your musket and carry it with the rest. Uncock your match and put it between your fingers.

It was important that the muzzle of the musket was always kept up, otherwise there was a danger, if it dipped below the horizontal, that the 'rolling' ball might roll out, followed by the powder,

leaving the musketeer with a useless weapon. With a good charge, well loaded and a ball well rammed home, it was reckoned by Sir John Smythe, writing in 1590, that the ball had an effective range of twenty-four to thirty yards.

When the musketeer had discharged his 'Twelve Apostles' he had to refill them. He was instructed to hold the glowing match between finger and thumb and one cannot help but wonder how many times a forgetful musketeer, in the midst of battle, must have gone to a powder keg to replenish his stock of powder from the barrel, with a glowing match in his hand. The result must have been spectacular if not pleasant!

The great weakness of the musketeer as an effective fighting man lay in the time that he took to reload. During this period he was virtually defenceless, a liability to the rest of the army. If attacked he could do nothing. The usual solution to this dilemma was to intersperse the musketeers with groups of pikemen. These troops were armoured and carried an ash pike which might be sixteen to eighteen feet in length. The whole unit was commonly drawn up in a formation known as the Swedish Brigade. Units comprising some 2,000 men each were split into groups, each formed up in six ranks, and these were placed in an oblong formation, headed by a body of pikemen followed by two smaller groups of musketeers. At the rear this formation was repeated and on each side were pikemen and on the flanks two groups of musketeers. They advanced towards the enemy, the pikemen engaging if the need arose or the musketeers opening fire. Should they be attacked they could then move in amongst the pikemen during the time it took them to reload.

Engraving of an early seventeenth-century pikeman and musketeer. The musketeer's rest has a fitted loop through which he passed his hand so reducing the chances of loss. Note the 'twelve Apostles', spare match and bullet bag.

Details from *The English Military Discipline* (about 1675) giving instructions in musket drill.

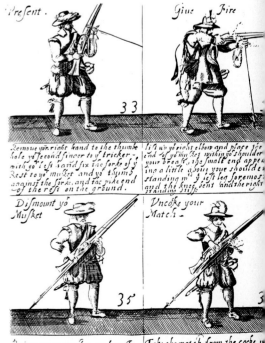

Afridi warriors of the Khyber Pass area, about 1865. They are carrying the conventional, long-barrelled flintlock jezail.

The advent of the musket had a tremendous impact on warfare in the sixteenth century. One of the first commanders to realize the potential of the new weapon was a Spaniard, Gonzalo de Córdoba, and his tactical use of firearms devastated his enemies. He had been sent to Italy in 1495 and had there suffered a defeat by a combined force of men-at-arms and pikemen. The defeat rankled and Córdoba sought means to combat the very effective mixture of troops. He decided that the solution was to increase the number of firearms among his men, to reduce the number of conventionally armed soldiers, and to intersperse them with pikemen. At Serignola in Italy in 1503 he had his first opportunity of trying out his new system against a determined French army. He arranged for a comparatively small number of arquebusiers and pikemen to take up their positions at the bottom of a hill. In front of them was a ditch or trench with a fairly simple rampart. The French attacked in their normal echelon formation, confidently expecting to break through the apparently frail Spanish line. The well-trained arquebusiers held their fire until the French were close enough for them not to miss. They then opened a steady barrage causing heavy losses among the advancing French. Their confusion was increased as the leading troops encountered the trench and rampart. To confound matters even further the French commander was killed by a bullet and the battle ended as an overwhelming defeat for the French.

The Spanish continued to exploit their superiority and similar victories were gained over the Swiss at Bicocca in 1522, when the power of the Swiss pikemen, who for long had been considered some of the finest mercenaries in Europe, was smashed. The victory at Bicocca was against infantry, but the Spaniards repeated their success against French cavalry at the battle of Pavia in 1525.

The military minds of Europe needed no further convincing. Men-at-arms. bowmen and crossbowmen gradually begin to disappear from the lists of troops. In Europe the matchlock was to remain the prime military weapon until early in the eighteenth century when it was superseded by more efficient and reliable firearms.

In the East the matchlock musket continued as a 'working' weapon long after it had been abandoned in Europe. Its first appearance there was in the hands of Portuguese explorers whose vessels reached India in 1498, Malaya by 1514 and then Japan in 1543. There is little doubt that the new weapon impressed the native inhabitants, who examined them and were soon able to copy them. Their simple construction would naturally recommend itself to the craftsmen of these countries with their basic technology, and until industry developed in Eastern countries in the nineteenth century the matchlock was supreme.

The subcontinent of India developed its own peculiar forms of matchlock. Although in such a vast area there were variations, the majority of Indian matchlocks, known as *toradors*, are straight-stocked, with a narrow butt which is near-rectangular in section and slopes only slightly. The barrels are frequently very long and this may well be the result of using rather poor quality powder which needed a considerable time for its combustion to be completed. The other feature found on almost all Indian matchlocks is that the arm which holds the match moves forward to the touch-hole and pan rather than backwards as on European examples. The mechanism and part of the arm are normally enclosed in the stock. Triggers are frequently decorative and there is usually no trigger guard.

One very distinctive type of Indian matchlock is that made in the northern regions of the subcontinent and in Afghanistan, which has a butt somewhat reminiscent of the early French petronel, with a very pronounced curve. Another feature common to most Indian matchlocks is that the barrels are secured to the stock, not by pins and lugs as with European weapons, but by metal bands or thongs encircling barrel and stock. Many of the Indian weapons are highly decorative, with the stock inlaid with ebony, ivory, lacquer work, enamel and semi-precious stones.

The further east one travels the more common becomes a version of the old European snap-lock, which is found in Burma, Java and Japan. It will be recalled that this was the type of lock with the arm pressing down into the priming pan and touch-hole in the rest position. The Japanese in particular favoured this style of lock and the very considerable skill of the Japanese metalworker was applied to the production and copy of early snap-locks. The barrels, usually octagonal in section, were frequently fashioned by layer upon layer of tempered steel, wrapped one about the other.

Japanese matchlocks are usually substantial but strangely enough, despite their great skill, the Japanese smiths seem not to have favoured the use of screws. Wherever possible the barrels and other parts of the mechanism are secured to the stock by pins, and even the pan cover is folded so that a pin can go through from top to bottom and hold it in position. Moreover, despite their un-doubtedly superiority in metallurgy the Japanese smiths were apparently unable to produce a really good-quality spring. The

Indian matchlocks.
Left. Torador with painted wooden stock and silver fittings. The barrel has some gold decoration. Late eighteenth century.
Right. Matchlock with mahogany stock and fine decoration overall; the barrel with gold decoration. The matchholder is shaped into a monster's head. Wallace Collection, London.

Hunting with matchlocks in the latter part of the sixteenth century. The shooters went after sitting birds. Shooting 'flying' at birds on the wing did not appear until much later. From a drawing by Stradanus.

To the Honble Sr Henry Goodricke of Ribston Parke in Yorkeshire Knight & Bart his Majesties Envoy Extraordinary, to the King of Spain. Anno Dom 168⅔. This Plate is humble dedicated by Richard Blome

Arthur Soly fecit 1683

In order to approach their prey these seventeenth-century hunters are using a 'stalking horse', hoping that the birds will not be alarmed. From *Gentleman's Recreation* (1686).

action of Japanese matchlocks has a distinctly soft and imprecise feel about it, since the spring is usually of brass. The impact of the matchlock in Japan was particularly great and led to very marked changes in the political structure of the country.

Matchlock muskets were retained as hunting weapons by the peasants of Europe for some time, but by the mid-eighteenth century they had virtually been forgotten except in the East, where some may still be found in use in the more remote areas. Although outmoded the matchlock had ushered in a new style of warfare and in many ways marked the end of the old concept of war.

34

The wheel-lock: the hunter's weapon

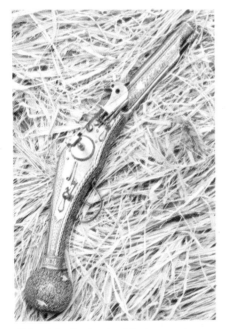

Wheel-lock pistol with the stock almost completely covered with inlay of ivory. Made in Nuremberg. Overall length 18½ inches (47 cm). T. Porter.

Although the matchlock musket remained the main infantry weapon until the seventeenth century, other developments were taking place. The gunsmiths were only too well aware of its inadequacies, and from the beginning of the sixteenth century at least they had been seeking a system which would overcome these. One of the major tasks was to somehow replace the burning match which was so inconvenient and unreliable and such a danger wherever gunpowder was to be found. An alternative means of igniting the priming powder was essential.

The usual method of providing fire in the home was by tinder and steel. A piece of hard rock could be struck by a specially shaped piece of steel to provide sparks. These fell into a piece of dry moss or similar combustible material and, with gentle blowing, could be coaxed into flame. Gunmakers experimented to see whether this method could be applied to firearms.

One solution was produced by an unknown maker at an unknown date. The available evidence indicates that the device could have been made at any time between the latter part of the fifteenth century and the middle of the sixteenth century. It is known as the Monk's Gun, a throwback to the old tradition of Black Berthold and his connection with early firearms. The device consists of a barrel about eleven inches long, with the wall thickened at the closed or breech end. Fixed on the side of the barrel is a narrow box, the rear end divided to make a small pan, which is situated by the touch-hole. An arm is hinged at the front end of the box and this arm, the cock, has a jaw fitted at the free end which holds a piece of mineral called pyrites. There is also a rectangular rod with one surface roughened, and this rod is pushed into the box passing through the pan compartment.

The barrel was loaded with powder and ball and a pinch of powder was placed in the pan compartment. The cock was swung forward and the pyrites pressed down on the roughened surface of the rod. A finger was put through the ring at the end of the rod and it was then pulled smartly backwards, striking sparks between the steel and pyrites. The spark ignited the priming powder and so fired the shot. Beneath the barrel is a hook-like rod with which the gun could be hung from the belt.

The Monk's Gun works, but it is obviously limited in its application, probably wildly inaccurate, awkward to handle and of little

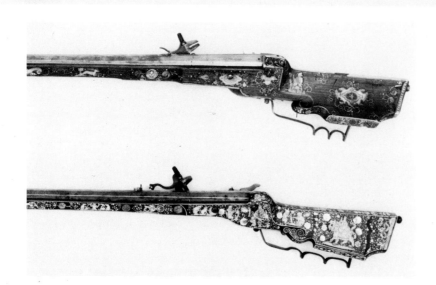

Above:
Types of ignition mechanisms of the seventeenth century.
Top. Wheel-lock musket with very large lock.
Centre. Musket with snaphaunce lock, with steel separate from pan cover.
Bottom. Matchlock musket with serpentine.

Left:
Views of two wheel-lock pistols.
Above. German with octagonal barrel and walnut stock inlaid with engraved horn showing hunting scenes, monsters and walled cities. Overall length 45¼ inches (115 cm). About 1600.
Below. This was made by Hieronymus Jager of Regensburg. The weapon is dated 1644 and the walnut stock is inlaid with engraved horn and mother of pearl plaques. Overall length 37½ inches (95·3 cm).

Above right:
Engraving from the *Art Militaire à Cheval* by J. J. de Wallhausen (1616). The heavily armoured cuirassiers of the period are discharging wheel-lock pistols.

Right:
Top. Made in Thuringia in Germany during the last quarter of the sixteenth century, this wheel-lock pistol has a stock covered with engraved horn. Overall length 22 inches (55·9 cm).
Centre. This pistol was probably made by Klaus Hort of Wasungen in Germany about the same period. Overall length 23 inches (58·4 cm).
Bottom. Priming powder flask decorated with silver and horn. Diameter 3 inches (7·6 cm). Late sixteenth century.

real use. However, the principle was sound and it does indicate a move towards producing fire mechanically.

The evidence suggest that by the first decade of the sixteenth century some weapons were using a mechanical means of ignition. The system which was to prove the most practical is known as the wheel-lock and, although there were many variants, it consists basically of a device to produce sparks. The heart of the system is a thick steel disc, the edge of which has been grooved. This is connected, usually by means of a short linked chain, to a strong V-shaped spring. The other important component is a metal arm known as the dog's head and this held, between jaws, a piece of pyrites. The entire mechanism was usually attached to the inside of a steel plate, which in turn was fitted into the side of the weapon's stock. The disc or wheel was so placed as to form the floor of the priming pan and was fitted adjacent to the touch-hole.

The sequence for firing the wheel-lock was far less complex and dangerous than with the matchlock. After the barrel had been loaded with powder and ball, a key with a square-shaped recess was fitted over the axle or lug of the wheel. This was then turned and, since the wheel was connected by means of the short chain to a strong spring, the spring was compressed. When the spring was fully compressed a small spring-operated arm moved forward and engaged with a hole on the inside of the wheel, so locking it in position. The metal key or spanner was then removed. A pinch

36

of fine-grained powder was now placed in the pan and a sliding cover was moved forward to protect this priming.

To fire the wheel-lock the dog's head arm was swung forward so that the pyrites now pressed quite heavily on to the pan cover. When the trigger was pressed the arm which locked the wheel was withdrawn. Under the thrust of the main spring the wheel rotated rapidly and the pan cover was automatically pushed clear, so allowing the pyrites to drop on to the rotating wheel. The sparks produced fell into the priming powder and ignition was sure and fast.

The wheel-lock had several advantages, but one of its greatest

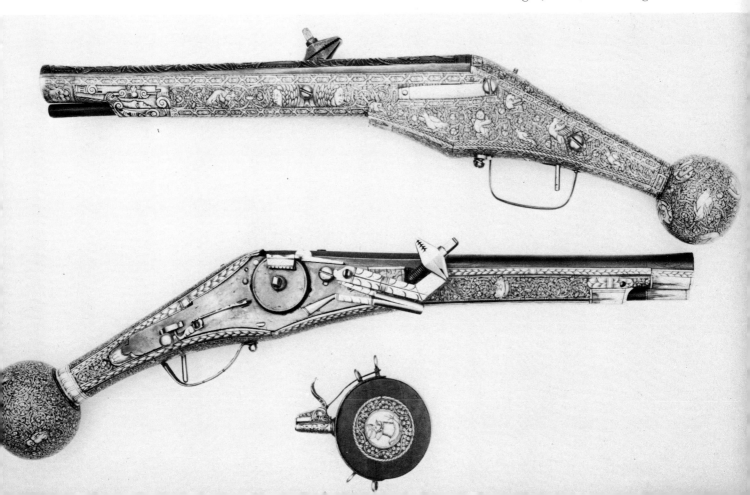

assets was that, provided the dog's head was clear of the pan cover, the weapon was completely safe even when loaded and primed. Even if the trigger was pressed the wheel was not in contact with the pyrites, no sparks were produced, and the chances of an accident were nil. All that was required to prepare for a shot was to pull forward the dog's head.

The wheel-lock opened up a new and exciting field for the gun-makers. Because matchlocks had necessitated the use of inconvenient lengths of burning match, horsemen had found it extremely difficult to handle them. It could, however, be done, and in nineteenth-century India one group of irregular cavalry was armed with full-sized matchlocks. Small matchlocks were produced and there are examples of matchlock pistols, but they are rare. The match made it impossible to manufacture a weapon which could be ready for instant action and yet be carried in a holster or secreted about the person. Now the wheel-lock pistol was a small weapon, ready to be fired, and one which could be carried in a holster, a pocket or concealed beneath clothing. Many of the rulers of Renaissance Europe realized the dangers implicit in this new firearm. It was an ideal assassin's weapon, and numerous ordinances were passed restricting the carrying of wheel-lock pistols.

The place of origin and the name of the inventor of the wheel-lock are not known and surviving examples do not predate the first decade or so of the sixteenth century. The earliest known wheel-locks are in the Venice Museum. They are, ironically, a combination weapon, consisting of a crossbow fitted with a wheel-lock pistol. Evidence suggests that these weapons date from about 1510–20. Other records appear to confirm that this was the period when the wheel-lock first appeared.

It was often claimed that the wheel-lock was invented in Nuremberg in 1517, the statement first appearing in a history of that city printed in 1697. The chronicle from which this statement

Pair of ball-butted wheel-locks, the stocks inlaid with horn. They are unusual in having a safety catch mounted on the side of the stock and not on the lock plate. The barrels are dated 1590. Overall length 23 inches (58·4 cm). Barrel 12¾ inches (32·4 cm). Bore ·63 inches (16 mm). Diameter of ball 3 inches (7·62 cm). T. Porter.

is supposed to have been copied has not been traced and there is ample evidence that the invention predates 1517 by at least ten years.

Leonardo da Vinci left amongst his *Codex Atlanticus* papers sketches which are of a practical if somewhat inefficient mechanism for a wheel-lock ignition system. Leonardo da Vinci's drawings are tentatively dated about the last decade of the fifteenth century. A manuscript held in Berlin before the Second World War, a quarto volume bearing the arms of a Nuremberg elder named Martin Loffelholz, contained a variety of technical drawings and recipes. These included two illustrations of a wheel-lock tinder lighter. This manuscript was actually dated 1505. Buried in various archives which are all from the first two decades of the sixteenth century there are other references to wheel-locks, or rather to mechanisms which are not described as wheel-locks but leave little doubt that this is what is referred to. Limited in number though the references are, the context of many of them suggests that the wheel-lock of this period was widely distributed, but that it was still a novelty.

Under normal circumstances the wheel-lock with the dog's head in the withdrawn position was completely safe but mishandling could lead to accidents. One story related by a writer in Augsburg in Germany describes a young man, Laux Pfister, who had such an accident. On the 6th January, 1515, he invited up to his room a young whore. While she was with him he produced a pistol. This is described as having a lock which functioned so that when the firing mechanism was pressed it ignited itself–surely a clear indication that this was a form of wheel-lock. Apparently Pfister was playing around with the mechanism and the gun went off. The bullet hit the young woman under the chin and passed out through the back of her neck but, despite the apparent seriousness

Designs for decoration on wheel-lock weapons from a French book of the mid-seventeenth century, engraved by C. Jacquinet.

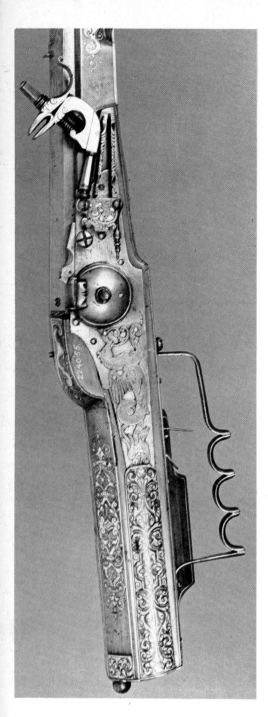

of the wound, she survived. The passionate but careless Pfister had to pay compensation. The accident cost him forty florins then, twenty florins per annum for life, and some seventy or eighty florins in various other expenses!

Taking all the available evidence into consideration it is reasonable to conclude that the wheel-lock was probably invented in Italy or Germany in the latter part of the fifteenth century or very early in the sixteenth. By the second decade of the sixteenth century it was no longer a rarity, although it was not yet in the hands of a large number of people.

The construction of the wheel-lock presented certain problems. The matchlock could be put together by any competent blacksmith, but this was not the case with the wheel-lock. It involved a fairly complicated system of levers and springs and required a degree of skill beyond the scope of many metalworkers. Its very complexity was an additional handicap. A snapped link or a broken spring and the weapon was utterly useless.

This fact was appreciated by some and it is not unknown for firearms of this period to be fitted with both a wheel-lock and a matchlock. Should the wheel-lock break the matchlock could be brought into play so permitting continued use of the weapon. The wheel-lock's complexity meant that it was also liable to jamming. Dirt, a broken screw or a bent pin could all lead to the clogging of the mechanism. Even a comparatively simple fault required some skill in stripping down the lock and far more tools were required than for the old matchlock.

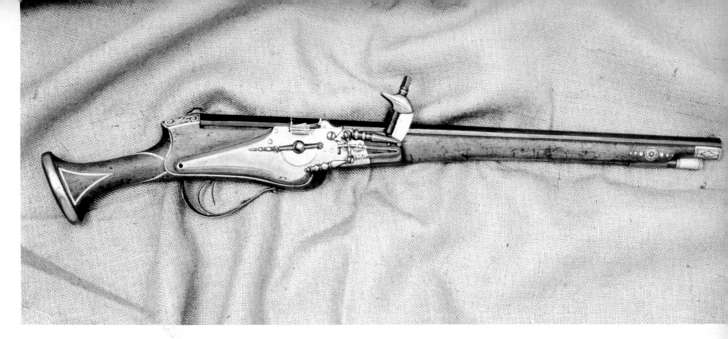

Unusual, breech-loading wheel-lock. The weapon carries the mark of Hans Stockmann who worked in Dresden about 1610. Victoria and Albert Museum, London.

Opposite:
Two views of a wheel-lock of usual form with pearwood stock inlaid with staghorn and some applied decoration to the steel lock plate. The butt has the inlaid arms of Marquard Von Hatstein Zu Weilbach and the date 1605. Victoria and Albert Museum, London.

Quite apart from the problems of repair the mechanical complexity of the wheel-lock made it a difficult item to produce and in consequence the cost was, for its period, quite high. The enormous expense of equipping an army with wheel-locks meant that only a comparatively small number of military units ever received them as standard issue. Cavalry commanders realized the tremendous potential of the weapon. It meant that for the first time horsemen could be equipped with firearms, but again expense was a limiting factor although certain select units were indeed armed with wheel-lock pistols.

However the high cost of the wheel-lock encouraged its purchase by the gentleman, the rich merchant and the nobleman of the sixteenth and early seventeenth century, since the possession of such a fine-quality weapon would have undoubtedly carried a certain status. Although very plain, serviceable wheel-locks were produced, the majority of surviving examples are high-quality, richly decorative hunting weapons.

One of the most popular pastimes of the leisured classes has always been hunting, and in the sixteenth and seventeenth centuries it became something of a passion. By present-day standards many of the hunts should more aptly be described as massacres. The assembled hunters adjourned to a clearing in the forest which had been carefully divided off by nets or by screens some nine to twelve feet high and thirty feet wide. In the centre of one side of the enclosure formed by these decorative screens there was a pavilion which was protected from sun and rain and well equipped with refreshments. A large group of beaters would sweep the forest, driving the quarry, usually deer, in towards the enclosure. Here the hunters, plentifully supplied with loaders to maintain a constant supply of weapons, were able to shoot down their deer in comfort.

The whole sordid business was hemmed in with conventions, and writers of the period emphasize that incorrect use of technical terms and any breach of etiquette would lead to ritual punishment. Serious breaches of etiquette required the offender to lie across the body of a freshly killed deer and be whacked hard with the flat of a hunting knife. To complete the farcical picture these hunting parties were often turned into fancy dress events. One such occasion in 1662, held to mark a princely wedding, included giants, satyrs, nymphs, bagpipers and lion-tamers, and the entourage was completed by a large orchestra which played sweet music.

Top. Austrian wheel-lock by Johann Krach of Salzburg, with brass rear sight. The stock of fruitwood is inlaid and dates from about 1680, but the chiselled and engraved lock is mid-eighteenth century.

Above. German wheel-lock rifle with octagonal barrel dated 1680. The lock plate is engraved and the stock is carved and dated 1681. Signed 'Borg Ball 1680' on the lock plate.

Left:
German wheel-lock pistol of good quality. The wooden stock is inlaid and it has the typical large-diameter ball pommel. The lock plate is fitted with a safety catch – a feature later discarded. Mid-sixteenth century.

Some idea of the scale of the slaughter at such an event is given by the records of one hunt at Mainz in 1764, when within an hour 104 stags were killed. The account states that the hunt then stopped, there being no targets left alive! Stags were not the only animals subjected to these terrible massacres. Wild boar were similarly treated and on one occasion alone about 1,000 were killed. A book published in Copenhagen in the seventeenth century sets down the incredible fact that the Elector John George I of Saxony (1585–1656) managed during his lifetime to destroy 116,906 animals. His son, later John George II (1613–80), reached the equally remarkable total of 111,141 animals.

Since it would have been embarrassing to miss one's aim when surrounded by lesser mortals, the rich or titled hunter wanted a weapon which would give him a very good chance of scoring a hit. In the old musket the ball, particularly the rolling type, had been very loose-fitting, and this meant that the weapon was basically rather inaccurate. When the charge started burning pressure was built up and the bullet began its journey along the barrel. Since it did not fit tightly there was some random side-to-side movement, and the ball was, in fact, almost bouncing along the inside of the

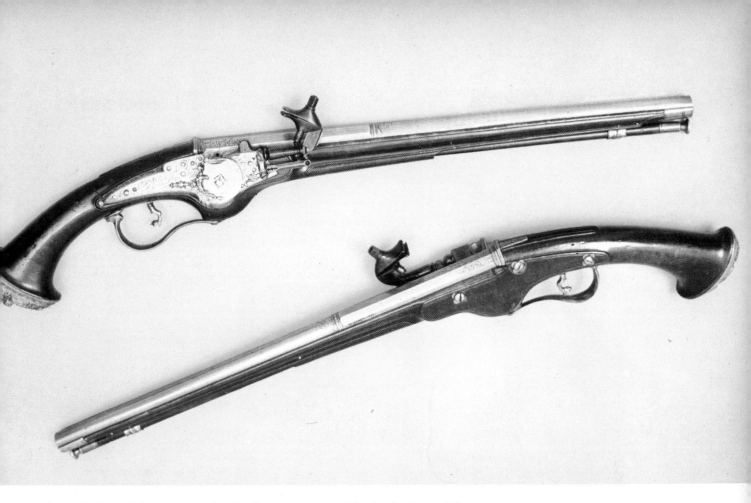

Pair of wheel-lock pistols by Felix Werder of Zurich, made in 1640. The lock plates and barrels are of brass. This shape is typical of military wheel-locks of this period. Victoria and Albert Museum, London.

barrel. As it left the muzzle the last contact with the inside of the barrel was totally unpredictable, but this slight contact produced a drag which threw the bullet marginally off course in one direction or another. Although this displacement was only very little at the muzzle, by the time the ball had travelled up to 100 yards it made a significant variation.

In 1800 one French expert gave the figures for a French musket on a fixed base and claimed that at a range of 150 yards the bullet struck anywhere in a rectangle 30 inches high and 24 inches wide. Since the ball was loose-fitting the amount of gas escaping from around it as it travelled along the barrel was also variable. This meant that its velocity varied and consequently the path or trajectory of the bullet was never constant. Even with the musket held firmly in some fixed stand, it was unlikely that the bullets would strike the target in a consistent pattern.

These variations, in addition to those produced by differences in the weight of the bullet, in amounts of powder, in quality of powder and even in the shape of the ball – all could affect the line of flight of the bullet.

With the military musket there was little that could be done to correct these variables and, in fact, they were not of any great importance. The basic way of fighting a battle was with volleys of fire, and a barrage of several hundred bullets meant that a proportion must hit their targets. The hunter wanted something better and the means of correcting some of these defects were known from the earliest times. If the ball could be made to spin in its flight, the spinning created a gyroscopic effect, which tended cancel out variations from the axis of flight. If the ball was slightly misshapen there was a tendency to veer off course, but if it was spinning, then this veering was immediately cancelled out, since the ball would try to veer in all directions and thus follow a straight course.

The problem was how to make the bullet rotate, but a solution was found very early on in the history of firearms. First the bullet was made to fit tightly inside the barrel, which helped reduce loss of powder due to gas leakage and also reduced the bouncing effect. If the inside of the barrel was cut with a number of grooves of just the correct depth and the bullet was of the right material, it would bite into the groove. If the groove twisted in a spiral fashion then the bullet would be turned as it travelled along the barrel and would be spinning when it left the muzzle. The rate of spin depended on the degree of twist of the grooves, which were known as the rifling. With rifled barrels a high degree of accuracy was obtainable, although factors such as powder content and bullet weight could still affect the flight.

Traditionally the credit for the introduction of rifling goes either to a gunmaker of Vienna or to an armourer of Nuremberg, but there is little or no proof of this. One of the earliest-known barrels with rifling dates from the turn of the fifteenth century. It seems reasonably certain that by the 1540s the properties of rifling were well-known, because many examples dating from this period have survived. If the principle was understood, it may be asked why it was not adopted on a wider scale. The answer is to be found in the limited technology of the period. In order to be effective the grooves cut on the inside of the barrel must be of a consistent depth and width, and need to be accurately spaced around the circum-

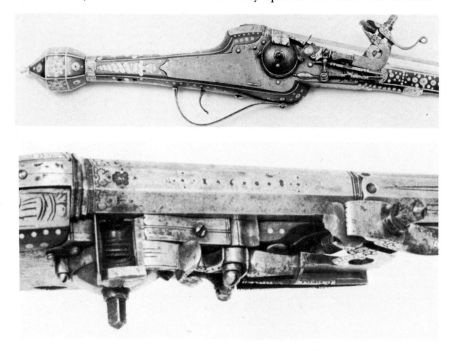

Left:
This wheel-lock carbine, which was probably made in Dresden between 1600 and 1608, has a straight, inlaid stock with a small ball pommel.

Left:
Detail of the lock showing the pan cover open and the grooved wheel against which the pyrites rubbed. Peter Dale, Esq.

Below
French wheel-lock pistol with walnut stock with some silver decoration. The lock is the French style with the mainspring fitted inside the stock and not on the lock plate. Overall length 22$\frac{2}{5}$ inches (56·9 cm). About 1615. Wallace Collection, London.

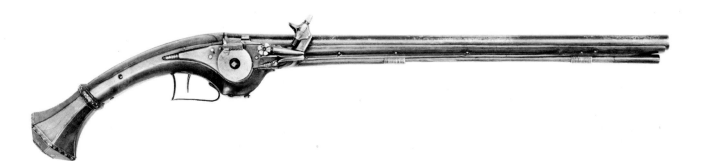

The butt of a wheel-lock rifle made by Christoph Dressler of Dresden and dated 1602. The patch-box cover carries an engraved illustration showing a hunter firing the wheel-lock from the cheek.

ference. These requirements involved a degree of mechanical skill beyond the ability of many craftsmen and even those who possessed the ability often did not have the facilities to carry it out on a large scale. Consequently in the sixteenth century – indeed until the mid-nineteenth century – rifles were rather a luxury.

In the sixteenth and seventeenth centuries the skill of the barrel-maker producing rifles was at a premium and the price was high. However cost did not deter the nobility and rich merchants and they demanded these latest weapons. The rifle barrels were usually substantial with very thick walls, for there was an advantage in having a heavy barrel. The rifling was often multi-groove, with far more grooves than many of the later rifles.

The wheel-lock owner wanted a weapon which was not only accurate but also impressive and spectacular, a weapon which was not only effective but also good to look at. The decorative quality of some of the wheel-locks of the sixteenth and seventeenth centuries is quite outstanding. Inlay of ivory, horn and mother of pearl was used to embellish the plain surfaces of the stock. The inlay could be fairly simple, with lines and volutes, or it could be far more elaborate, with hunting scenes, classical motifs, military trophies or, in the case of titled owners, their coats of arms and perhaps their initials. On later models the stock itself is quite frequently carved as well as inlaid.

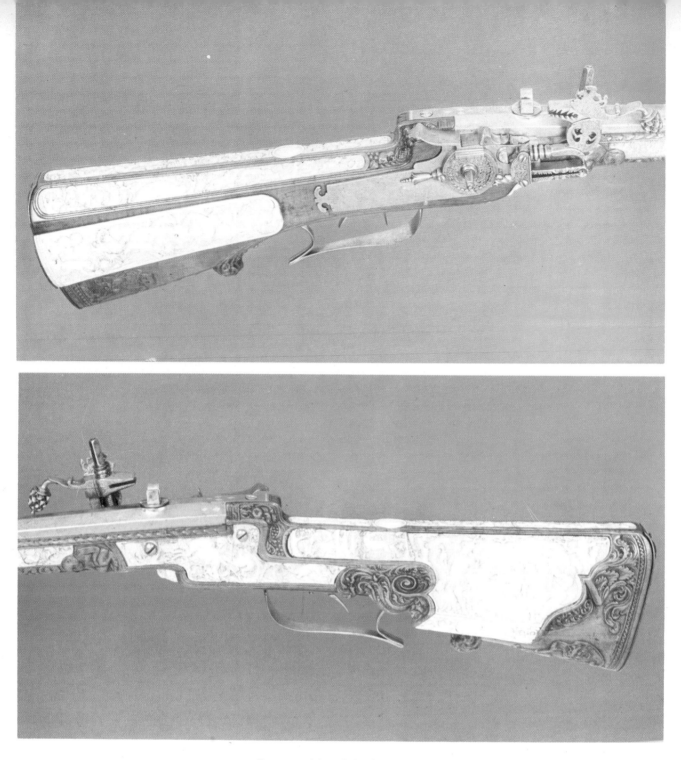

Top and above:
Wheel-lock rifle seen from both sides
The stock of pearwood was shaped
by Johann Michael Maucher and
inlaid with ivory plaques carved with
the stories of Diana and other
classical themes. South Germany.
About 1680. Victoria and Albert
Museum, London.

On one side of the butt there is often a patch-box for holding the waxed pieces of cloth which were wrapped around the bullet before it was rammed home to bite tightly into the rifling. The lids of these patch-boxes were themselves a favourite surface for decoration and are sometimes of solid horn or inlaid with the various materials in use. Not only the stock was decorated but later weapons were carved and chiselled on the barrel, on the lock-plate and any other metal surface.

One obvious feature of the German hunting rifle is the apparent lack of a butt. The stock, usually substantial, ended in a rather truncated, square-cut section, which is obviously quite unsuitable to be held against the shoulder. The majority of wheel-locks were designed to be held with the butt pressed against the cheek, not the shoulder. Although this might appear a rather hazardous process the very heavy barrel absorbed the recoil, so that the danger of a blow in the face was small.

Many of these hunting rifles will be found to have two triggers. One is often very thin and almost wirelike while the other is the conventionally shaped trigger. The accuracy of a shot must be affected by any movement of the weapon at the moment of firing, and excessive pressure on the trigger could move the rifle very slightly just as it was fired. To overcome this problem the gunmaker produced a hair trigger. An ingenious system of levers and springs could be set by means of this second trigger, so that only the lightest pressure was needed to operate the lock.

Early examples of wheel-lock rifles are frequently to be found with the wheel mounted on the outside of a very plain lock-plate. As the skill of the gunmaker increased during the seventeenth century the typical style of the period changed. Most of the mechanism was then mounted on the inside of the lock-plate and the surface became very flat and devoid of any protuberances, so offering ample scope for the attention of the steel chiseller.

During the seventeenth century one particularly delicate and graceful form of wheel-lock rifle was produced in the area around Teschen in northern Bohemia. The Polish form of the name became attached to these rifles and they are known as Tschinkes. They are easily recognizable by their peculiar form of lock. The mainspring is not fitted inside the stock but hangs from the base of the external lock-plate. This method of construction was adopted because it enabled the stock to be made very light and slim, and this particular form of rifle was much favoured by huntsmen whose prime quarry was birds.

At this time most shooting was at sitting birds and as they could not be driven it meant that the hunter had to stalk his prey. The heavy rifle favoured by the Austrians and Germans would have been rather unsuitable, and the hunter naturally preferred the much lighter Tschinke. Most Tschinkes are rather well decorated, with walnut stocks inlaid with stag horn and mother-of-pearl, and they frequently have the lock and trigger guard embellished with chiselling and carving. Sometimes the metalwork is also gilded.

A light hunting wheel-lock of the type known as a Tschinke and made during the second half of the seventeenth century. The stock is decorated with inlay and there is a peep-sight fitted above the breech. Royal Scottish Museum, Edinburgh.

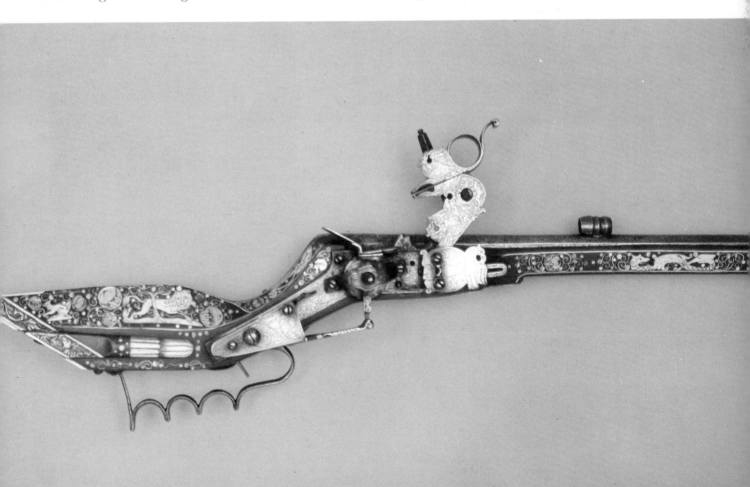

Left. Tschinke, with walnut stock inlaid with mother of pearl and stag's horn. Overall length 50½ inches (128·3 cm). About 1630.
Centre. Similar weapon with an overall length of 47·7 inches (121·2 cm).
Right. Light German wheel-lock rifle. Overall length 36·7 inches (93·2 cm). About 1600. Wallace Collection, London.

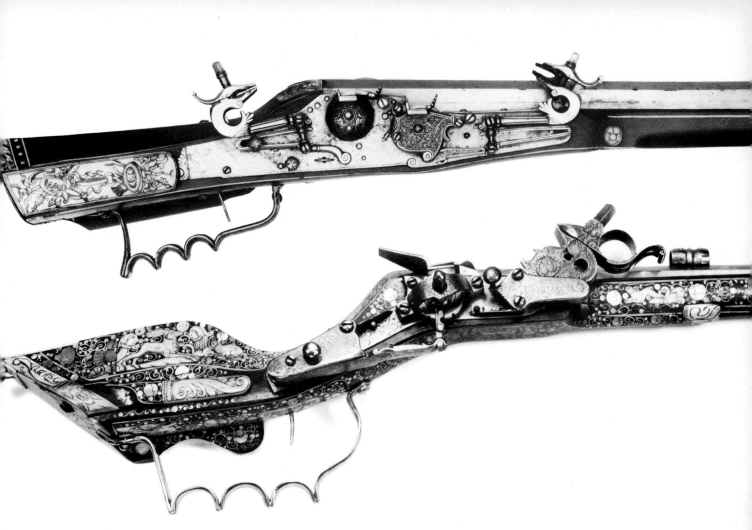

Top:
Superimposed load wheel-lock with two wheels mounted on a single lock plate. The forward lock was operated first and then the rear one. The barrel was double-loaded in such a way that the two shots could be fired independently.

Above:
Butt and lock of a Tschinke made in Silesia during the second quarter of the seventeenth century. The walnut stock is inlaid with mother-of-pearl scroll work. It has a rear sight mounted above the breech.

It will be remembered that in order to prepare the wheel-lock for firing the wheel had to be rotated and the spring put under pressure. This action, known as spanning the lock, could only be done with an appropriate key to fit over the spindle of the wheel. The spanner was itself frequently an example of the metalworker's craft and often served a double function, being also used as a powder measure. The weapon was vulnerable: the loss of the spanner meant that it could not be used, and a few locks were produced which were self-spanning. This was achieved in a variety of ways, the most usual being that the pulling forward of the cock or dog's head to the firing position over the pan activated a series of gears and levers on the inside of the lock to span the mechanism.

Wheel-lock rifles were not only used for hunting. From the sixteenth century onwards it was a popular pastime to shoot on a range. It is a comment on the accuracy of the weapons that in many cases any hit on the target was valid and rated the same no matter how near or far it was from the centre. Most of the targets were plain boards, usually between thirty and forty inches in diameter, although in the latter part of the eighteenth century it became the fashion to use targets painted as a whole range of subjects.

The idea of a special target was, however, not new, and there is a full written account of the range of Archduke Ferdinand of Tyrol (1529–97). The account includes engravings showing a life-sized model of a rider which apparently moved backwards and forwards between two huts at the end of the range. The contestants were awarded the article on the target hit by their shot. A hit on the sword by the Emperor Rudolph won him a rapier and dagger, and the chamberlain of Archduke Ferdinand won the horse.

Seventeenth-century wheel-lock hunting rifle with typical trigger guard and hair trigger. The lock plate and cover over the wheel are gilt and the stock is carved with hunting scenes and volutes. Bayerisches Nationalmuseum, Munich.

German powder flask dating from the middle of the seventeenth century. Its decoration is similar in style and fashion to that used on the wheel-lock rifles. Victoria and Albert Museum, London.

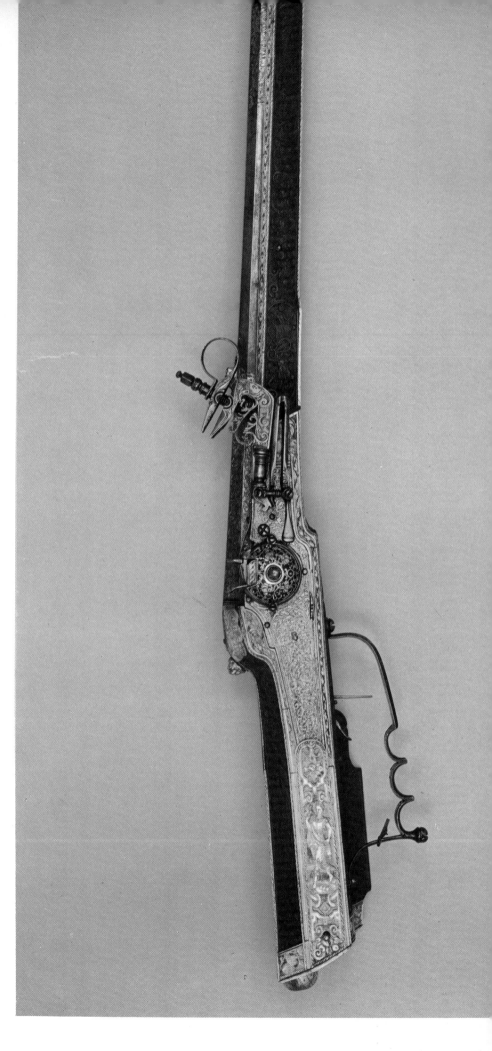

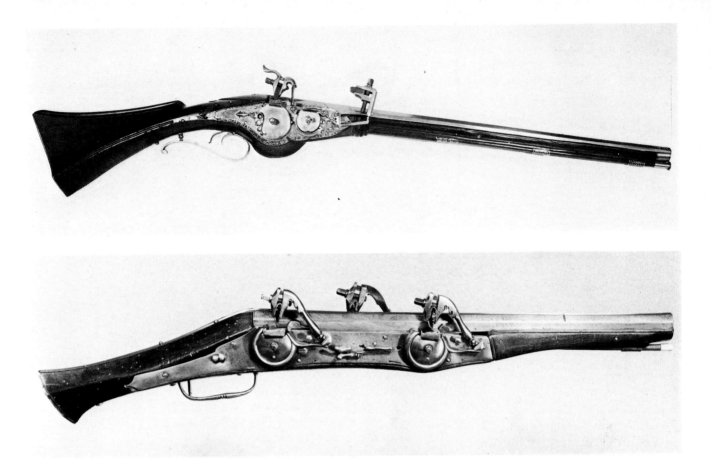

More elaborate targets than this were used. One castle at Lysice in Moravia had at the end of a 600-foot range two targets, and between was a large wooden model of a castle. If the centre of the targets was hit this activated a mechanism which opened the gate and a model of a beautiful girl carrying a bunch of flowers appeared. If the contestant missed a devil appeared instead.

The records of some of these ranges go back to the beginning of the sixteenth century and indeed one of the earliest known references to a wheel-lock occurs in the rules and regulations of just such a range. Frequently they were situated in castle moats, now disused, where the depth offered some safety against accidental hits beyond the confines of the range.

Most of the ranges conformed to a basic pattern. They were usually about 500 feet long and 300 to 500 feet wide, with five or six shooting bays all sheltered by a wooden roof. Behind the targets was a 16-foot-high wall. Many of these ranges are to be found even today, scattered over Germany, Austria and Czechoslovakia.

The fine decoration of the wheel-lock rifle is also to be found on the wheel-lock pistols. The earliest evidence for the existence of pistols is probably an order from the Emperor Maximilian dated 1518. It mentions guns carried secretly under clothing and there is also a reference to guns that ignite themselves, which would argue that some form of pistol was available at this date.

References to them begin to increase from 1530 onwards as pistols became more common. The origin of the word 'pistol' has exercised the imagination of experts, with suggestions ranging from the Italian word for pipe or whistle to the connection with the town of Pistoia in Italy. On balance it is likely that the name came from the town, although the word does not seem to have been used much until late in the sixteenth century. Before this pistols were generally referred to as small arquebusses, although in England they were frequently known as dags.

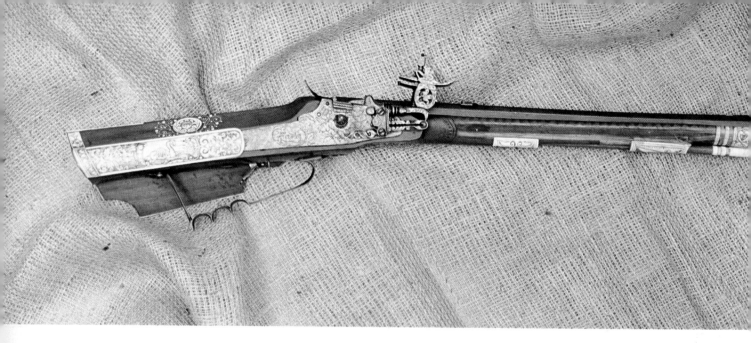

Wheel-lock carbine or pistol with straight walnut stock and some inlaid staghorn decoration. Dated 1680. It was made in Germany by Peter Pock. Victoria and Albert Museum, London.

Despite the almost certain derivation of the name from an Italian source, it was Germany that dominated in the production of pistols, particularly the towns of Augsburg and Nuremberg. Some of the earlier examples of the 1540s were small versions of the arquebus or wheel-lock rifle, even down to the flattened butt. By the middle of the century the majority still had a fairly straight stock, but they were more slender and more elegant, with a rather sword-like pommel at the end of the butt. In Germany the popular form of pistol was known as a 'puffer' and is easily recognized by the acutely-angled, straight butt terminating in a large ball shape. It has often been suggested in the past that the object of this was to enable the owner to use the empty weapon as a club. This is extremely unlikely for two reasons. The heavy metal barrel would have made a much more effective bludgeon. Moreover, the large ball-shaped terminal was normally quite flimsy in structure and often beautifully decorated – hardly an encouragement to hit somebody on the head with it!

The true purpose of these large balls was almost certainly to provide an easy grip when drawing the pistol from the holster, where it was normally carried at the pommel of the saddle. Not all pistols, however, were carried in holsters and a number of small versions are fitted with a belt hook which is a bar standing clear but running parallel with the side of the stock. This could be slipped over a belt allowing the pistol to hang ready to hand.

During the seventeenth century when the construction of the lock had been simplified and greater skill was available, a number of very workmanlike wheel-lock pistols with plain wooden stocks and simple locks were produced for military purposes. They were particularly popular in northern Europe and were used in the English Civil Wars and the Swedish Wars.

The wheel-lock mechanism represented a great step forward but it was limited because of its high cost and complexity of construction. For the wealthy patron its decorative features outweighed any limitations and, although for military purposes the wheel-lock was largely superseded by the middle of the seventeenth century, hunters continued to order their highly decorative wheel-lock rifles well into the eighteenth century. Examples dating from the 1730s are known but possibly the very latest wheel-locks are a pair of pistols made in 1829 by the famous gunmaker, Le Page, of Paris. They are a superbly engineered piece of craftsmanship, but the reason why they were made or who owned them is not known.

52

Brown Bess

The English are not a military race despite some apparent evidence to the contrary. The standing army dates from 1660 and was created only in the face of strong opposition from many influential people of the period. The British had suffered the effects of civil wars from 1642 to 1649 and the experience had not been pleasant. After that Oliver Cromwell's Major-Generals had ruled England almost as a series of small police states, and this had reinforced the strongly anti-military attitude of the people. In 1697, some thirty years after the army had been officially founded, John Trenchard wrote a pamphlet setting out his reasons for believing that 'A Standing Army is Inconsistent with a Free Government and Absolutely Destructive to the Constitution of the English Monarchy'. His was not a lone voice; many others felt the same.

England had had no army as such, apart from volunteers, until 1645 when Cromwell's New Model Army was created. Before this time the country's military might had consisted of the Trained Bands, which had been established in 1573. These were composed of some 100,000 men, who were called up for training in the use of military arms and military drill. In 1641 Parliament had debated a Militia Bill and many members had argued strongly that the king should not be given command, but that Parliament itself should exercise control over the military forces of the crown.

Then came the Civil War and the whole situation changed. In 1645 a Self-Denying Ordinance was adopted by Parliament, which effectively debarred members of the House of Commons and the House of Lords from holding any 'command military or civil granted or conferred by both or either of the Houses'. This meant that the army would have to find a whole new group of officers to command the New Model Army, which was being built up by pressing large numbers of men to join existing regiments.

The cavalry was the more popular arm. Men gladly volunteered for service and received 'back, breast, head piece, pistols, holsters and a considerable advance'. There were eleven regiments of horse (some 6,600 men) and one regiment of dragoons, who were really mounted infantry, riding to battle but fighting on foot. There were twelve regiments of foot–14,400 men made up of pikemen and musketeers. The pikemen carried a 16-foot pike which some shortened to reduce the weight–quite contrary to orders, of course. They also carried a sword, which General George

Engraving from the *Instruction of the Principles and Foundations of Cavalry* by J. J. de Wallhausen, written early in the seventeenth century. Cavalry, arquebusiers and mounted infantry or dragoons are shown.

Monck, a seasoned commander, suggested should be a rapier (tuck) for if they had cutting swords half would be broken 'with cutting of boughs'.

The musketeer had his matchlock musket with all its inherent faults and attendant risks. Contemporary memoirs mention occasions when a spark from one musket fired an unprepared companions weapon. Even more disastrous were the times when a spark set off a bandolier! These accounts also carry many references to the inaccuracy of the muskets. General Monck proposed that six men from each company be armed with the much more accurate 'birding piece' to pick off enemy officers. Some military writers offered suggestions as to how the efficiency of the weapon could be improved and in 1637 William Bariffe suggested a 'half-pike' combined with the musket but, despite some enthusiastic comments, it was never adopted.

Right:
Snaphaunce musket from the
Cabinet d'Armes of Louis XIII and
numbered 138 in his inventory. The
patch-box lid has been removed to
show the retaining clip. This weapon
was sent to England on the orders of
the Duke of Wellington in 1816.
Victoria and Albert Museum, London.

Below:
The lock of the above showing the
separate steel and priming cover
typical of these weapons. Victoria
and Albert Museum, London.

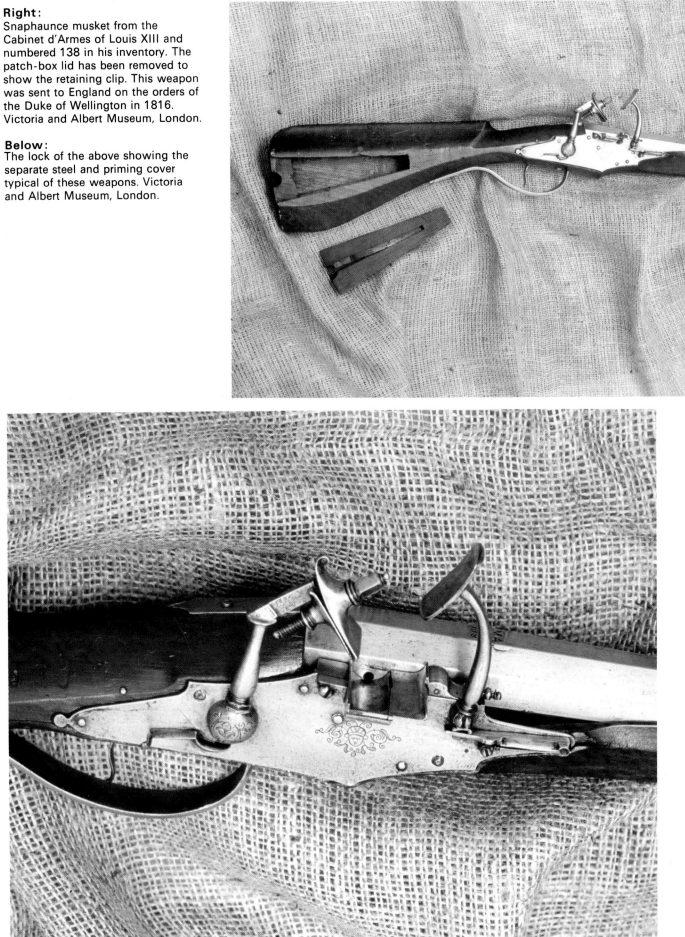

Charles II, during whose reign the British army was formed. National Portrait Gallery, London.

The soldiers of the New Model Army were trained to fire in three ranks, the front rank kneeling, the second leaning forward in a kind of stoop, and the rear rank standing. At one period each rank fired in turn, but it was the general opinion that a massed volley of all ranks was far more effective.

The Self-Denying Ordinance meant that the officers of Cromwell's army were selected purely for ability and not because of their social background. This was viewed with some suspicion at the time, for it was felt that, lacking the aristocratic tradition, some of these officers could not be relied on to act in a normal, civilized manner. However, the majority of the members of the New Model Army were filled with a 'godly spirit' and viewed their job almost in the light of a holy task. Numerous tracts and pamphlets appeared arguing the pros and cons of a standing army, but it was not until the Restoration in 1660 that any further effective action was taken.

One of the first tasks of the Restoration government was to disband the army, since it represented a constant danger. The Disbanding Act of September 1660 laid down that Cromwell's army had to be dispersed, but it did allow King Charles II to raise as many soldiers as he required providing he paid them, and that they were primarily intended as a guard for the king. Some urgency was given to the question of the king's forces when, in January 1661, there was a minor but frightening revolt against Charles. It was led by Thomas Venner, a London wine cooper and religious fanatic. His supporters, calling themselves Fifth Monarchy

56

Men, marched through London, causing a great deal of disturbance, although there were only about thirty of them. They spent some time on the outskirts of London and then stormed back into the city. They were confronted by some of General Monck's guards and, at the end of a brief, confused fight, they were either killed or captured. This pathetic rebellion stirred fears that had lain dormant and it was felt by many in authority that the disbanding of Cromwell's army should be either halted or at least slowed down for fear of further rebellions. A compromise was reached and, with the king's approval, on February 14th, 1661, Monck's regiment of foot and horse marched to Tower Hill. There they paraded and laid down their arms, so officially carrying out the policy of disbanding Cromwell's army. They then immediately took them up again, this time not as Cromwell's men but as the Lord General's Regiment of Foot Guards, better known as the Coldstream Guards. Their prime duty was to serve as guards for the king.

Although the army had tacit approval it did not really become constitutional until 1689 when the Declaration of Rights in effect authorized the king to maintain an army but only with the approval of Parliament. It also stated that henceforth there would be no billeting of troops on private citizens—a change which was welcomed by the people as a whole. In 1689 the first Mutiny Act was passed by Parliament, which really only created a martial, as opposed to civil, code of laws. However, the acceptance of the need for a law for the army in effect gave the army a legal and constitutional existence approved by Parliament.

Britain's new standing army was equipped with the old matchlock musket and the musketeer still carried his bandolier. However, by the last quarter of the century a considerable number of the matchlocks were being withdrawn and replaced by newer weapons. The matchlocks were used to equip units considered as second-line forces, and numbers went to the colonies such as Virginia, where they were received with a certain amount of grumbling and complaints.

Two views of a flintlock carbine bearing the cypher of James II and made by Brooke. The weapon has the slightly heavy look common to seventeenth-century flintlocks.

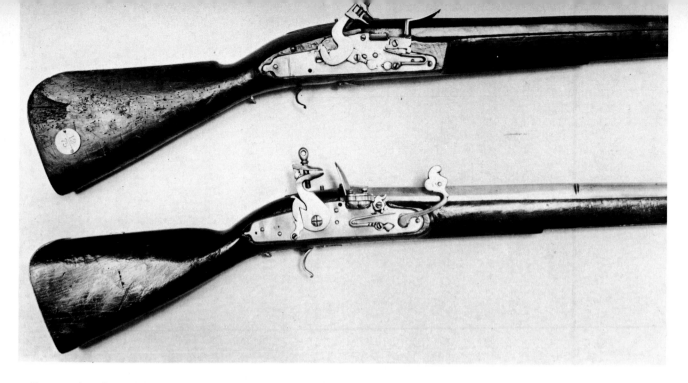

It was in the 1720s that the British army acquired what has
become probably the best known of all eighteenth-century
military weapons—the Brown Bess. The name has provided a point
of discussion. Some argue that Bess is a corruption of *Busche*, the
German word for gun, others that it is an affectionate nickname.
Some claim that the 'brown' applies to the barrel, others that it
applies to the stock. Whatever the origins of the name may have
been, the weapon was not referred to by this title for some considerable time. The earliest reference so far traced appears in
1785, over fifty years after it had been introduced into service.
The earliest dated examples of Brown Bess carry dates between
1725 and 1730.

The first type of Brown Bess was known officially as the Long
Land Musket. It was a pretty substantial weapon, although not
quite as heavy or as awkward as the old matchlock musket. It
was fitted with a barrel forty-six inches long, only two inches
shorter than the old matchlock musket, and fired a ball ·75 inches
in diameter. The stock was almost invariably of walnut and extended the length of the barrel to within four inches of the muzzle.
The stock at the muzzle end was fitted with a brass cover to prevent the wood splitting. The ramrod was housed in a channel cut
into the stock beneath the barrel.

Spaced along the length of the ramrod slot were four pipes of
brass, with a trumpet-shaped one at the muzzle end, which was
usually longer than the other three. The one nearest the breech end
had a long tail which was let into the stock. On the early Brown
Besses the ramrod was of wood, but all the Long Land models were
fitted with steel ramrods by the middle of the eighteenth century.

Steel ramrods are first mentioned in 1724, but their general
adoption came only gradually. They were preferable since they
were far less liable to breakage and could be used much more
vigorously if the ball proved to be a very tight fit. Trigger guards,
ramrod pipes, nose caps and butt plates, known collectively as the
furniture, were originally of iron, but from the mid-1720s there
was a gradual change over to brass. By the late 1730s brass was the
invariable rule.

The biggest difference between the old military matchlock
musket and the new Brown Bess was in the method of ignition.
Most of the troubles which had plagued the matchlock had been
overcome by the more complex wheel-lock, but expense had

prevented wholesale production of this much superior lock. However, the use of a mechanical means to provide ignition (as opposed to actual fire itself) had been established, and the gunsmiths of Europe had turned their attention to the new idea. Struck against a piece of steel, flint would produce incandescent sparks, and it was this combination that the gunsmiths developed. Moreover, flint could be found over the greater part of Europe in reasonable quantities.

The lock fitted to the Brown Bess was the commonest form of the so-called flintlock which used this principle. It was basically a French-designed lock and its creation has been credited with a fair degree of certainty to Marin Le Bourgeoys, a royal gunmaker working in Paris. The earliest known-example of the 'French lock' or flintlock dates from around 1610. Le Bourgeoys was not the inventor of the flintlock, for its principle had been known for many years before he produced his famous lock. He was, nevertheless, an innovator in that he took several of its features and put them together to produce a simple, efficient, hard-wearing and reliable mechanism, which would, with a fair degree of certainty, produce sparks when activated.

Mechanisms using the principle of striking flint against steel had been in use as early as the middle of the sixteenth century. These mechanisms had a long metal arm, rather like the dog's head of the wheel-lock, which held a shaped piece of flint, or in the earlier models, a piece of pyrites. This was gripped between two jaws which could be tightened by means of a screw traversing both jaws. Above the priming pan was attached a small, vertical steel plate, which was in turn fitted at the end of a pivoted arm. These weapons were loaded and primed in the normal fashion, and then the arm with the steel plate was swung forward so that the plate stood vertically above the priming powder. When the trigger was pressed the long cock, or arm, swung forward and scraped the flint down the face of the metal plate. At the same time as the incandescent sparks fell into the pan to fire the charge, the steel plate at the end of the pivoted arm was pushed clear. The pan cover was designed to swing out sideways and, like the matchlock, had to be operated manually.

The earliest recorded appearances of this type of lock were in Sweden in 1547, Norway in 1562, and Denmark in 1565, but it was probably first developed by the German gunmakers. The power to operate the mechanism was provided by a mainspring fitted to the outside of the lock plate. The cock, the arm holding the flint, had a forward projecting 'toe', which pressed down on the spring. When this was fully compressed at the full cock position, a small arm, the sear, which passed through the lock plate from the inside, engaged with the 'heel' of the cock. This sear was withdrawn when the trigger was pressed and the cock released. The mechanism, usually called the Baltic lock, was fitted to many weapons all over Europe, and remained popular until the eighteenth century.

The Baltic lock was only one of a group known as snaphaunces. The name is usually thought to be derived from two Dutch words meaning 'snapping hen'—from the pecking movement of the cock. Variations on this particular type of lock were developed. In Italy the style remained popular long after the rest of Europe's gunmakers had abandoned it and examples from early in the nineteenth century are found. In Spain another variation, known today as the Miquelet lock, also remained in use until well into the nineteenth century.

In northern Europe, perhaps as early as 1570, an improved form evolved, which incorporated a mechanically operated pan

Blunderbuss of the late seventeenth century with a brass barrel which widens towards the muzzle. The wide muzzle was thought to spread the shot but, in fact, had little real effect. Overall length 30¼ inches (76·8 cm).

cover. An internal lever ensured that as the cock fell forward the pan cover was automatically pushed clear—an obvious improvement. This type, usually known as the Dutch style, had the pan set in a rather deep, square compartment which, at one end, had a large circular disc. The steel was fitted on an angular arm, and the cock itself was large and similarly angular. It is an interesting, if inexplicable fact that, although the Dutch snaphaunce was abandoned in Europe during the seventeenth century, in Africa it remained in use until the nineteenth century. The trade guns which were exported in quantity from Belgium to Africa were fitted with the lock. The only distinction between original seventeenth-century guns and the later models lies in the quality and craftsmanship.

The basic concept of the snaphaunce was simple and had advantages over the wheel-lock, but one great weakness lay in the design of the pan cover. Without the cover the priming was at the mercy of wind and rain, but the closed pan cover represented a potential drawback. If the linking arm broke or if the firer forgot to remove the pan cover, the sparks struck by flint on steel fell on to the pan cover and did not discharge the weapon. What was required was some foolproof system of opening the pan cover at the same time as sparks were struck. The gloriously simple solution was to combine pan cover and steel into one L-shaped piece. This had been done in Italy as early as 1580, but it was not until the latter part of the seventeenth century that it became fairly common practice.

This L-shaped steel, usually called the frizzen by present-day collectors, was hinged at the rear of the pan and was held closed by a spring. The action was simple and foolproof since, as the cock swung forward and struck sparks from the upright steel face, the impact pushed the steel back, automatically exposing the priming in the pan. In this way there was virtually no danger of mechanical breakage or forgetfulness preventing the pan cover from being opened.

This type of flintlock was far simpler in construction and operation than any previous form of ignition. However, in its early days it had suffered from one great disadvantage. With both the wheel-lock and the snaphaunce it was safe to carry the weapon loaded and primed. If the dog's head on a wheel-lock was pulled back, there was no possibility of accidental discharge. In the case of the snaphaunce, if the steel was raised the same principle applied. However, with the flintlock, once the pan had been primed and the steel (or frizzen) closed, the weapon was potentially fireable. In order to raise sparks the cock needed to swing forward and strike against the steel. This meant that when the weapon was primed and the steel had been closed the cock had to be pulled back or else the flint fouled the steel and prevented its closure. With the cock pulled back it was obviously potentially dangerous, because any jarring or accidental touch of the trigger could discharge the firearm.

One of the earliest methods of overcoming this problem had been to cut in the rear of the cock a V-shaped notch and to secure to the lock plate behind the cock a small hook, the point of which could be engaged with the notch. This so-called dog-catch would hold the cock safely in a midway position. To fire the weapon all that was needed was to pull the cock back to the firing position, which would automatically disengage the dog-catch. The internal mechanism was similar to that of the wheel-lock, with a large V-spring to provide power and a sear operating through the lock plate to hold the cock in position.

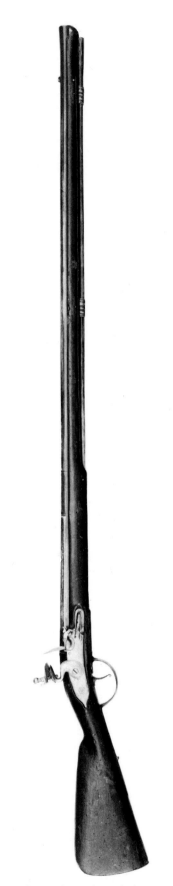

English flintlock musket of about 1690 with 'chunky' style butt and wooden ramrod. A plug bayonet would have been used with this weapon. Tower of London Armouries.

Bayonets were not restricted to military muskets and blunderbusses. Some pocket pistols were fitted with them. This brass-barrelled flintlock of about 1780 by Twigg, a London gunmaker, has a short, triangular bayonet fitted under the barrel. It is released by pressing back the trigger guard. Private Collection.

About 1610 Marin Le Bourgeoys, who has been mentioned earlier, introduced a new, simpler system. The cock was secured to a spindle which passed through the lock plate where it ended in a tumbler which was basically a fairly thick metal disc. Into the edge of this tumbler two slots were cut and, as the cock was pulled back, the toe of the tumbler compressed the mainspring. At the same time another sear, situated on the inside of the lock plate and pressed down by a spring, slid along the face of the tumbler and locked the movement. Pressure on the trigger would not move the sear in this position (known as half-cock) and consequently the weapon was safe. If the cock was pulled back further the sear disengaged and continued to ride over the edge of the tumbler until it engaged with the second notch. In this, the full-cock position, the trigger would remove the sear and so allow the cock, impelled by the spring, to fly forward and strike sparks from the steel. This was the effective French lock but, despite its simplicity, it was not immediately popular. Its use spread slowly until by the second and third quarters of the seventeenth century it had become fairly generally accepted.

During the seventeenth century the old matchlock was gradually replaced by these new types of lock, but it is not always clear which type is meant, for all were referred to indifferently as firelocks, shaphaunces, or fuzees. Available evidence suggests that the snaphaunce was the gun with the combined steel and pan. There is no doubt, however, about Brown Bess, which had the normal French-style flintlock. The rather graceful, almost banana-shaped lock plate was slightly rounded in section, unlike

Early flintlock musket with a stock of the typical wheel-lock form, but the dog-lock suggests a date around 1650–60. It has a little inlaid decoration. Tower of London Armouries.

Far left. Flints—large for a musket, very small for a pocket pistol.
Centre. Nipple from percussion revolver and percussion caps.
Left. Conversion block for changing from flintlock to percussion fitted with a nipple. This was secured into an enlarged touch-hole and the end block was then removed.

earlier plates which were mostly flat. The cock was of the elegant, goose-neck variety, with two jaws secured by a screw which passed through both. The lock plate was fastened by two screws which passed through from the other side of the stock. This was given a little extra strength by means of a curved, rather serpentine, brass or iron side plate. Behind the cock the lock plate was engraved with the word 'Tower' or the name of the manufacturer and the date of production—a practice which, unfortunately for collectors, was stopped in 1764.

To indicate that the weapon was an official issue the lock plate was engraved with a crown and royal cypher, and with the traditional government ownership mark of a broad arrow. The broad arrow had been in use since at least the fourteenth century, although it does not seem to have been commonly engraved on arms before the reign of Queen Anne. The cypher varied with the monarch: G. R. for George, W. R. for William, V. R. for Victoria, and E. R. for Edward.

Weapon production, a rather involved operation, was under the control of a government body known as the Board of Ordnance. Previously it had been for the officer commanding the regiment, a colonel, to purchase weapons for his own unit. It was decided that this system was open to abuse and could also lead to problems in that different regiments might well have different-calibre weapons. It was, therefore, decided in 1715 that in future locks and barrels would be purchased in quantity from gunmakers who worked mainly in Birmingham and London. The barrels would be kept in store and then, as required, handed over to contractors,

Blunderbuss pistol with brass barrel and spring-operated bayonet— patented by J. Waters in 1781. Overall length 12½ inches (31·8 cm). Barrel 7½ inches (19 cm). Bayonet 6 inches (15·2 cm).

usually the London gunsmiths, to be stocked, finished, and put together as a complete weapon. This system offered a number of advantages since supplies could be held in reserve. Consequently there was no problem of delivery when weapons were urgently required and suppliers could not, as in the past, raise their prices at a time of great demand.

The barrels and locks, which came from Birmingham, were accepted only after they had been examined and approved by government inspectors. If satisfactory they were then forwarded to London. This work was under the control of the Ordnance Office, which had its headquarters in the Tower of London. The man in charge was the Principal Storekeeper and one of his departments was the Small Gun Office, where his men were busily engaged in looking after and repairing arms and, if necessary, assembling them.

The barrels of the Brown Bess were proved by the Ordnance in the Tower. Proving was a system of testing a barrel, whereby it was loaded with an extra charge of powder and then fired. It was then examined for any signs of damage, wear, cracks or pinholes. If satisfactory the barrel was said to have been proved and it was stamped with the Ordnance view and proof marks. These varied over the years, but from the reign of Queen Anne (1702–14) they incorporated the Royal Cypher and the broad arrow, as well as crossed sceptres and a crown. These marks normally appeared at the breech of the barrel.

A noticeable feature of the Brown Bess was a square lug on top of the barrel, set back some two or three inches from the muzzle. This is frequently thought to have been a foresight but, in fact, it was primarily a means for attaching a bayonet. In order to accommodate this new weapon the wooden stock stopped short

some four inches from the muzzle. It will be recalled that one of the problems of the musketeer was his lack of protection against cavalry, particularly when his weapon was empty. Attempts to overcome this had been made by the use of a knife with a circular wooden grip which tapered towards the pommel. When threatened by cavalry, the musketeer could force the wooden grip of this knife into the muzzle of his empty weapon, so converting it into a kind of half pike some six or seven feet long.

The name bayonet is generally taken to be derived from the French town of Bayonne, noted for the production of hunting knives. The bayonet was apparently in use on the Continent around the middle of the seventeenth century, but the earliest reference in British records appears in 1663. The dagger-like weapon was known as a plug bayonet and was issued to most troops. The great disadvantage of this system was that once the bayonet had been placed in position the musket was useless as a firearm.

Obviously some steps had to be taken to overcome this deficiency, and there were experiments during the latter part of the seventeenth century to devise some alternative means of attachment. After several had been tried the one which proved the most satisfactory was the replacement of the wooden grip with a socket. The socket bayonet was composed of a metal cylinder just big enough to slip over the barrel. To the top of this cylinder was fixed a curved neck, and to this was attached a triangular blade some eighteen inches in length. The socket or cylinder was held in place by means of an angled Z-groove, which fitted over the lug on top of the barrel. When not in use, the bayonet was carried in a leather scabbard fitted to a shoulder belt. Socket bayonets are mentioned as far back as the 1680s, but they were not issued until the early part of the eighteenth century.

Top. Blunderbuss with brass barrel made by F. Smart, probably early in the eighteenth century. *Above*. A later brass-barrelled one with a spring-operated bayonet which snapped down into position on releasing a catch. Made in London by H. Mortimer, probably at the beginning of the nineteenth century. Private Collection.

The loading and firing sequence of the Brown Bess was simpler that that of the matchlock. One factor which had made things easier was the adoption of the cartridge. This was not a new idea: cartridges had been used by sportsmen as early as the sixteenth century, but they were not adopted for military use until the mid-seventeenth century, and did not become general until the eighteenth century. Cartridges were manufactured quite quickly, and at the time of the American Revolutionary War (1776–83) they were made from white or whitish-brown wrapping paper. The paper was made to a special shape, a rectangle six inches by five inches, with the top section cut off diagonally to within two inches of the base.

A wooden former, with one end slightly recessed to seat the ball, was laid on the bottom edge with a ball in place. The paper was rolled around the ball and the former, and the end with the ball in folded or twisted to hold it in place. A loop of twine or thread was then tied around the rolled cartridge to keep the ball in position. The former was withdrawn and a correct charge of powder, plus a little extra for priming, was poured in and the end twisted tight.

The soldiers of the British army and most Continental armies carried a supply of cartridges in a large leather case, frequently lined with tin, which was divided into a series of compartments, each holding a single cartridge. The cartridge case was suspended from another shoulder belt which crossed with that one supporting the infantryman's sword and bayonet.

The sequence of movements for loading the Brown Bess varied slightly but that given in 'New Manual Exercise as Performed by His Majesty's Dragoons, Foot Guards, Foot, Artillery, Marines and by the Militia' (third edition, 1760), is fairly typical. After firing the musket the commands were:

Open your pans.
Handle your Cartridge.
Open your cartridge.
Prime.
Shut your pan.
Load with cartridge.
Draw your rammer.
Ram down your cartridge.
Return your rammer.

The cartridge was opened by biting off the top and then covering the powder with the thumb. Some powder was shaken into the pan and then, with the cartridge still in the hand, the pan was closed. Powder, ball and cartridge paper were then put into the barrel and rammed home. The manual points out that there are only twelve words of command for the priming and loading part but, in fact, the number of movements is twenty-one. The Brown Bess suffered from a rather slow rate of fire, but this was somewhat minimized by the system of rank firing.

In a set-piece battle the troops formed three ranks, with the front one kneeling. This ensured that the maximum number of muskets were presented within a given length of line. Controlled fire by platoons, allowing time for other units to reload, enabled a fairly continuous volley of fire to be maintained. The British troops acquired a reputation for their steadiness under fire, and most battles of the period degenerated into slogging matches in which the side able to sustain the most casualties for the longest time before breaking was the winner.

Below:
Late eighteenth- or early nineteenth-century French flintlock with a brass pan. The frizzen is in the open position. The cock is of the ring-neck form.

Opposite, above:
Pair of fine quality flintlock holster pistols with gilt furniture. Made by Wilson of London, the barrels are decorated with gilt. Overall length 15 inches (38 cm). Barrel 9 inches (22·8 cm). Bore ·64 inches (16·3 mm). R. H. Thornton.

Opposite, below:
Seventeenth-century Scottish snaphaunce weapons. The pistol (below) is unusual in that it has a left-hand lock – a feature found on early Scottish weapons. It is dated 1619. The musket has nail decoration incorporating a thistle motif. Tower of London Armouries.

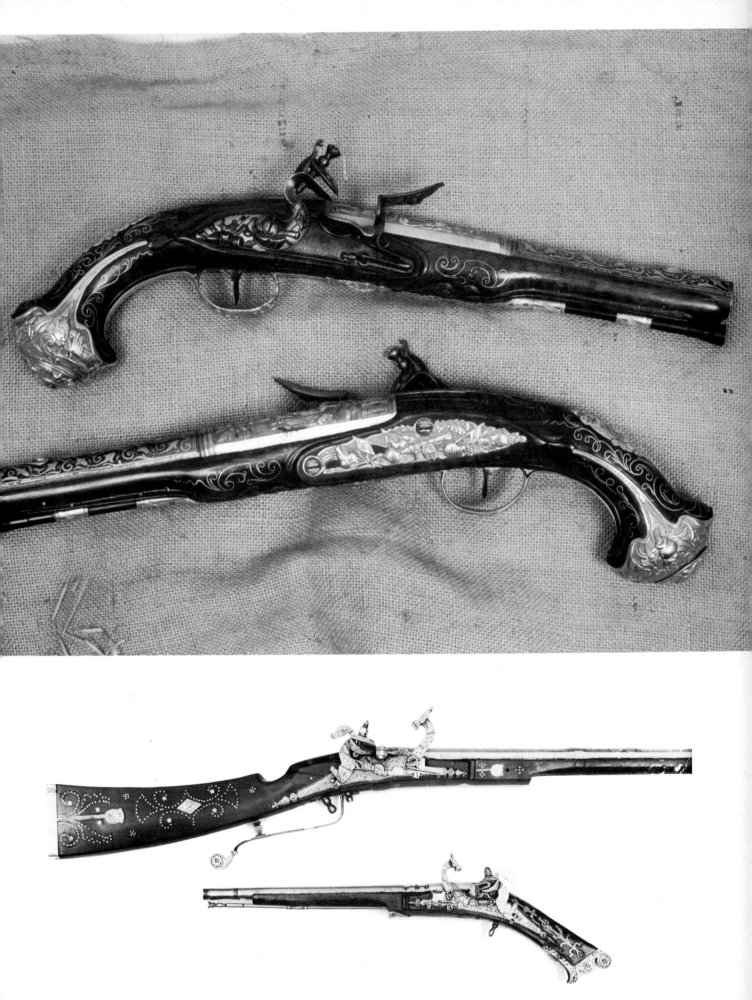

Right:

Top. Musket with a dog-lock and on it the cypher of Queen Anne. The butt is very heavy. Made by Richard Wooldridge and fitted with iron furniture.

Centre. Later version by Farmer and dated 1745. The catch has been discarded.

Bottom. Another later version by Galton.

Tower of London Armouries.

Below:

Seventeenth-century flintlock by Jean Paul Cleff. The shape is characteristic of the period and the engraved lock has a typical flat cock. Museo Stibbert, Florence.

At the famous battle of Quebec in 1759 General James Wolfe's troops held their fire until the French were nearly upon them. Then, with one or two volleys, they broke the attack and sent the French reeling back. The use of volley fire was in part necessitated by the inaccuracy of the Brown Bess, since the bullet leaving the muzzle was subject to a number of variables and accuracy consequently suffered. The bullet issued was a rolling ball and the difference in diameter between the ball and the internal measurement of the barrel was something in the region of one-twentieth of an inch. This gap was deliberate to ensure easy loading. As the gunpowder burned it left on the inside of the barrel a deposit known as fouling, which built up with continuous firing. Fouling reduced the internal diameter of the barrel, so that it would have become progressively more difficult to load a tight-fitting ball. Fouling also cut down the speed of loading. Although a well-trained soldier could probably get off a maximum of five rounds a minute, after a number of shots this number was reduced. With volleys, when it was necessary to wait for the slowest reloaders, the rate of fire was probably down to two or three volleys a minute. The spherical bullet, nearly three-quarters of an inch in diameter, was both heavy and large, and consequently lost velocity fairly quickly. By present day standards it was a very slow-moving bullet, something in the region of 1,000 to 1,300 feet a second, compared with around 2,000 feet a second for a modern service rifle.

On the march Brown Bess was carried at the slope over the left shoulder or by means of a sling, usually of buff leather, attached to two sling swivels, one on the front of the brass trigger guard and the other one along the stock near the forward ramrod pipe. The length of the sling could be adjusted and when marching at ease the musket could be slung across the shoulder.

The actions for priming a flintlock as illustrated in *Military Instruction* by David Roberts (1798).

Long Land Pattern musket with the 46-inch (116·8-cm) barrel. The lock bears the name Farmer and dates from about 1750. Tower of London Armouries.

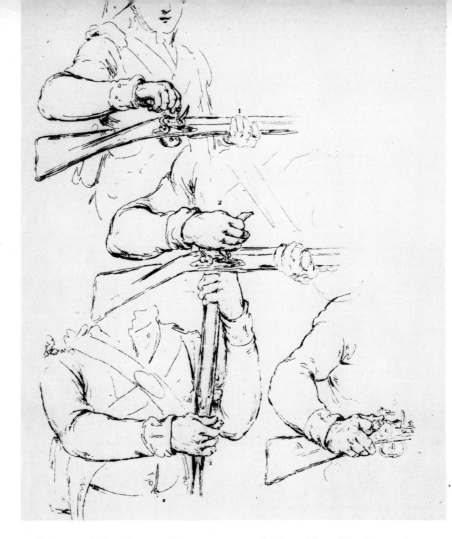

Many of the Brown Bess were marked to identify the regiment. In the British army the tradition was that the unit was generally known by the name of its colonel. In 1751 a Royal Warrant ordered colonels to cease putting their personal crest or coat of arms on items belonging to the regiment. Two years later they were ordered to use the regiment's number. Weapons marked prior to 1753 therefore carry the colonel's name, but after this date the regimental marking is either a number or an abbreviation of the title.

Barrels for the Long Land pattern, 46 inches in length, continued to be made until at least 1790, but in fact these were the last examples of what was then an old-fashioned weapon. By 1765 muskets held in government stores with 46-inch barrels which were wearing thin at the muzzle end were ordered to be cut down to 42 inches. In 1768 a Royal Warrant adopted a shorter musket with a 42-inch barrel as the standard weapon for British infantry. This model was known as the Short Land New Pattern. The idea was not a new one and, in fact, certain units in the British army had been using the shortened barrel for a considerable time.

The reduction of some four inches did not present any great problems. Existing Long Land Patterns were cut down and quite easily modified by having a new lug brazed on the barrel and the stock adapted at the muzzle end. Experiments had shown quite clearly that it was not essential to have 46 inches and that a musket of 42 inches performed equally well. Indeed, in experiments carried out by Major-General La Fausille barrels had been cut to a mere 20 inches and the effect on their range and capability was very limited.

The Short Land Pattern had been issued to dragoons, marines and militia, and had therefore been well tested. Thus the Ordnance Office and the government knew that they were not taking any

69

A box-lock flintlock pistol by
Ketland. This arrangement was
commonly used on pocket pistols,
since it has far fewer projections
than the usual pistol and was,
consequently, easier to draw from a
pocket without snagging. Private
Collection.

An engraving of the Tower of London
when it was the main British arms
depot and factory.

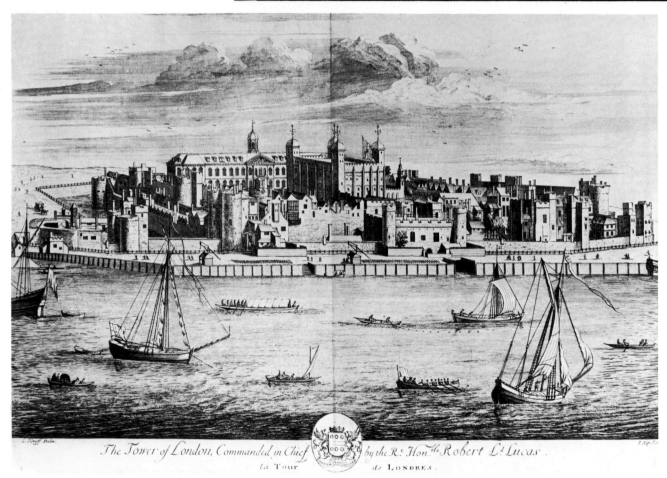

The Tower of London, Commanded in Chief by the R.t Hon.ble Robert L.d Lucas.
la Tour de LONDRES.

serious risks by changing to this shorter version. No doubt the
soldiers were quite delighted with the loss of some 4 inches of
musket barrel, which must have reduced its weight appreciably.
About the same time the infantry were also deprived of their
swords – yet another piece of largely useless equipment which they
had been obliged to carry around with them.

The Short Land Pattern closely resembled the earlier weapon,
although at least three variations of the model were issued. It
remained the principal arm of the British infantry until 1797,
when it was replaced with a new but very similar weapon. The
main reason for the alteration in pattern was essentially practical.
In 1793 France, in the throes of post-revolutionary enthusiasm,
declared war on Spain, Holland and Great Britain. Britain had
been at peace since 1783, when the Americans had achieved their
independence, and the demand for muskets had been met by the
normal means of supply. The average life of a musket had been
reckoned to be about ten to twelve years, so that replacements
could be amply supplied from stock.

When war came in 1793 there was a constantly growing demand
for new muskets. The British army was now fighting in many
parts of the world and was steadily increasing in numbers. There
was, moreover, a growing fear of a French invasion, which
stimulated the growth of militia and volunteer units, all of which
had to be armed. The Ordnance soon realized that the demand
was far outstripping supply and that unless some drastic action
was taken supplies would cease altogether. Efforts made to purchase
muskets from abroad met with little success and it was soon obvious
that Britain must depend on its own manufacturers.

71

13 Handle your Cartridge

14 Open your Cartridge

Military flintlock of James II's reign with brass fittings. The lock plate is engraved with the cypher of J.II.R. Overall length 21 inches (53·3 cm).

The Ordnance was not the only large-scale purchaser in the market for muskets. Almost by accident the East India Company had developed an empire of its own. Beginning in a small way in 1600, it had grown steadily. It had fought against the French for possession of India and now ruled much of the country in a semi-official capacity. The Company hired soldiers from the British government but also maintained a large standing army of its own. Soldiers protected its factories and trade routes, and, on occasions, mounted punitive expeditions against Indian princes who transgressed its rules or imperilled its profits.

The Company bought muskets ready-made from British gunmakers and it was realized by the government that they were a serious competitor in the purchase of firearms. In 1794 it was agreed, after various pressures, that the government could purchase the entire output of muskets made for the East India Company. The Company's warehouses were emptied. Muskets en route for the docks and even those loaded in ships were diverted to the Ordnance. By December of that year the Company had passed over nearly 32,000 muskets and carbines as well as over 1,300 pairs of pistols.

The India Pattern musket, as it was called, was generally a cheaper and less well made weapon than the Short Land Pattern. The biggest difference was in the length of the barrel. The New Land Model had been 46 inches, the Short Land Pattern 42 inches and now there was a further reduction to 39 inches. Although the basic shape of the musket was much the same as the Short Land Pattern there were minor differences. It had only three ramrod pipes instead of four and a different side plate, which held the lock screws, as well as other differences of construction. The walnut for the stocks was generally of a slightly inferior quality and the whole musket was accepted on a lower standard of viewing and proof. However it met an emergency and from 1793 until 1809 the India Pattern was produced in quantity to fill the gap.

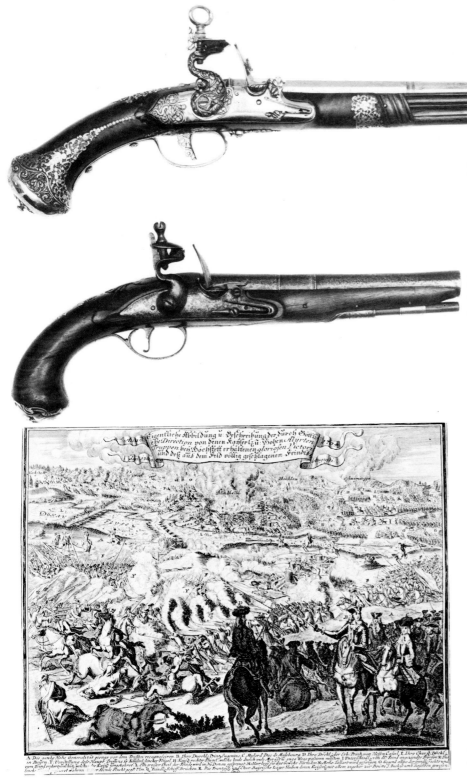

Above. Good-quality Italian flintlock holster pistol with the barrel signed 'Lazarino Cominazzo', a famous gunmaker. The steelwork is chiselled in the typical style of the craftsmen of Brescia. Overall length 20¼ inches (51·4 cm). About 1680.

Left. Belt flintlock pistol signed on the lock 'E. North' and on the barrel 'London'. The butt has a typical grotesque silver mask. Overall length 13 inches (33 cm). About 1740.

Below left:
In August 1704 the Duke of Marlborough gained a great victory over the French at the battle of Blenheim. The smoke from the muskets is clearly portrayed in this German print.

In 1809 the cock which held the flint was changed from the rather graceful goose-neck to a flatter, reinforced ring-type. Locks still carried much the same markings as on the earlier models, but the New India Pattern was also supplied to large numbers of volunteer units which sprang up all over Britain especially following the Peace of Amiens in 1802. These muskets are usually marked on the butt plate with identifying letters and numbers. India Pattern weapons are also to be found bearing the East India Company mark on the lock plate. The Company mark was a heart divided into quarters enclosing the letters 'E V I C' and surmounted by a figure 4 or a rampant lion holding a crown.

In the brief breathing space afforded by the Peace of Amiens the Board of Ordnance considered the whole problem of weapons for the British army. It was decided that a new pattern should be manufactured. This was basically the same as the Short Land Pattern, with a 42-inch barrel, but there were to be a number of changes in the construction. This New Land Pattern was a very plain weapon, which used many of the components found on the India Pattern. The side plate was very similar to the India Pattern, although it differed in having a wood screw through the centre to hold it permanently in place on the stock. There was also a change in the manner of attaching the barrel to the stock. The pin and lug method had been used on the earlier patterns of Brown Bess, but removing the pins could be a little awkward, and so, in place of the small pin, a flat bar-type fitting was used. This bar was far easier to remove, thus enabling an armourer to change barrels or mend stocks with a minimum of trouble.

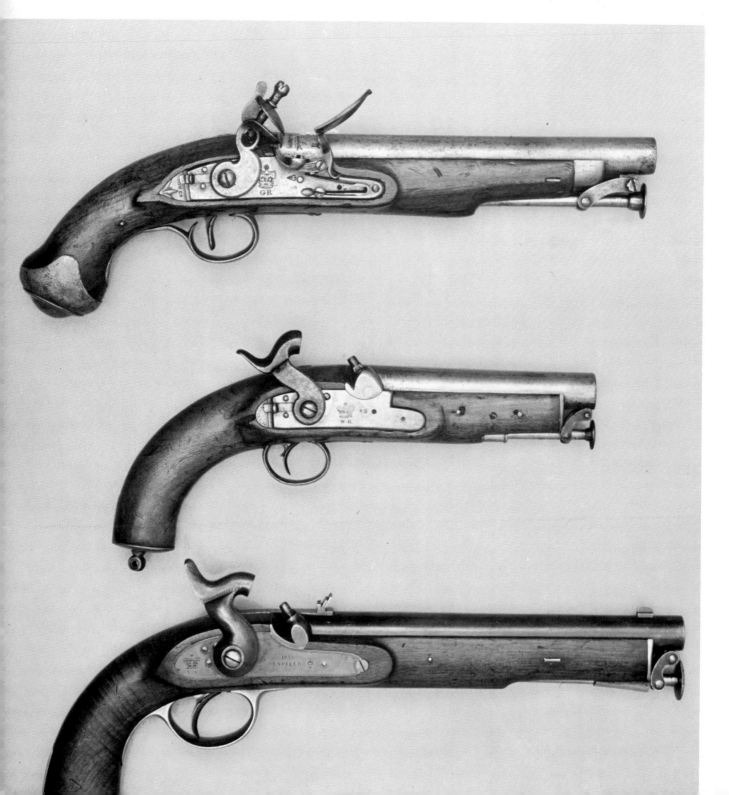

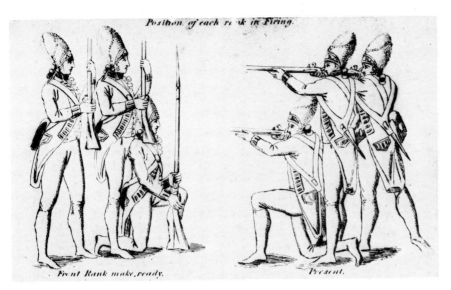

Firing in three ranks as shown in
*The British Soldier's Guide and
Volunteer's Self-Instructor* (1803).

Battle scene during the Peninsular
War, showing the vast amounts of
smoke generated by the firearms of
the period.

British military flintlock pistol bearing
maker's name WILITS, the date 1758
and the royal cypher on the lock
plate. The furniture is of brass.

Although the matchlock and flintlock were abandoned in Europe by the mid-nineteenth century, in the East both types continued in use until quite recently. This musket has the stock typical of the Scinde and Afghanistan. The lock bears the East India Company mark and the date 1814. The powder flasks held ordinary powder and fine priming powder. Private Collection.

Apart from the details of the uniform these Polish soldiers of 1794 are representative of all Europe's armies. They are armed with flintlock muskets and socket bayonets. Muzeum Wojska Polskiego, Warsaw.

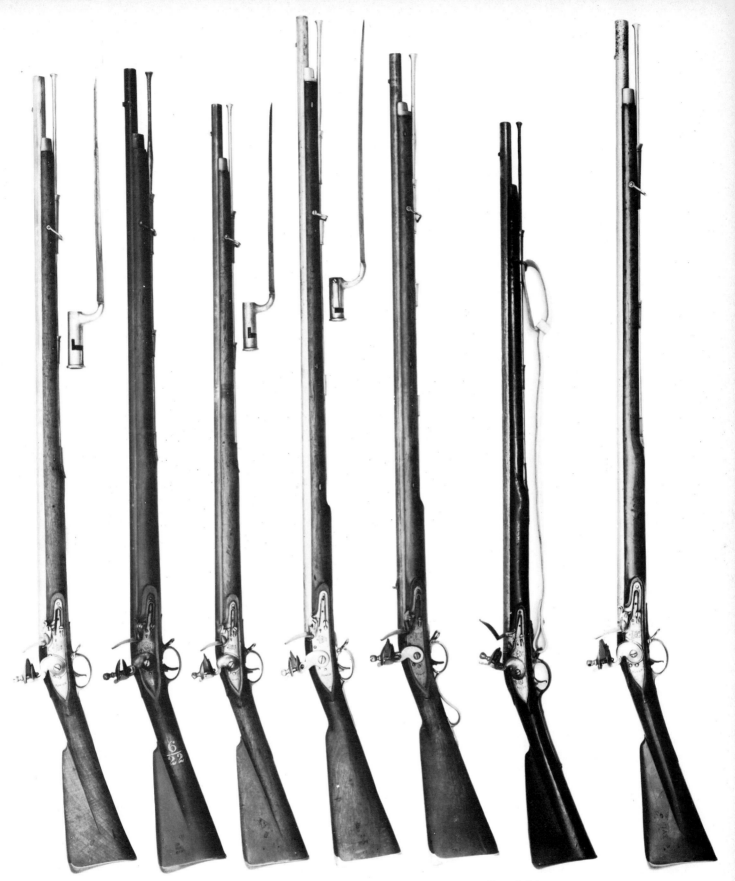

From left to right:
Five British army muskets of the
Napoleonic Wars. Far left is an
India Pattern musket and the
remainder are New Land Pattern
muskets, although the fifth from the
left was intended for light infantry
and has a 39-inch (99-cm) barrel.
Tower of London Armouries.

Second from the right:
A volunteer's India Pattern musket of
about 1800. The buckskin sling is a
later addition. Overall length
39 inches (99 cm).

Far right:
British army flintlock musket of the
India Pattern with a 39-inch (99-cm)
barrel. It has three ramrod pipes and
a steel ramrod, and the shape of the
cock suggests that it was
manufactured before 1809 when a
ring-necked cock was introduced.
Tower of London Armouries.

These two muskets, the New Land Pattern and the India Pattern, saw service throughout the greater part of the Napoleonic Wars. They were not the only weapons used by the British army, being essentially weapons of the Line regiments. There was, for example, a light-infantry version in the New Land Pattern style but with a 39-inch barrel. Since this weapon was intended primarily for men who were expected to be skirmishers and to maintain an aimed fire, the barrel was fitted with a slot backsight. It also had a trigger guard with a rear scroll fitting which gave a firmer hold, serving rather like a pistol grip. There were also shorter carbines for the cavalry.

It was not until 1815 that it became standard policy of the British army to have the barrels of its muskets browned. Before this date regulations had, in general, insisted that the barrels were polished bright. Quite apart from the dangers of reflection betraying the presence of any troops to the enemy, polished barrels were obviously susceptible to rust. Browning is a chemical process which produces a controlled and stable layer of rusting on the barrel and effectively prevents any further rusting. It can be done in a variety of ways, but the method used by the Ordnance was to soak the barrel in, or to cover it with, a special acid solution. When the correct colour was obtained the barrel was dried and varnished. Protection for the Brown Bess used by the Royal Navy was achieved by painting it with black paint to make it resistant to the ravages of sea and salt air.

The Brown Bess musket was not dissimilar to those used by other armies, but there were differences in detail. For example the French muskets were actually produced by national arsenals and fired a smaller-calibre bullet than the British. The first well-known

Below right:
An uncommon flintlock, made in Switzerland about 1660. The flintlock plate and the style of the cock are typical of the period. The butt cap is very ornate and the furniture is all gilt. Peter Dale, Esq.

Bottom right:
A Brown Bess of the 62nd Regiment of the British army, dated 1760 on the lock plate. The maker's name, Gover, is also on the lock and the regimental number is engraved on the barrel. The barrel is 43½ inches (110·5 cm) long and it fires a ball ·725 inches (18·4 mm) in diameter. Cranmer Collection.

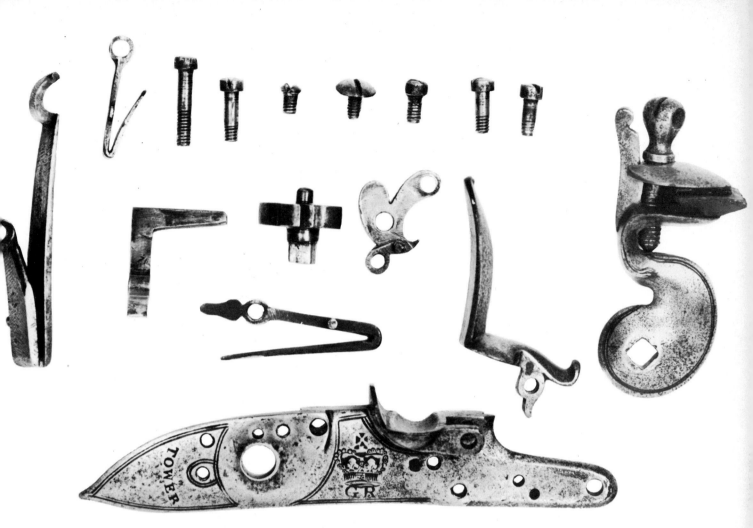

French type of musket was the Model 1717. It had a 45-inch barrel and fired a bullet ·69 inches in diameter, 16 to the pound.

One big difference between the later versions of the French musket (or indeed most of the Continental muskets) and the British ones was the use of bands to secure the barrel in place and the positioning of a large noseband near the muzzle. The differences, however, lay in detail rather than basic design. The Austrian and the New Land Pattern shared one feature in common: they both used a steel ramrod which had a swelling a short way down from the end with the button. This was to afford an easy and firmer grip when loading.

The Brown Bess was to stay in service until well on into the 1850s. As newer weapons were developed and put into production they were issued to the Line regiments, whose older weapons were put into store or issued to volunteer or colonial units. The last of the Brown Bess models to see service were the veterans of over a century of steady, reliable action.

The Brown Bess was a weapon which changed little because it was basically well-designed and well-made. It had its faults but they were common to all weapons of similar design. It was sometimes blamed unfairly, as when one soldier was describing his experiences at the Battle of Waterloo. He claimed that his musket refused to function because the stock was of unseasoned wood. When it became wet, it swelled up, so that the mainspring could not work, but since he obviously did not strip the weapon he was only guessing and it is most unlikely that he was right. The Brown Bess saw service in every continent and on most of the oceans of the world, and memoirs of the period frequently mention it with respect and affection.

The component parts of a flintlock. Although this particular example is from an India Pattern musket the pieces are typical of most locks of the late eighteenth and early nineteenth centuries.

The long rifles

Opposite, top:
Above. Bohemian-made fowling piece with typical long curving trigger guard. The piece is finely decorated with chiselling on the lock plate and barrel. Barrel length 51½ inches (130·8 cm). About 1700. *Below*. German sporting rifle with carved walnut stock and chiselled steel furniture. Barrel length 41½ inches (105·4 cm). About 1750.

Opposite, centre:
German fowling piece with octagonal, blued barrel inlaid with silver. The butt has some inlaid mother-of-pearl decoration and applied silver nails. About 1820.

Opposite, right:
Shot, which consisted of small lead balls, was made by pouring molten lead through a sieve and allowing the drops to fall into water where they hardened.

Opposite, left:
Print of 1804 showing woodcock shooting. The man on the right is priming his pan from the powder flask.

The great increase in accuracy obtained by rifling the barrel ensured that, for those who could afford them, rifled weapons were the only choice. Throughout the seventeenth century and part of the eighteenth century wheel-lock rifles continued to be very popular with hunters who shot for pleasure but not necessarily for survival. Accuracy was, of course, demanded even by those unable to afford the ornate and elaborate wheel-lock rifles, and during the seventeeth century there was a gradual extension of the use of rifling to flintlock weapons. However, it was not until the latter part of the eighteenth century that rifled weapons became at all common.

There was an interesting divergence in the lines of development between the weapons of the hunter in Britain and those of the hunter on the Continent. In Britain there were very few wild animals which were so large that they had to be killed by a bullet, and consequently the hunting rifle was never in great demand. Most eighteenth-century hunters used what would today be described as a shotgun, a smooth-barrelled weapon firing a large number of small slugs. On the Continent, however, there were bear, deer, boar, and even wolves, all of which would be largely immune to shotgun slugs. The only missile capable of stopping and killing such quarries was a fairly substantial musket or rifle ball. For long-distance shooting the musket was unsatisfactory, but for close work its accuracy was perhaps acceptable. However, when dealing with a dangerous animal such as a charging boar, it was vital to score a hit with the first bullet, since there would be no time for a second shot. These factors stimulated a growing market for hunting rifles in Europe.

During the latter part of the seventeenth century in central Europe, mostly in the areas of Karlsburg, Vienna and Prague, the gunmakers began to change their style and so started the long evolution of the flintlock rifle. The changes they made set the pattern for the hunting or Jaeger rifle for the next century or so. The weapon retained some of the features of the wheel-lock. Its barrel was normally very substantial, frequently octagonal in section, and fired a medium-sized ball, usually about ·6 inches in diameter. The stock had something of the rather stubby look of the earlier wheel-lock weapons, although it was generally less elaborately decorated.

There was also a gradual change in the method of aiming the rifle, the wheel-lock having been held with the butt resting against the cheek. Experience showed that a steadier aim could be obtained with the butt held against the shoulder, and consequently flint-lock rifles were almost invariably made with the longer shoulder butt. One feature which they retained from the wheel-lock was the patch-box. Normally positioned on the righthand side of the butt, this consisted of a hollowed-out section closed with a sliding panel. It was essential in a rifle that the ball should fit tightly enough to bite into the rifling. If the ball was made to fit exactly into the barrel, it was just a little too tight and difficult to push down. It could be forced down by using the ramrod, perhaps with the help of a mallet, but this could distort its shape and thus affect its accuracy. If the fit was too tight and the lead ball was hammered down the barrel the rifling stripped a thin outside layer from the ball until it was, in effect, shooting as a smooth-bore weapon.

A satisfactory compromise was to take a ball which was a reasonably close fit and wrap it in a piece of waxed linen or similar material. The patch, as the material was called, was laid across the muzzle, the ball placed in the centre, and the two were then pushed down with the ramrod. This ensured a fit which was sufficiently close to impart a spin on the ball as it left the barrel, but did not make the weapon too difficult to load. Ready-cut patches, waxed or greased, were kept in the patch-box.

The Jaeger barrel was fairly long, which helped to improve its accuracy. A line drawn between the backsight and the foresight

Flintlock fowling piece fitted with a barrel by Pedro Esteva of Barcelona. Spanish barrels were of extremely good quality and highly prized.
The lock is by Delite of Paris and the silver mounts bear Paris marks for 1770. Victoria and Albert Museum, London.

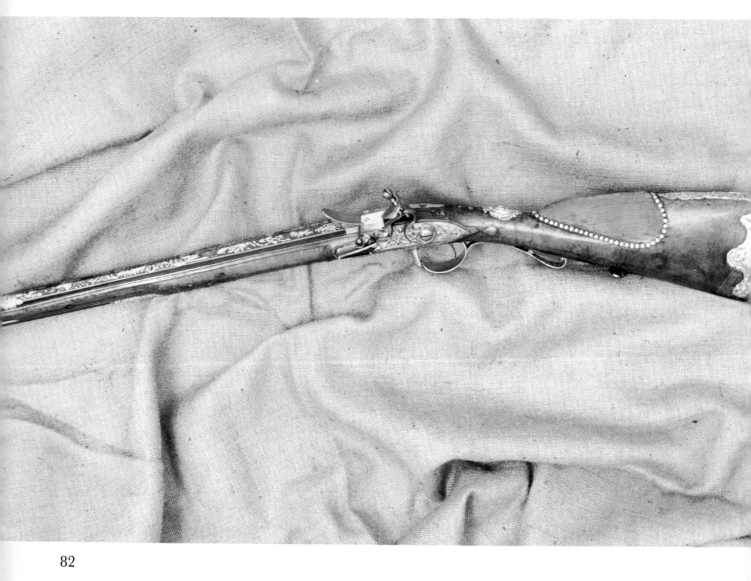

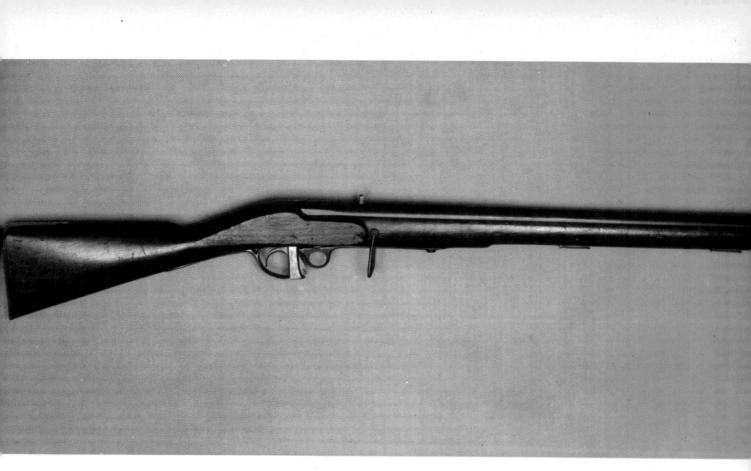

is known as the sight-line. Within limits, the longer the sight-line the more accurately the weapon can be lined up, as the possible degree of error in aiming is reduced. Since hunters were often firing at moving targets it was essential to follow the target and to hold the aim accurately. Anything which might cause the aim to waver had to be avoided. If the rifle could be secured by propping it up on a stone wall or against a tree, the chances of a miss were reduced. For a hunter firing from the shoulder in a free-standing position, it was useful to be able to reduce the amount of pull required on the trigger. It was, therefore, common practice to fit a hair trigger on these hunting rifles.

Another distinctive feature of the Jaeger rifle was the trigger guard. On most of the military firearms of the period the trigger guard was a cast, flat piece of brass or steel fitted beneath the stock and curved around the trigger. On the Jaeger rifle, as on the earlier wheel-lock rifles, the trigger guards tended to be far more elaborate and much bigger. They were commonly of steel and the bottom section was shaped to afford an easy fingerhold. More-over, since the guard had to accommodate both triggers it was much larger than those found on military weapons.

As the seventeenth century progressed there was a gradual reduction in the size and in the use of contoured finger holds. In order to afford a more comfortable and secure grip and so help achieve greater accuracy, the butt end of the trigger guard was often scrolled backwards and extended along the bottom of the butt. Many of these weapons were fitted with stocks that were fairly plain apart from some simple scroll or leaf carving around the breech or around the trigger guard and ramrod pipes. Others were decorated almost to the same degree of excellence as the early wheel-locks.

One very popular style of decoration was that of inlaid silver wire. The desired pattern was marked on the stock and narrow grooves were cut around the outline. The grooves were made slightly wider at the bottom and then soft silver wire was placed in

To allow a clear, uncluttered sight-line some percussion weapons were fitted with underhammer locks situated under the stock. This example was made about 1850 by a London gunsmith, Wilkinson. The percussion cap was placed on the nipple below the breech. The front ring, which formed the hammer, was pulled down and locked until released by the trigger. Pattern Room, Royal Small Arms Factory, Enfield.

A fairly typical example of the Pennsylvanian Long Rifle, with sloping butt, brass patch-box, long barrel and scrolled trigger guard. Late eighteenth century. American Museum in Britain, Bath.

them and gently tapped into position. As the wire expanded it was automatically locked into the groove and stayed firmly in position.

Jaeger rifles were not confined to Europe. In the seventeenth century and even more so in the eighteenth century an increasing number of people were emigrating to America. During the early period of colonization of the east coast of North America the majority of the people there were English. Further south (and in Canada) the French were strong in numbers and, of course, in Central and South America the colonizers were predominantly of Spanish and Portuguese origin. However, numbers of German and Swiss also emigrated to America.

With a growing demand for weapons there were the beginnings of a small but expanding gun trade. Most North American firearms at this period were supplied by the home countries. Canada drew largely on the French gunmakers, while settlers of English origin preferred the products of Birmingham and London.

In the western colonies of Pennsylvania and Kentucky the hunters were, in many ways, in a similar position to those of Western Europe. Game consisted of many large mammals which needed a powerful bullet to bring about a clean kill, and consequently there was a demand for hunting rifles rather than smooth-bore muskets. Some of the German and Swiss gunmakers undoubtedly settled in this area, but by the second quarter of the eighteenth century, Pennsylvania, and especially the part known as Lancaster County, had begun to establish itself as an important centre of rifle production. The Jaeger rifle, some examples of which had no doubt been brought into the colonies by their proud owners, was found to be not completely satisfactory. The heavy barrel, thick stock and comparatively large bore made them rather inconvenient.

The situation in America was very different from that in Europe. Apart from those in a few big towns, the people were living on a frontier. The country was enormous, with very few places where supplies could be obtained. Hunters and travellers were well advised to ensure that they had sufficient stores for, should these run out, there was little chance of replenishing them.

This limitation applied just as much to powder and bullets as to any other commodity. From the colonist's point of view it was preferable to have a weapon which fired a small bullet needing only a small charge of powder. In this way he could get a larger number of shots for a given weight of powder and lead. This is one of the reasons why these early hunting rifles used a comparatively small bullet, about ·45 inches, compared with the ·75-inch ball of the Brown Bess. With the smaller bullet he could cast thirty to forty to the pound, as against only sixteen or so to the pound for a Brown Bess ball. On some rifles the bore was as small as ·36 inches. The largest was normally ·58 inches and there were one or two exceptional weapons that were even bigger than this.

The majority of the barrels were octagonal in section. Some of the earlier ones had an octagonal breech, changing gradually to round section, although this was not a common feature. Barrels tended to be rather long, usually between 40 and 60 inches. Obviously weapons with the potentially high accuracy of these long rifles needed sights. The majority had a small bead fore-sight made up of a little sphere raised above the muzzle on a small pillar. The rear sight, perhaps surprisingly, was set not at the breech where it might be expected to give the longest sight-line, but usually along the barrel some 12 to 18 inches from the breech.

Each rifle was usually the work of one gunsmith, who carried out every part of the process except, perhaps, the making of the

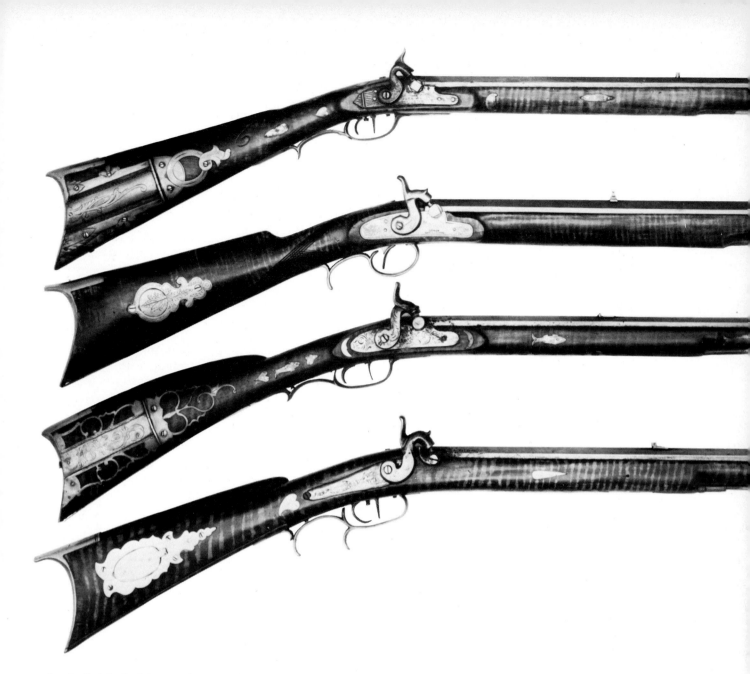

lock. Pride in his product and the need to advertise led him to put his name on the weapon, usually along the flat surface on top of the barrel. Sometimes the name is in block capitals, sometimes it is in script, and it has been suggested that these were facsimiles of the gunsmiths' signatures. In the few cases where it has been possible to compare written and engraved signatures there is some indication that this is so. Large numbers of names have been recorded and it is interesting to note how many of them suggest a Continental European origin. Some selected at random include Tannabecker, Jacob Metzgar, Henry Hunsicker, George Eyster, Jacob Dickert and John Bonawitz. In some cases the gunmakers are known to be of foreign origin, one being Henry Albright who came from near Suhl in Germany, a town which became famous for its its arsenal. He was born there in 1718 and went to America in 1750.

The barrel was obviously of great importance to the quality of the weapon as a whole and its manufacture was a long and complicated process. First a block of metal, known as a skelp, was chosen and then heated over the fire until it was white hot. It was next placed in a groove on a specially shaped anvil known as a buffalo head, and the end piece was hammered around a metal

A group of percussion Pennsylvanian Long Rifles. The top one has been converted from flintlock and the one beneath it carries the name of Leman of Lancaster County. About 1840. All have the gracefully drooping butt together with the decorative patch-box.

rod called a mandrel. When the skelp became cool the mandrel was removed. The skelp was then reheated and a further section was hammered and shaped around the mandrel. This process was repeated until the skelp had taken the form of a long tube with a comparatively small hole running through the centre. This rather complicated process was necessary since, at that time, the gunsmith did not possess the technical equipment necessary for drilling a small hole through a very long block of metal. With the tools and processes which were available it was easier to ream out, that is, to scrape out, a hole which was already there until it was of a suitable diameter.

The rough barrel was now ready to be reamed and for this task the gunsmith used a long bench adapted and specially strengthened to house a movable carriage. On to this the barrel was clamped. The carriage could be moved backwards or forwards between two special guide blocks and at one end of the bench was the chuck, or vice, to hold the reamer. This could be rotated, either by hand or, should the gunsmith be lucky enough to have a convenient stream near at hand, by water power. With the barrel clamped in position and the reamer rotating, the barrel was carefully centred and pressed steadily against the reamer. The size of the reamer was gradually increased until the hole was of the correct diameter. The very last reamer used, which was rectangular in section, did no cutting but simply gave a fine, mirror-like polish to the inside of the bore.

Typical hunting scene. The huntsman is using his double-barrelled, percussion shotgun to bag some woodcock. Painting is by William Jones about 1830.

86

The gunmakers now carefully checked the bore in order to make sure that it was drilled evenly and that there were no weaknesses. If there were any black spots visible in the bore it meant that there were slight irregularities in the surface. The outside of the barrel was hammered with a copper mallet until the metal had been pushed forward to fill any depressions and the whole thing was repolished. When the bore satisfied the gunsmith, the outside of the barrel was held in a special clamp and ground to shape by two large-diameter grindstones.

The next important step was the cutting of the rifling on the inside surface of the barrel. The process was similar to the original bore-cutting, but this time the barrel was fixed solidly to a bench. Facing it was a movable frame which consisted of a horizontal, large-diameter rod with spiral grooves cut into the face. These grooves were, in effect, the pattern for those to be cut on the inside of the barrel. At one end of the rod was fitted a pair of handles and at the other a bit with a cutting edge. The handles were firmly grasped and the whole moving section was pulled back, and as it did so it passed through a vertical plate with a hole in the centre. Around the edge of the hole were teeth which engaged with the grooves of the wooden pattern.

The rod and the bit were now ready for use and the two handles were gripped and slowly pushed forward. As the rod moved forward the teeth in the vertical plate engaged with the rod and slowly turned it. The combined forward and turning movement resulted in a spiral motion. As the cutting edge engaged with the inside surface of the barrel a thin sliver of metal was removed and one shallow groove was cut. The process was repeated several times, if necessary, until the groove was of the correct depth. When one groove was completed the barrel clamps were loosened, it was turned through the appropriate angle, and the process repeated until the rifling was complete. In the early days the job was done by hand, but in the nineteenth century mechanically operated devices took over and eliminated much of the hard labour.

The next step was to close one end of the barrel by fitting a breech plug. Threads were cut on the inside at the breech end and a solid plug with a matching thread was made. The plug had a long 'tail', known as the tang, which was used to secure the barrel to the stock. When the threads were completed the plug was screwed home firmly and a hole drilled through the tip of the tang. There only remained the fitting of the foresight and rear sight, the drilling out of the touch-hole and any engraving or stamping of names. To finish off, the barrel was usually browned to reduce the chances of rusting.

The next stage was the fitting of the barrel to a wooden stock, and it is the shape of the stock which is such a characteristic feature of these weapons. The early models had rather thick butts. However, from the latter part of the eighteenth century the more elegant shape became common. The American long rifle was normally fully stocked, which meant that the wooden body extended from the butt right the way along the underside of the barrel, virtually to the muzzle. The stock is graceful and slim, and slopes just behind the lock not as on many long arms acutely, but with an elegant curve, to a rather long slender butt.

The shoulder end of the butt was cut with a deeply indented curve to fit firmly and securely against the shoulder. There is a slight step, level with the trigger guard, the whole section being shaped and smoothed so that it fits comfortably into the right hand in the aiming position. The wood most often used was maple,

One of the last steps in the manufacture of a gun barrel was the polishing of the outside. Most makers polished them against large rotating wheels as shown here in the Birmingham Small Arms Factory (1851).

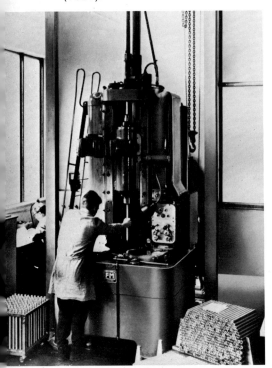

Much of the hard labour needed to produce rifled barrels has been reduced by modern methods. This machine used by the British firm of Parker-Hale cold forges barrels in one operation.

simply because if was easily available to the gunsmiths. Walnut remained the most popular wood in Europe, but in the New World supplies were meagre, and only a few long rifles were fitted with walnut stocks.

The gunmakers cut down the trees, sawed them into planks and, judging by a few surviving examples and contemporary records, cut them roughly to shape. They then left these planks for a period up to seven years, ensuring that the wood was thoroughly dried and seasoned. The final shape and angle of the butt were no doubt determined by the purchaser, for most of the guns were custom made. As with top-quality guns today, the customer was probably given a number of specimen stocks to try for comfort and size. When the best fit had been chosen the rough shape was drawn on a plank of wood and then cut out. Any minor changes were made at this stage.

The preliminary shaping was carried out and a groove cut to house the barrel. Since it was essential that the barrel should sit securely in place, the bottom of the barrel was coated with oil, chalk or any other suitable material that would leave a mark. The barrel was laid in the stock, left for a while and then removed. Any places where the wood stood out would be shown up by the marking substance and they would be rubbed down to ensure a perfect fit. The barrel was then secured by means of pins and lugs.

The next part of the process was to cut the recess to house the lock. Little is known about the manufacture of locks by the Pennsylvanian gunsmiths. Although the locks frequently bear the name of gunsmiths it is likely that they were imported ready-made from Europe. Care was necessary when cutting the recess, for too large a hole weakened the stock. Next to be fitted was the trigger. At this stage of development it was mounted on its own small plate, which had to be recessed into the stock beneath the lock. The next step was the fitting of the parts known collectively as the furniture of the gun: the trigger guard, the plate to protect the end of the butt, the band at the front of the stock near the muzzle, the ramrod pipes and, most important, the patch-box cover which was a distinctive feature of these American long rifles.

The wheel-lock patch-box had usually been covered with a sliding wooden lid and some of the American rifles, particularly the earlier ones, retained this sytem. In a short time it seems that a less complicated arrangement was adopted. The recess was cut in the same way but in place of the sliding lid a hinged metal cover became the standard fitting. It was held closed by a little thumbnail catch, usually operated by a small button set into the butt plate. The patch-box covers and their often elaborate surrounds were of brass and were frequently cast, together with other brass furniture, by the gunmaker, although some pieces are known to have been imported. The design of the patch-box was very variable and was probably made to the customer's specifications. A few long rifles were fitted with silver inlay and one or two had silver furniture, but these were very much the exceptions.

The colony which dominated the field of arms manufacture was Pennsylvania. It was originally divided into three counties, Bucks, Philadelphia and Chester, a fourth, Lancaster County, being formed in 1729. The majority of the earlier inhabitants were of English stock, mostly of Quaker origin. There were also large numbers of Swedish and Dutch colonists. However William Penn, who had founded the colony, visited Germany and Holland in 1686, and his glowing accounts of the New World encouraged many Germans and some Swiss to leave Europe and make their homes in Lancaster County.

There are records of gunmakers at work in this county as early as 1740. So prolific was the manufacture of these particular weapons that they acquired the name of the Pennsylvanian Long Rifle. However, through one of those accidents of history the name of another state, Kentucky, became associated with the rifle, and many writers refer to them as Kentucky rifles.

These long rifles saw service during the American Revolutionary War, but not in the hands of the regular troops, who were mostly equipped with muskets similar to the British Brown Bess. In fact the first weapons officially issued to the American forces were virtually straight copies of the Brown Bess. Many of the American troops were also armed with French muskets, since France assisted the colonists in their struggle against Britain. It was in fact the volunteer and irregular units who were equipped with the long rifle. These troops were often woodsmen with long experience of hunting and of fighting the elusive Indian in his own environment.

Dreyse needle guns.
Below. Model of 1862. Overall length 53½ inches (135·9 cm). Barrel 32½ inches (82·5 cm).
Bottom. Jaeger model Overall length 45 inches (114 cm). Barrel 26 inches (66 cm). Bore ·47 inches (11·94 mm). Pattern Room, Royal Small Arms Factory, Enfield.

Their method of warfare was considered by regular British army officers to be ungentlemanly, indeed almost cowardly, for they emulated the Indian and made use of every scrap of cover.

The American colonists soon realized that an army bereft of officers is an army largely lost and British officers were, therefore, prime targets. It is on record that many officers, not from cowardice but from sheer self-protection, would remove any indication of rank before going to attack an American position.

There are numerous accounts of the effect of these long rifles. No doubt many of them were exaggerated, but on the other hand the general picture emerging from contemporary references is of a highly accurate weapon in the hands of men well qualified to use it. To troops accustomed only to the relative inaccuracy of the Brown Bess they must indeed have seemed very impressive. In 1814 in his book *To all Sportsmen* Colonel George Hanger claimed that he 'never in my life saw better rifles (or men who shot better) than those made in America; they are chiefly made in Lancaster, and two or three neighbouring towns in that vicinity in Pennsylvania. The barrels weigh about six pounds two or three ounces, and carry a ball no larger than thirty six to the pound; at least I never saw one of a larger caliber, and I have seen many hundreds and hundreds'.

If his last statement is accepted at face value then the Pennsylvanian Long Rifle was presumably fairly common at the time of the Revolutionary War. Colonel Hanger also has some interesting details about the loading of this weapon and says that the riflemen never used more powder 'than contained in a woman's thimble'. He describes how they took a piece of antler and used it as a container as they experimented with the load for their rifle. When they found a load which gave a recoil then 'They draw off a small quantity of the powder, cut the horn off, and use it for actual service before an enemy'.

While the accuracy of the Pennsylvanian Long Rifle was remarkably good, the rifleman did not have everything in his favour. Writers of the period stress that the lack of a bayonet was a serious handicap. Caught with an empty weapon, riflemen were defenceless and accounts speak of them fleeing before bayonet charges by British troops.

Below. Canadian target rifle by W. P. Marston of Toronto, fitted with a telescopic sight made by Morgan James, Utica, N.Y. Barrel length 33 inches (83·8 cm). About 1860. *Bottom*. Pennsylvanian Long Rifle, but marked 'Charleston So.CA' (South Carolina). With ornate patch-box lid. Barrel length 36¾ inches (91·9 cm). About 1850.

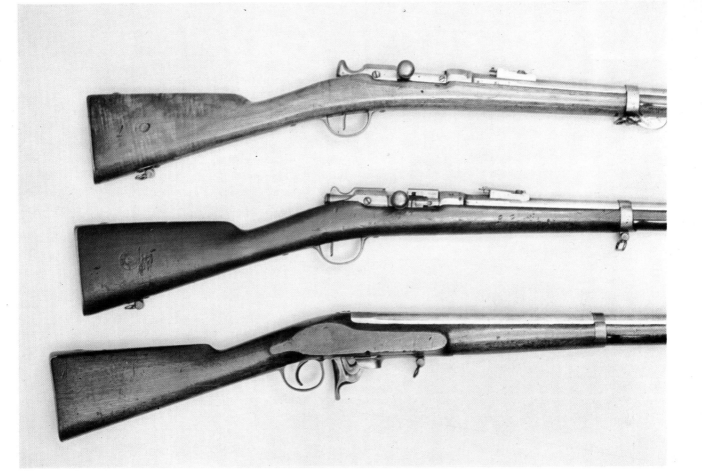

The skill of riflemen in general seems to have earned them a special hatred on previous occasions. Hanger relates how during the Battle of Minden in 1759, some Jaegers (riflemen) hidden in a wood wrought such execution on the French officers that artillery was brought up to clear them out. Some wounded Jaegers captured by the French were promptly buried up to their chins in the ground and left. A British officer was also quoted in 1776 as saying 'a rifleman is not entitled to any quarter'.

Pennsylvanian Long Rifles were in demand by hunters, but they were custom-made firearms available only in limited amounts, and by contemporary standards were fairly expensive. However, simpler, plainer versions of the Pennsylvanian Long Rifle were to be produced in quantity. In 1796 the U.S. Office of Indian Trade, which would barter rifles for pelts, was set up and there were also large fur companies employing many hunters. Thus there was a ready-made market for hunting rifles. While craftsmen producing high-quality Pennsylvanian Long Rifles were not greatly concerned with this trade, there were others who were prepared to enter the commercial field. The general quality of these weapons was inferior and they also lacked the fine finish and decorative features.

The cheaper versions were produced in considerable quantities. J. J. Henry was commissioned to supply 1,325 rifles between 1835 and 1842, and Henry Derringer's firm produced 5,000 rifles for the Indian trade in the 1830s. One contract in 1837 was for 2,750 rifles at a cost of $13.50 each. For production on this scale some standardization was required and these Indian fur trade guns are all basically the same. They are full-stocked with a long barrel and, although there are variations in the style of butt, they are generally a recognizable form of the Pennsylvanian Long Rifle. The fittings

French rifles.
Top. The Chassepot of 1866 used a paper cartridge of 11-mm bore and was based on the Dreyse.
Centre. Gras of 1874 which was a Chassepot modified to take the 11-mm metallic cartridge. Overall length 51 inches (129·5 cm). Barrel 32½ inches (78·5 cm).
Bottom. Heurteloup's rifled musket with his special lock using an under-hammer system and a tube primer. Overall 52½ inches (133·4 cm). Barrel 38½ inches (97·8 cm). About 1833–4. Pattern Room, Royal Small Arms Factory, Enfield.

are commonly of iron rather than brass and the rifles are normally of a calibre about ·45 to ·55 inches.

Military versions of the long rifle were produced in America. The model 1803 had a 32-inch barrel with seven-groove rifling, a plain brass patch-box and butt plate, and a trigger guard rather resembling the Pennsylvanian style but less elaborate. In 1817 a new variety but with a 36-inch barrel and oval iron patch-box, was adopted. In 1841 yet another version was produced.

The Pennsylvanian Long Rifle was essentially light, and a much heavier rifle for use on the Western plains of America was very popular. Two brothers who gave their name to this type of rifle were Jake and Sam Hawken. In 1815 they set up a shop in St. Louis, Missouri. The rifle they developed was basically a Pennsylvanian Long Rifle, but with a thicker stock which gave it a sturdier, more substantial form. The brass decoration on the stock often included a buffalo. Its bullet was about thirty-two to the pound. The barrel of this so-called Plains Rifle was heavy and thus permitted the use of a fairly large charge of powder. This, in turn, ensured that the bullet followed a nice flat path, giving

Page from Diderot's *Encyclopaedia* showing a French gunmaker's workshop around 1770, with manually operated drill.

Arquebusier,
Machine à Caneler les Canons de Fusil.

English flintlock rifle with long barrel, patch-box and scroll trigger guard – all typical of these weapons. Tower of London Armouries.

'The Battle of Lexington', an engraving by C. Tiebout (1798). The Americans are firing at the British with their long-barrelled rifles.

improved accuracy at ranges of 150 to 200 yards. The increased thickness and greater weight of the barrel also reduced the recoil produced by the heavier charge. The Hawken brothers supplied quantities of rifles, mostly stocked in maple, for the Indian trade.

Both Pennsylvanian and Plains rifles were fitted first with flint-locks and later with percussion locks. They were widely used in the eighteenth and nineteenth centuries and have become part of the legend of the West. They were reliable and accurate weapons and much of the legend that has grown up around them has a solid foundation of fact.

During the heyday of the flintlock Pennsylvanian Long Rifle the great majority of the British line regiments were still armed with the Brown Bess, thought to be a perfectly satisfactory weapon by most authorities. However, there were some who saw great advantages in having an accurate, rifled weapon. In 1775 Viscount Townshend had asked that 1,000 German rifles should be purchased and issued (five to a company) to the Highland regiments. Some 200 were ordered from Hanover and 800 were to be supplied by Birmingham gunmakers. The weapons lived up to expectations and there are reports of some very good shooting.

On April 27, 1776, a new rifle was demonstrated by Captain Patrick Ferguson in adverse conditions of rain and wind. His performance was outstanding: he fired at targets and hit them consistently. He soaked the weapon and still it functioned, and his rate of fire was four times a minute even when he was on the move. The secret of his new gun was in the method of loading, for he had produced a breech-loading rifle. Instead of pouring powder and ball down the muzzle and then ramming them home, he had a plug which could be unscrewed to give direct access to the breech. Powder and ball were inserted and the plug closed (the trigger guard operated it), the pan was primed and the weapon was ready. Ferguson patented his design in December 1776 and 100 of his rifles were produced by Birmingham gunmakers.

Ferguson's idea was not new. Earlier gunmakers had used the system but he had introduced several improvements. A unit of 100 men from the 6th and 14th Regiments was formed, Ferguson took command and the unit began training. In May 1777 he landed in America with his corps of riflemen, complete with green cloth for their uniforms. The first action in which they took part

A trapper priming his flintlock rifle—an early Plains Rifle—which was basically a shortened version of the Pennsylvanian Long Rifle. Painting by A. F. Tait. Yale University Art Gallery, New Haven, Connecticut. Whitney Collections of Sporting Art.

American soldier of the Continental Army during the Revolutionary War. The accuracy of detail in the flint-lock leaves much to be desired. Radio Times.

was at Brandywine Hill and they acquitted themselves well, but
Ferguson was wounded in the arm so badly that it was feared he
would lose it. The riflemen were disbanded and dispersed to join
light companies with the 6th and 14th Regiments. Ferguson was
later killed at the Battle of King's Mountain in October 1780.
With his death the driving force in the rifle movement was lost,
and rifles were largely to disappear from the British army for the
next twenty years.

When peace came in 1783 any great incentive to adopt the
rifle was lacking and it was not until war broke out with the
French in 1793 that the British army found itself once again under
pressure. Napoleon Bonaparte was to make considerable use of
light skirmishers, many of whom were equipped with a rifle, and it
was thought that similar units could be raised in the British army.
As a result of experiments and tests a rifle manufactured by a
London gunmaker, Ezekiel Baker, was adopted in 1800. The rifle
was seen as being special, in fact so special that the ordinary troops
were not to be armed with it, but only a select group of riflemen
whose task was to scout, harass the enemy and act as skirmishers.
The same year the first steps were taken to raise a new body, the
Corps of Riflemen, which eventually became the 95th Foot or
Rifle Brigade.

The Baker rifle was nearer the Jaeger rifle of Europe than the
Pennsylvanian rifle of America. Although the butt had a patch-
box, it was quite severe in design and lacked the colourful brass
embellishments of the American model. Early rifles had a patch-
box with two compartments. Later ones had a single compartment only, which held tools not patches. This difference suggests
that cartridges rather than patches were then in use. Some Baker

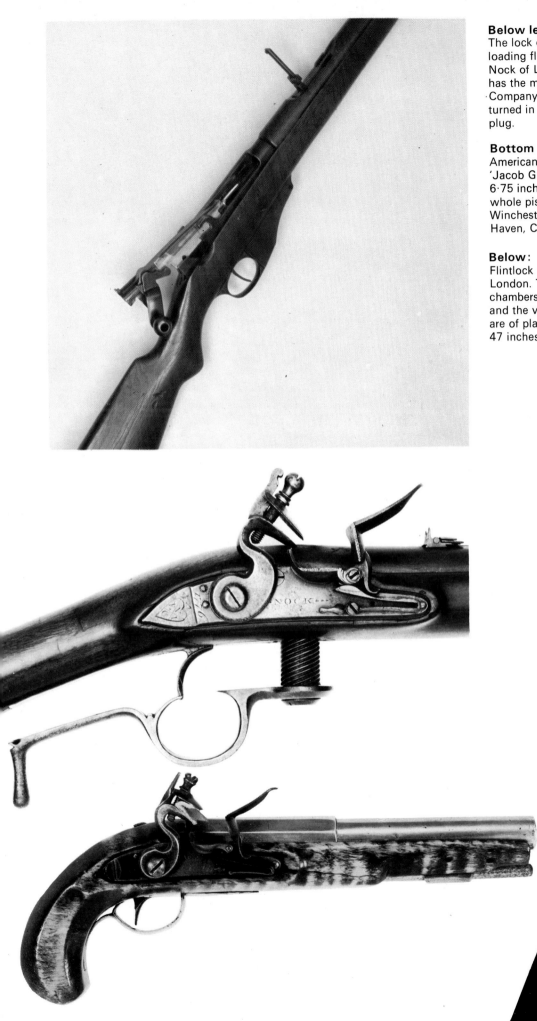

Below left:
The lock of a Ferguson breech-loading flintlock rifle made by Henry Nock of London. It is dated 1776 and has the mark of the East India Company. The trigger guard has been turned in order to lower the breech plug.

Bottom left:
American-made flintlock marked 'Jacob Grubb'. It has a brass barrel 6·75 inches (17·2 cm) long, and the whole pistol rather lacks finish. Winchester Gun Museum, New Haven, Connecticut.

Below:
Flintlock revolving rifle by Collier of London. The cylinder with five chambers has to be rotated by hand and the vents with the touch-hole are of platinum. Overall length 47 inches (119·4 cm). About 1820.

95

Rifled flintlock pistol by I. Christ Kuchenreiter of Regensburg which was skilfully converted to percussion early in the nineteenth century. Overall length 10 inches (25·4 cm).

French army officer's flintlock pistol, known as Model 1777, of simple construction and rugged quality. It was a good example of military firearms of the latter part of the eighteenth century. After the American Revolutionary War the United States produced pistols largely based on this pattern.

Illustrations from *Art Militaire* showing some of the drill movements with the flintlock musket about 1750. At the top right the system of three-rank firing is shown.

rifles lack the butt- or patch-box altogether. The 30-inch barrel was rifled with seven grooves and fired a ball ·7 inches in diameter, although some models were produced with a smaller calibre. The ball was extremely tight-fitting and, with the patches, was often quite difficult to ram home. To overcome this problem a comparatively heavy, wide-headed ramrod was adopted and at first a mallet was also issued.

The Baker rifle was not intended to be used in volley fire but for single, aimed shots. For this reason, like the Pennsylvanian rifle, it was fitted with sights, but these raised a problem. If the fore-sight was to remain carefully positioned and accurate in use, it was essential that it should be protected from damage. However, it was equally necessary that the rifle, as a military weapon, should be able to take a bayonet. The sight had to be fitted or protected in such a way that it would not be knocked when the bayonet was fixed or unfixed. A bar was attached on the right-hand side of the barrel, and a special bayonet, which had a brass hilt cut with a slot fitted with a spring clip, was issued. The hilt slid comfortably over the bar and locked in place well clear of the sights.

Many volunteer units armed themselves with Baker-type rifles. They continued in the service of the army for many years, with only minor changes of detail in the design. They were apparently still in use as late as 1851 in South Africa, although no new ones were made after 1838.

The Baker was replaced in 1837 by the Brunswick rifle, which was based on a rifle designed by Captain Berners, an officer with the Duke of Brunswick. It too had a 32-inch barrel and fired a ball which was nearly as large as one fired by the Brown Bess. The distinctive feature of this weapon was that it used a rather special

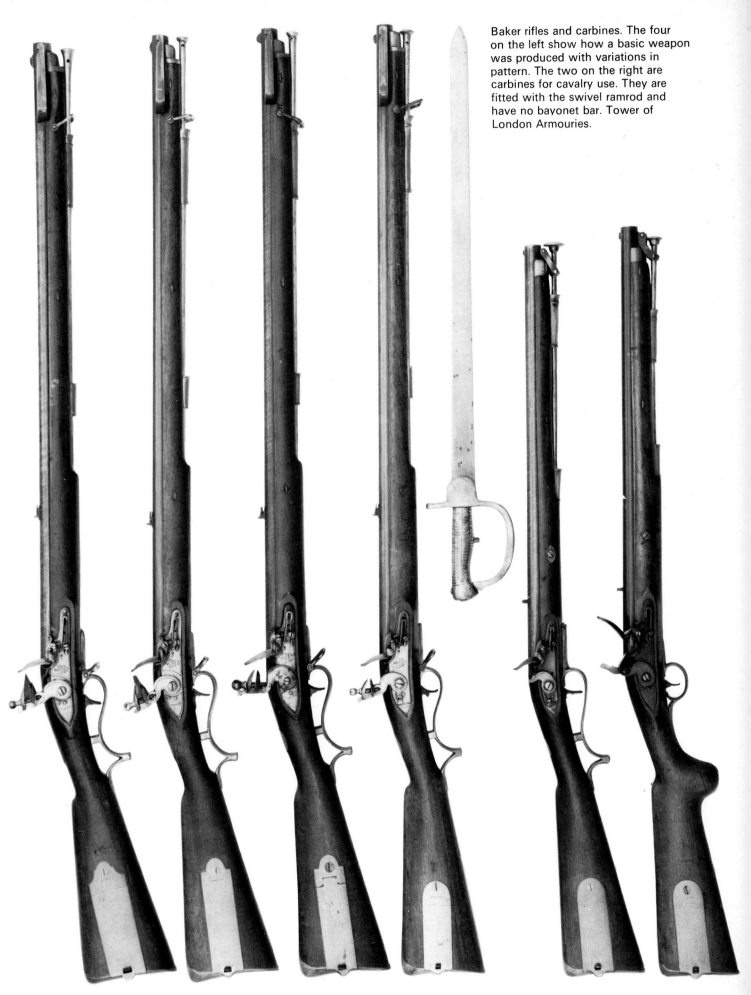

Baker rifles and carbines. The four on the left show how a basic weapon was produced with variations in pattern. The two on the right are carbines for cavalry use. They are fitted with the swivel ramrod and have no bayonet bar. Tower of London Armouries.

Making barrels for high-quality shotguns is still very much a craftsman's job. Each is inspected and checked at each stage of production, as shown here at Cogswell and Harrison, the London Gunmakers.

American Civil War army sniper using a rifle with a long sighting tube which served as a telescopic sight.

Target shooting was very popular during the later part of the nineteenth century and international competitions were not uncommon. A match between America and Ireland in 1875 is shown here.

form of rifling consisting of two grooves only. The ball had a raised ridge running around the circumference and, when loading, the ball was slotted into the grooves and then pushed down. Many advantages were claimed for it, including long-range accuracy, easy loading, and fewer problems due to fouling. Moreover, since there were only two grooves, the wear on the barrel was small. The Brunswick rifle incorporated features of the Baker in its design. It had a patch-box in the butt and a side bar for the bayonet.

Despite the high hopes held out for this weapon it was not popular, and after a comparatively short life steps were taken to produce a new one. The main trouble was that fouling soon clogged the two grooves and made loading difficult. Ironically, ease of loading had been one of the advantages claimed for it when it was first adopted. Anything which could reduce fouling, which so hindered loading and accuracy, was to be encouraged. Associated with this was the problem of finding easier ways of loading a rifle. How could the bullet be made to fit tightly and yet still be easy to load? Numerous suggestions were offered, but one which seemed to offer most hope was devised by two Frenchmen. The basic idea was to use a bullet smaller than the bore, which was then expanded to fit tightly into the grooves. Such a system would speed up loading and yet retain the accuracy given by the rifling.

In 1826 Captain Gustave Delvigne used a breech which was slightly narrower than the bore. When the bullet was dropped down the barrel it rested on the shoulders of the breech and was then struck heavily by the ramrod so that it expanded and fitted into the rifling. The expansion was not always satisfactory and in any case led to distortion of the bullet, affecting its accuracy. A Captain Claude-Étienne Minié developed the concept further and in 1849 produced a lead bullet with a hollow base, into which was fitted a small iron cup. When the bullet was driven forward by the expanding gas the iron cup was pushed into the base broadening it sufficiently to grip the rifling.

In 1851 it was decided that the Minié rifle would be adopted as the official British weapon. The 1851 model had a barrel 39 inches long with four grooves and fired a ·702-inch diameter bullet, weighing (with the iron cup) 680 grains. Later versions

Top. Winchester rifle Model 1886 No. 29406, with a half magazine. This model is a 'take-down', which means that it can easily be separated into two parts. Overall length $44\frac{1}{4}$ inches (112·4 cm).
Centre. Double-barrelled flintlock by Carr & Cooper, with waterproof pans. Overall length 45 inches (114·3 cm). About 1820.
Bottom. Flintlock rifle with a lock of the type known as miquelet. It is from the Caucasus and has a great deal of silver decoration of various forms. Overall length $43\frac{1}{2}$ inches (110·5 cm). Nineteenth century.

Left:
Sergeant Oscar Ryder of the 7th New York State Militia. In addition to his percussion rifle he carries a revolver holster at his belt.

Right:
A soldier from the period of the American Civil War, with full equipment, including percussion musket, bayonet, bent scabbard and a sword of a type carried by militia non-commissioned officers.

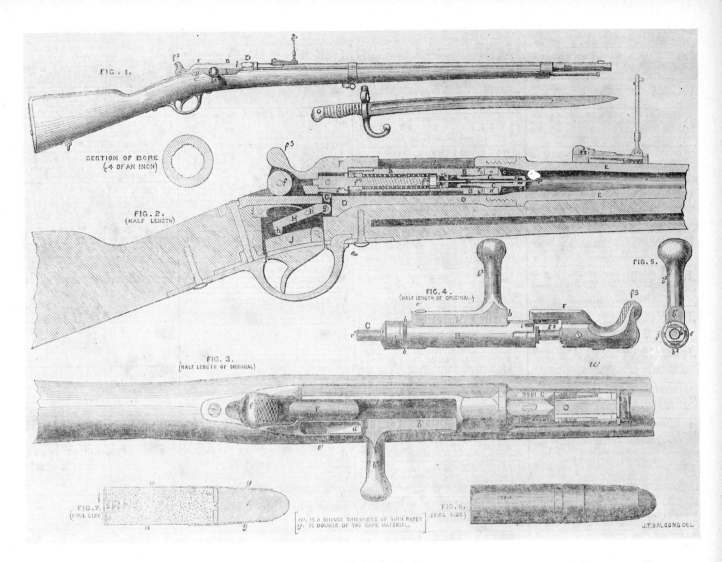

Details of the French Chassepot rifle as shown in the *Illustrated London News* of March 1867.

omitted the iron cup and the wooden base which had been adopted by the British. A number of muskets were converted to the Minié system, because all that was required was some quite shallow-grooved rifling.

Development did not stop there and tests continued to find a new and better weapon. As a result of these tests an 'ideal' rifle was conceived and the outcome was the 1853 Enfield rifle. It had a number of new features including the reintroduction of bands to secure barrel to stock. Its barrel was at the now fashionable length of 39 inches, and it fired a much smaller bullet, only ·577 inches in diameter. It was a good weapon and one that is still in demand today.

Despite the gradual changeover to rifles there were those who refused to be convinced, and as late as 1864 military writers felt obliged to justify the 'new' weapon. One of the staff at the British School of Musketry at Hythe, writing in *The Rifle*, pointed out that during the Napoleonic Wars it was calculated that an average of 3,000 cartridges were fired for each casualty caused. At the Battle of Vittoria in 1813 the Allied troops fired 800 cartridges for each casualty they caused. He gave several more figures and finished by claiming that during one battle in the Crimean War the Russians, using smooth-bore weapons, fired 1,500 rounds for every casualty. The British, using rifles, were getting a rate of one hit for every eighty rounds. Most of the British troops had by then been armed with the Enfield rifle but this was to be the last of the 'old' weapons. Developments in firearms were about to usher in great changes.

101

Duelling pistols

From the beginning of recorded history it seems that many men have held two qualities higher than their own lives: one was the abstract concept of honour, so difficult to define, and the other was bravery. No doubt in the Ancient World to call a man a coward was to invite retribution, and certainly from the Middle Ages onwards to call a man's honour or bravery in question was the gravest insult that could be offered. Such an insult placed life at risk, for it inevitably led to a challenge to a ritual, rigidly controlled fight, and often to death. To refuse a challenge meant ostracism at least and quite possibly banishment or worse.

The placing of one's life at risk in defence of a principle was also used in the Middle Ages to test the question of guilt. If a serious dispute had been dragged through the courts without a satisfactory solution, the final test was to put one's life at stake and to settle the matter by ordeal by combat. The two participants in the quarrel prepared to fight to the death. It was quite in order to employ someone to fight on one's behalf, since it was believed that even if the defendant involved was not actually engaged in combat the gods watching from above would not allow wrong to triumph and would send victory to the innocent.

During the sixteenth and seventeenth centuries the question of honour seems to have become almost an obsession. The slightest suggestion that one's conduct was lacking in honour was sufficient to call forth a challenge which, at this period, was usually settled with swords. This tradition was to continue until the nineteenth century. Death was no longer necessarily the outcome of the dispute and, indeed, modified forms of combat have continued. Fencing today is, of course, the emasculated version of the duel.

After the appearance of firearms it was not long before these too were being used to settle affairs of honour. From the sketchy evidence available it seems quite likely that some of the first duels using firearms were fought on horseback. This was possibly because the only large groups of men equipped with pistols were cavalry units. Although sets of rules do not seem to have been drawn up, contemporary accounts indicate that the normal procedure was for the contestants to ride towards each other and, on a shouted command, to fire their weapons simultaneously. Duels were not always fought on horseback. There are some reports of foot combat,

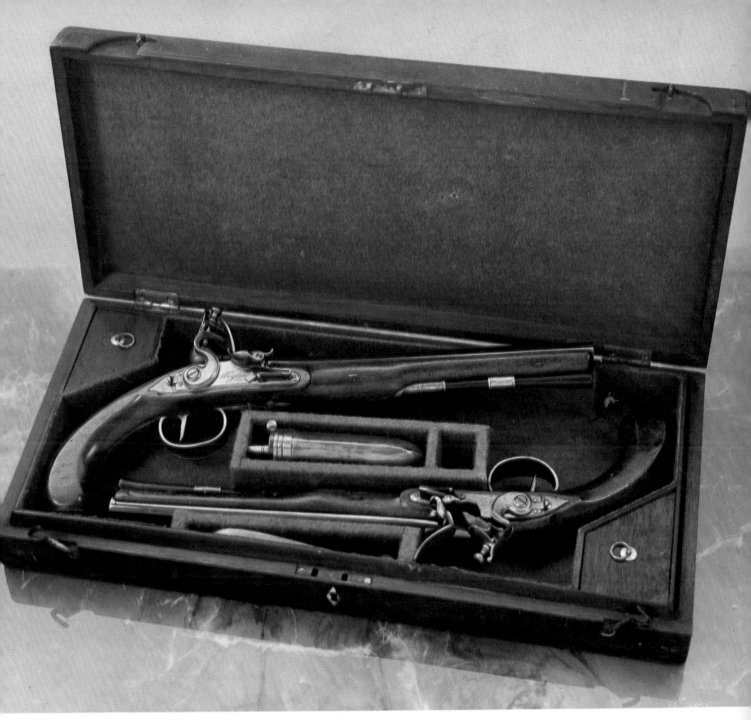

Pair of Wogdon flintlock duelling pistols in their original case with bullet mould and powder flask. Plain and serviceable, they lack the later refinements. Private Collection.

Satirical engraving of 1792 depicting the art of duelling. The contestants are prepared for both styles with pistol and sword. The artist's imagination may have been stimulated by the Chevalier d'Eon (1728–1810) who for years intrigued London society by wearing women's clothes.

Top. High-quality French flintlock pistol by Chasteau of Paris. The barrel is chiselled at the breech and the stock is inlaid with silver wire. About 1720.
Centre. Superbly decorated French flintlock pistol with silver wire inlay, chiselled metal work and, on the butt cap, a medallion portrait of Louis XV. The barrel and lock are marked 'La Roche à Paris'. About 1740–45.
Bottom. Ornate Turkish flintlock pistol with silver gilt furniture and chiselling. One of a pair. Early nineteenth century.
Wallace Collection, London.

As late as 1893 duels still took place in France. The one illustrated was between Deroulède and Clemenceau, two prominent politicians, and was occasioned by the infamous Dreyfus spy trial. The 'bent arm' stance is used.

Le Petit Journal
SUPPLÉMENT ILLUSTRÉ

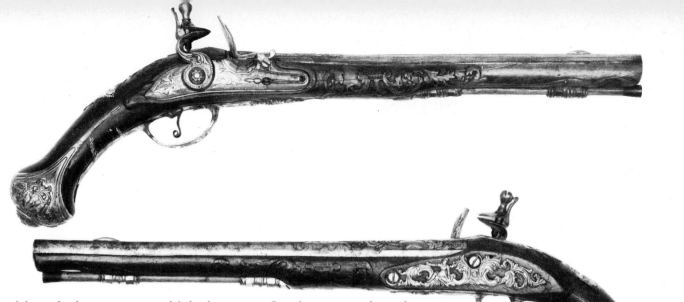

Pair of holster pistols by Thiermay of Liège. The stocks of walnut are carved and fitted with gilt metal furniture. The lock plate is of brass and all the furniture is finely chiselled. Overall length 19½ inches (49·5 cm). Early eighteenth century.

although the ranges at which they were fought seem to have been extraordinarily short.

Strange duels also took place and there is an account of one between a musketeer and a cavalryman told by Hans Grimmelshausen, writing at the time of the Thirty Years War. It is interesting to note that although honour was probably involved one participant, at least, was quite prepared to use subterfuge to win. It was agreed between the participants, a dragoon (mounted infantryman) and an ordinary infantryman, that the duel would be fought with standard military weapons. The dragoon was to have his two wheel-lock pistols, carbine and sword, and the infantryman would use his musket. The infantryman is reported to have loaded his matchlock musket with great care, using two bullets instead of the normal one. He then primed the weapon and covered the pan with lard, paying particular attention to the joints, so as to seal in the priming powder.

When the two opponents approached one another the musketeer pretended to empty away the priming powder, but left some on top of the pan cover. He set up his musket and as the cavalryman drew near, pressed the trigger. The glowing match touched the loose powder on top of the pan cover and flashed. There was obviously no explosion, and the cavalryman assumed that, as frequently happened, there had either been a 'flash-in-the-pan' and no shot or that the shot had missed. Believing his opponent was now defenceless he approached quite carelessly, and when he was so close that the musket could hardly miss, the infantryman opened the pan cover and shot him dead.

Probably one of the oddest of horseback duels was that which took place in England between Hudson, a dwarf in the service of King Charles 1, and Cross, one of the Queen's courtiers. Apparently the courtiers had been poking fun at the dwarf who, finally goaded beyond endurance, issued a challenge to a duel. In order to overcome the difference in size it was decided that the combat should be on horseback. Hudson, although small, apparently did not lack skill, for with his first shot he killed Cross.

Duels on horseback with pistols continued during the seventeenth century and even as late as 1759 there is a record of one such combat in Ireland between a Colonel Barrington and a Mr Gilbert. They were armed with pistols, broadswords and daggers, but despite their courage and determination they were apparently not good shots. After firing their pistols one was only slightly wounded, so they continued with swords. Gilbert's horse was killed and Gilbert himself was struck to the ground, where Barrington presented a dagger at his throat. Gilbert wisely submitted and it is recorded that they became good friends.

Although in the early days duels on horseback were quite common, later they were largely abandoned and duels fought on foot became the fashion. Indeed so prevalent was the custom that it became quite common for kings, nobles and commanding officers to issue statements forbidding the fighting of duels on pain of death – usually with little effect. The Austrian Emperor Leopold issued such an edict forbidding them as early as 1682. Anybody who took part in them was to be prosecuted and banished and their property confiscated.

During the late eighteenth and early nineteenth centuries it became common practice in various countries for gentlemen to draw up, quite unofficially, sets of rules usually referred to as Codes of Duel. These were not, of course, legally binding, but they were intended as guides for duellists to ensure that the matter was carried out fairly and with honour. As early as 1777 the Irish drew up rules known as the 'Twenty-Six Commandments' and in 1824 there was published anonymously in London a *British Code of Duel*. It dealt with a whole range of subjects relevant to the duel and went into considerable detail. Once an insult had been suffered the name and address of the insulter was obtained and then passed on to a friend who was prepared to act as a second. The writer suggested that the second should not be married or hold any official position but should be prepared to take a very active part in the duel should the need arise.

Each party chose seconds and it was they who made the arrangements for the meeting. The seconds were recommended to chose a place 'away from the haunts of men'. They were also to arrange for the attendance of a surgeon and, to create a legal fiction that they were not present, they were to remain out of sight but within calling distance.

Before the actual duel took place it was incumbent upon the seconds to make every effort to arrange some satisfaction without bloodshed. If both principals insisted on continuing their dispute the seconds were to examine the weapons. By the late eighteenth century swords had usually been discarded, so it was almost certain that the duellers would be using pistols. The seconds were to ensure that these were in good condition and that the flints were of good quality. They were then to examine the ground to make sure that the position chosen by either duellist did not confer on him an unfair advantage.

When all was arranged to their satisfaction they next had to decide the distance at which the duel was to take place. According to the *British Code of Duel* the minimum distance was to be ten paces of not less than 30 inches each (about 24 feet). The two positions were to be marked and the opponents were to stand a step or two behind the mark. When all was ready the signal had to be agreed upon. Sometimes it was word of command and sometimes the waving or dropping of a handkerchief. The loaded weapon was then presented to the principal in an uncocked position. The author of the *British Code of Duel* also states that in any one duel no more than three shots are to be fired. Furthermore, it was stressed, one suspects rather with tongue in cheek, that the seconds were still bound to make every effort to obtain satisfaction, even if a shot had been fired.

Some twelve years after the publication of the *British Code of Duel* came *The Art of Duelling* by 'A Traveller' (1846). This had a sub-title claiming that it contained much information 'useful to young Continental tourists', which suggests that travel on the Continent was not without its hazards. The writer goes into considerable detail about many things and much of his advice is

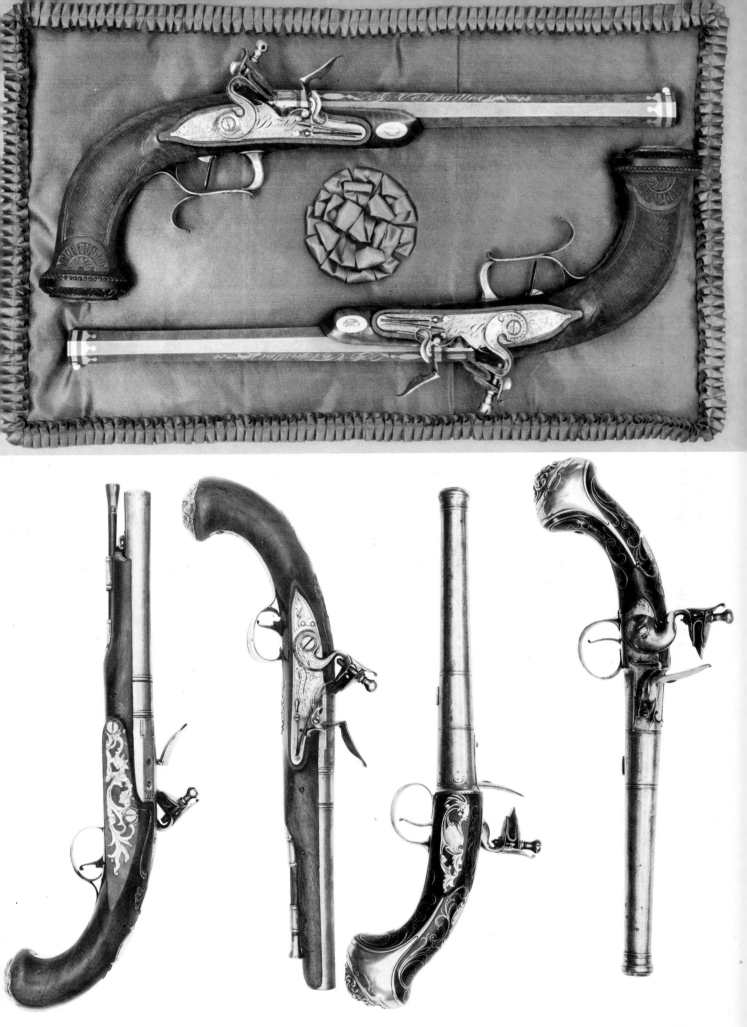

very sound. His opening sentence on the pistol applies well even today. 'Although it appears very easy to pull a trigger, and discharge a pistol, yet no one, until they make the experiment, can be aware of the difficulty in firing with accuracy and expedition'.

He goes on to say that to become a dead shot it is necessary first of all to have a good pair of pistols. He describes what he considers to be the best and states that the inside of the bore should be polished as brightly as possible. He evidently preferred pistols with 10-inch barrels, octagonal rather than round, firing a ball of forty-eight to the pound and equipped with a percussion lock. He did not approve of saw-handle pistols, claiming that they were clumsy. He also makes the very practical point that he does not like silver sights, for these can catch the sunlight and may well dazzle the marksman. Consequently, he prefers the metal to be blued.

Above:
A so-called officer's pistol, by W. Parker of London, fitted with swivel ramrod. It has sights and could have served as a duelling pistol or as a conventional weapon. About 1820.

From top to bottom:
Flintlock pistols by various British makers.
1. By Perkins of Salisbury—half-stocked.
2. Double-barrelled pistol by E. W. Bond, with attached swivel ramrod.
3. Saw-handled duelling pistol by Mortimer, converted to percussion.
4. Duelling pistol by Nock, with spurred trigger guard.
5. Half-stocked pistol by Joseph Manton of London.
All date from the late eighteenth or early nineteenth century.

Left:
Pair of duelling pistols by the London maker, Wogdon. With clean lines, no unnecessary decoration, and simple stocks, they are balanced to come up to the aim with maximum ease. Overall length $14\frac{1}{4}$ inches (36·2 cm).

The writer suggests that the rifling has little or no effect, especially the 'half' rifling which was supposed to have been introduced by a British gunmaker Joseph Manton. It was thought to be 'not quite the thing' to use rifled pistols, and the so-called secret rifling was introduced to give improved accuracy without betraying the fact that the barrel was in fact rifled. This was done from the breech to part of the way along the barrel, but not as far as the muzzle, so that the ridges did not show. The writer claims that they had no advantage over smooth-bore at twelve to fifteen paces, but that they were better for long-range shooting.

Meticulous instructions for charging the pistol are given, and again the author makes the very relevant point that much of the poor shooting that occurred was probably due to an incorrect load. His description of the charging of the pistol is worthwhile repeating in detail. Assuming that it has just been removed from the case, the first thing he recommends is to take the muzzle of the

Above:
Pair of fine-quality duelling pistols by Joseph Manton of London. The butts are hatched to afford a firm grip but all other decoration has been omitted. Overall length $15\frac{1}{2}$ inches (39·4 cm).

109

pistol, place it in the mouth and blow gently through the barrel to make sure that the touch-hole is clear and that any dust or dirt that might be blocking it will be moved. The hammer is then put to the half-cock and, if there is one, a safety catch should be applied in this position. The powder should then be measured and very carefully poured down the barrel. To judge the amount required he suggests that experiments should be made by firing the pistol against an iron plate as a target and examining the ball. If when flattened by impact it is about the diameter of a shilling (approximately one inch) that is the correct charge. If the charge is too large the ball will be destroyed on impact.

The next important component was, of course, the ball and again it is emphasized that the ball should be round, cast with great care, and filed till any ridges or obvious irregularities have been removed. The ball should then be wrapped in a piece of kidskin and inserted gently into the barrel. The writer also points out that some powder may be lost if the touch-hole is left unblocked. As the tight-fitting ball is pushed down it displaces air in the barrel, which could force some grains of powder out through the touch-hole. The ball should not fit too tightly: pressure with one thumb should be sufficient to drive it home, and with the other thumb the touch-hole should be blocked to prevent any accidental loss of powder.

The merits of leather over waxed linen for patches are also discussed. The author does not approve the use of waxed linen, since it may leave a deposit on the inside of the barrel, to which some of the grains of powder could become stuck, thus reducing the amount of powder deposited in the breech.

The correct stance for duelling is with the body turned sideways so as to present as small a target area as possible. The stomach should be drawn in and the feet should be almost touching each other. He recommends stamping the feet two or three times onto the ground to make sure that it is steady beneath them. He suggests, very wisely that some point of aim should be taken on the opponent, such as a button on the waistcoat. He advises firing with the arm bent at the elbow and the upper part of the arm pushed

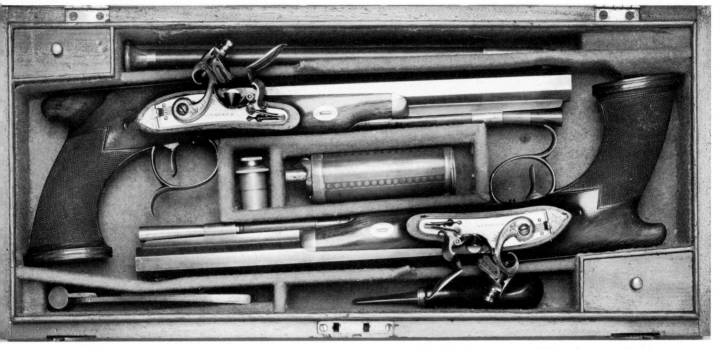

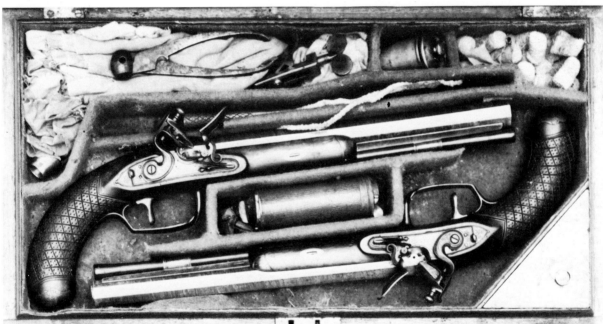

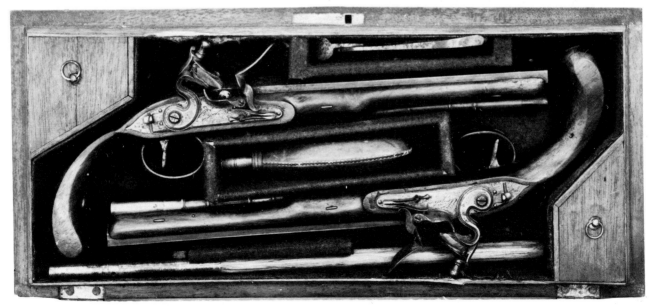

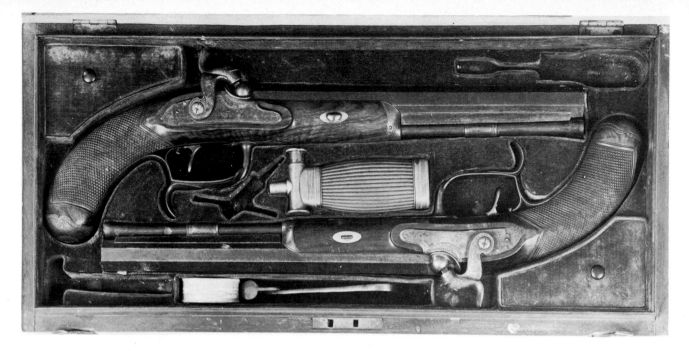

These pistols were the work of a London maker, Durs Egg, about 1800, but at a later date they were converted to the newer percussion system. The style of casing and the powder flask suggest that the conversion was done on the Continent.

firmly against the body – a stance which is certainly not in accordance with the present-day practice. Most experts believe that a much steadier aim is obtained if the arm is rigidly extended. The writer also stresses that the trigger should be squeezed and not pulled.

'Traveller' makes the rather obvious point that the courage to stand still and face an enemy's fire is not easily acquired. He goes on to suggest that in order to accustom himself to this unpleasant event the aspiring duellist should make a wooden model of a man with a strong bracket behind it which would be sufficient to hold a pistol. The trigger would then be fastened to a length of whipcord about thirty-six feet long, with a small hook at the end.

When the pistol had been charged with a good load of powder rammed tight, the duellist would then take up his position facing the model with the pistol pointing at him. He would come up to the aim, ready to fire, and the hook at the end of the cord would then be slipped over his belt. The duellist would then fire and at the same time step or lean backwards, putting pressure on the cord which would cause the pistol to fire.

The author claims that if he carries out this procedure for some months then he will be able to stand and receive fire! His standard of accuracy should enable him to hit twelve targets at fourteen yards in six minutes, loading the pistols between each shot himself. If he can do this he can consider himself proficient in pistol practice.

Some rather interesting figures are given, showing that the chances of a man being killed in a duel were about fourteen to one and, of his being hit, about six to one. 'Traveller' calculates these figures after having examined the results of nearly 200 duels. He also argued that if a man's body as exposed to his enemy is divided into nine parts, only three of them are areas where a wound would prove fatal. If he is hit the chances are three to one against his being killed. Modestly, the author then goes on to say 'that is, however, provided his antagonist has never read my work, or followed any of my practical rules: if he has, the case may be different'.

On the Continent the duel was to become far more elaborate. In 1836 a set of rules was drawn up and supported by seventy-six notable personages of France. This particular French code was adopted by a number of other countries and became more or less

Below:
German percussion rifled target pistol with spurred trigger guard and set trigger. The lock is marked 'S IUNG IN SUHL'. Overall length 15 inches (38 cm).

Left:
Cased set of percussion duelling pistols by Verney at Lyons. The accessories include nipple key, mallet, powder flask, ramrods and cleaning rod. The pistols have octagonal barrels and fluted butts. John Jarvis, Esq.

standard throughout Europe. It was reprinted many times in many countries and, like the *British Code of Duel*, it covered not only the actual duel but also the steps leading up to it. The offended party had the right to choose the weapons and the challenge could be made either on the spot or at a later date, verbally or in writing by means of the second.

The French code listed no less than six different forms of duel and the Austro-Hungarian version added an extra one. The simplest form of duel was that in which the duellist fired from a fixed point. In Europe the firing points were marked out somewhere between fifteen and thirty-five paces, and the offended man had the right to fire first. Once the two were in position facing each other, the signal to fire was given, and both parties then fired in the stated order.

A time limit was set and the first shot had to be fired within a minute of the command. If the second duellist was still on his feet he had to fire within the same time limit. In another slightly different form of duel the two opponents took up their positions twenty-five paces apart. They faced in opposite directions with their backs to each other. On the signal to fire they turned, cocked their pistols, aimed and fired.

More complicated still were the 'moving' duels. In one the opponents faced each other with a space of fifteen to twenty paces marked off between them. Each was then positioned ten paces further back from the lines marking the space. On the command 'march,' they cocked their pistols and, holding them with the muzzle upwards, advanced towards each other. They could fire at any time between starting and reaching the line bounding the space, which they were forbidden to enter.

In some cases the duellists had two pistols each, so giving a double chance, although there were time limits during which the shots could be fired. There were even more elaborate duels in which the two opponents advanced towards each other but did not have to progress in a straight line. They could weave about and even aim without firing. As soon as one combatant had fired both had to stop and the second duellist was allowed his shot. It was very much a matter of nerve and skill, for if the first shot missed the second duellist then had a stationary target. A similar, but more complex, form had two parallel lines twenty to twenty-five paces long, separated by a minimum of fifteen paces. At a given signal the opponents began to walk towards each other from opposite ends of their lines. Each could fire whenever he wished, but once he fired he was bound to stop. If one was wounded he had two minutes in which to fire.

The method which may have caused more fatalities than most was the one known as 'au signal', and it was normally used only when the cause of the duel was thought to be very serious. The seconds drew lots to decide which of them was to give the signal to fire. The opponents were in position twenty-five to thirty paces apart and signals were given by hand claps. The sequence began with the word 'attention', when the opponents took their places, cocked their pistols and stood ready, weapons pointing downwards. At the first clap they moved slowly towards each other. At the second clap they aimed their pistols, and at the third clap they fired. There were all manner of rules to cope with duellists who fired early or who did not fire at the signal and in some cases the seconds were placed in considerable danger if they enforced the rules.

Possibly the most bizarre of duels was the German style known as 'kukuk.' Only one revolver was used and the two duellists, one

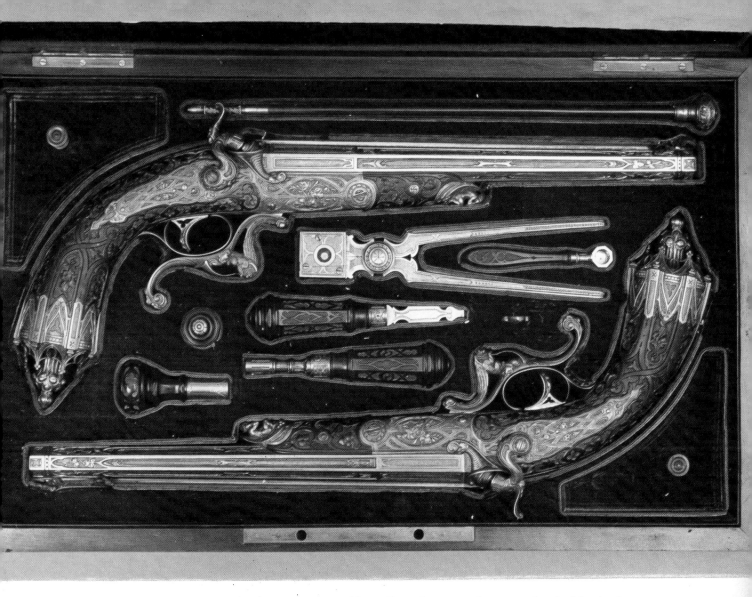

A pair of Austrian target/duelling pistols made about 1860. Although they look very much like percussion weapons they are breech-loading, centre-fire. The ebony and steel stocks are chiselled and carved and the case holds all the necessary accessories. Victoria and Albert Museum, London.

unarmed and barefooted, entered a completely blacked out room. The unarmed duellist was now obliged to call out 'kukuk' and his opponent tried to shoot him, guessing his position from the sound of his voice. It he was successful the duel was over, but if not the roles were then reversed.

These then were the rituals of the duel, but what of the weapons? Until about the last quarter of the eighteenth century the duel was fought with everyday weapons and no special preparation was made except perhaps for an attempt to ensure that both pistols were of comparable quality so that each duellist had a reasonable chance. From about 1770, particularly in Britain, there developed what were in many ways the most finely made of all single-shot flintlock (and later percussion) pistols. One or two London makers acquired a particular reputation for the quality of their specially made duelling pistols, but all good gunmakers could supply such weapons on demand.

Robert Wogden of London was regarded as one of the best suppliers of duelling pistols. His shop in the Haymarket provided the weapons for several famous duels, including those of a vice-president of the United States, Aaron Burr, and a member of the British royal family, the Duke of York. According to a later maker Wogden slightly deformed his barrels so that they shot dead straight at twelve yards enabling the bullet to hit the point of aim. Wogden was also the subject of a poem written in 1782 by 'An Irish Volunteer', which began with the immortal line 'Hail Wogden, Patron of that leaden death'!

115

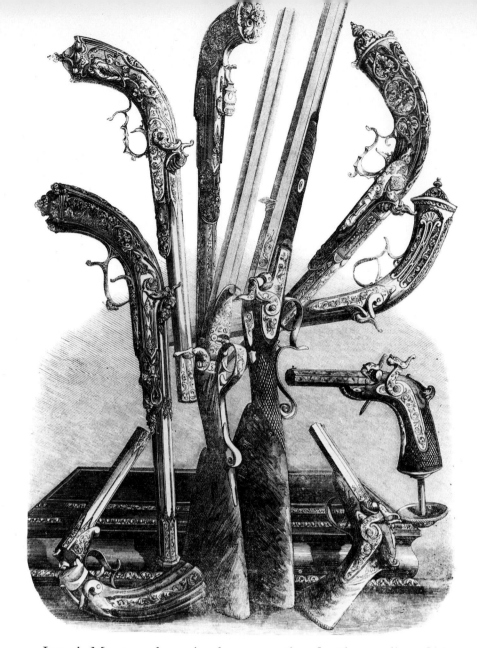

Engraving from a contemporary newspaper showing a display of weapons produced by French gunmakers for the Great Exhibition. The ornate percussion pistols are typical of the Continental target or duelling weapons of the period.

Joseph Manton also gained a reputation for the quality of his pistols. He claimed to be the inventor of the percussion cap and was regarded by many shooters of the period as the leading gunmaker in the country. Henry Mortimer was another famous maker of duelling pistols, which were usually characterized by a pronounced curve at the bottom of the butt.

It is always difficult to define precisely what is a duelling pistol, but basically it is one which is designed to function smoothly and shoot accurately, and which is largely devoid of all unnecessary extras and decoration. Good duelling pistols were made to sit comfortably in the hand, come up to the aim with ease and to be totally reliable.

The finely balanced pistol of the early nineteenth century evolved slowly from about 1770. From the early part of the duelling period, (from 1770 to about 1790) the distinction between an officer's pistol and a duelling pistol was not too obvious. In Britain the sword as a part of civilian attire had been discarded in the 1760s. It was, however, still carried by officers, but it was also usual for them to arm themselves with some form of pistol. The small pocket pistol favoured by gentlemen of quality for self-defence was not really suitable for military use. The officer's pistol usually had a fairly long barrel and a plain wooden stock, and was intended to give reliable service.

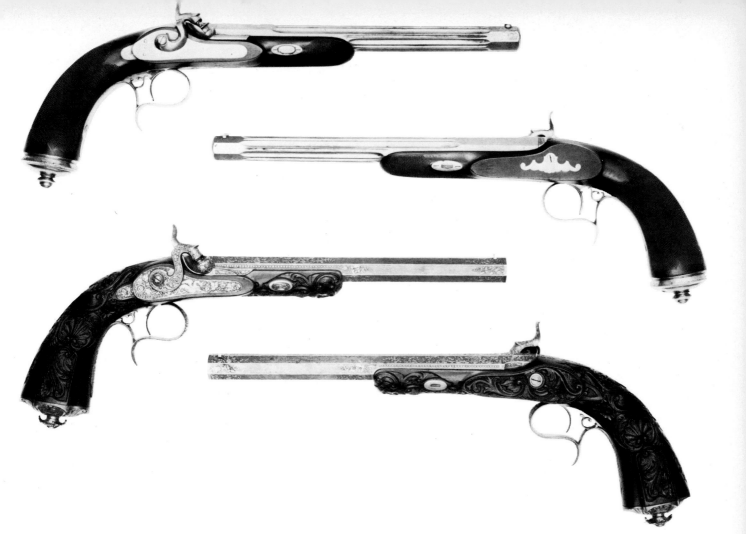

The flintlock duelling pistols of this period are quite similar, lacking frills and fripperies, the only obvious difference being usually in the quality of the workmanship. The typical 'dueller' of the late eighteenth century was usually fully-stocked in walnut, with a gracefully curved butt, which might have flattened sides. Some makers cross-hatched, cutting straight shallow lines on to the butt, so that the surface was roughened to afford a slightly more secure grip. Small shields or escutcheons were sometimes let in the top of the butt just to the rear of the lock. These might carry the numbers 1 and 2, the owner's initials or his coat-of-arms. The furniture, ramrod pipes and trigger guard, which were made of iron or brass, were usually quite plain.

Ramrods were sometimes more elaborate than those on ordinary pistols, with solid horn or brass-capped heads, and many were fitted with a gimlet-like tip, normally covered by a screw cap. This device, known as a jag, was used to draw a charge from an unfired pistol. It was pushed down the barrel until it engaged with the lead ball. It was screwed in and then pulled out with the bullet attached and the powder emptied out. Yet another type of jag was used as a powder measure and loading tool. The cap was unscrewed to reveal a cylindrical measure which was filled with powder. The pistol was held, muzzle down, and the rod pushed in until it touched the breech. Pistol and ramrod were then inverted and the full measured charge deposited directly into the breech, with no grains adhering to the inside of the barrel.

The barrels were usually round in section, about ten to twelve inches long, of medium bore and lacking any decoration. Sights were not always fitted. Since the burning gunpowder left a deposit and could corrode the metal it was important to make

Above. Pair of French rifled target or duelling pistols with fluted barrels, ebony stocks and spurred trigger guards. Overall length 16⅝ inches (42·2 cm).
Below. Two ornate target or duelling pistols by Le Page Moutier. The ebony stock and butts are elaborately carved. Overall length 16 inches (40·6 cm). Mid-nineteenth century.

sure that the touch-hole did not become blocked. Better-quality pistols had a gold or platinum plug set in the barrel around the touch-hole. These 'noble' metals were far more resistant to the corrosive effects of the priming. On some pistols the pan was also lined with gold.

Lock plates were of a shape typical of the period and, like the rest of the weapon, plain and unadorned except for the maker's name engraved on the lower part. The pan was often of the waterproof type, which was so shaped as to guide drops of water running off the barrel away from the pan and the priming powder. Cocks were almost invariably of the goose-neck variety.

Hair triggers were often fitted and, although they could help, they were also potentially dangerous. In September 1859 David C. Broderick, a U.S. senator from California, and David S. Terry, a former chief justice of the Supreme Court of that state, fought a duel over a speech about slavery. They used pistols fitted with hair triggers. When they had been loaded the triggers were set and the pistols were handed to the duellists. One of the seconds then gave the instructions about firing and the two men faced each other, their pistols pointing towards the ground. On the command 'fire' Broderick started to come up to the aim but before he reached it the pistol went off. Almost certainly in his haste he had touched the trigger, which was so light that he wasted his shot. His bullet struck the ground in front of his opponent, who was able to take his time, aim and fire his shot. Broderick was hit and died shortly afterwards. To avoid such disastrous accidents a safety device – a locking bolt – was often fitted to the lock plate just behind the cock. When the cock was upright in the half-cock position the bar could be pushed forward so that it engaged with a slot cut on the inside surface of the cock, thus holding it rigidly in the safe position.

Target Pistols.
Above. Single-shot target pistol made by Cogswell and Harrison 142, New Bond Street, London. It is numbered 58828 and is made to a patent of W. Tranter.
Below. Cheaper, single-shot target pistol – probably of Belgian manufacture. E. Kempster, Gunsmiths.

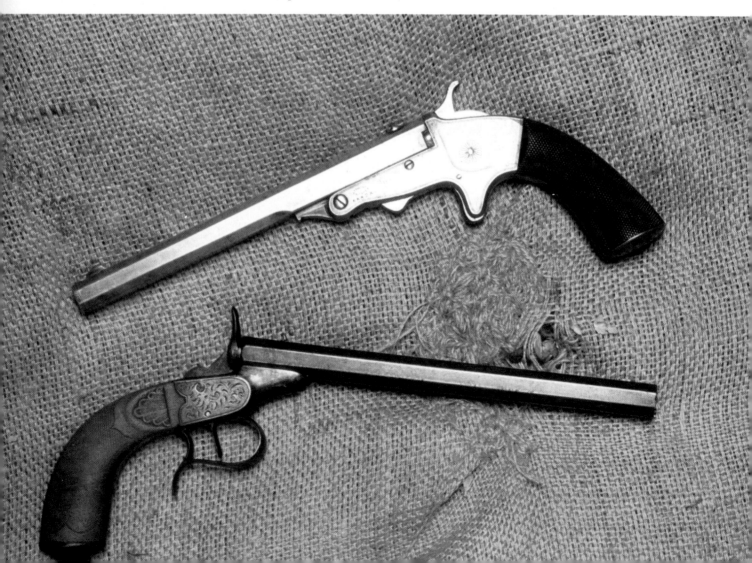

Target Pistols.
Above. The drop-down barrel has a
very simple, hand-operated slider
to eject the empty case. There are
German proof-marks on the barrel.
Despite its appearance it takes a
large-bore cartridge.
Below. A ·22-inch target pistol.
The barrel drops when the trigger
in front of the trigger guard is
operated. The fluted butt and finial
are very similar to those found on
earlier duelling pistols. E. Kempster,
Gunsmiths.

From the early part of the nineteenth century there were various
changes in the design intended to improve the performance of
pistols. Barrels were usually of a smaller bore and almost invariably
octagonal rather than round. Sights were now fairly standard
equipment. Locks were modified in order to improve their action
by reducing friction. Moving surfaces which bore down on each
other had always been carefully honed, but now the bearing
surfaces were reduced in area. The frizzen was often fitted with a
small roller at the tip of the arm, which pressed down on the
frizzen spring. Alternatively the roller could be fitted at the top of
the spring. The main internal bearing surface was between the
tumbler and the mainspring, and this was reduced by fitting a
tiny H-bar at their junction.

To improve the aiming and accuracy of the pistol the trigger
guard was fitted at the rear with a downward curving arm to the
spur. The butt could now be gripped with the index finger on
the trigger, the second finger around the spur and the other two
fingers firmly round the base of the butt. There was also a vogue
for extending the top of the butt into a flat-topped rear-projecting
spur, which rested along the top of the hand between thumb and
index finger – again helping to position the pistol and improve the
steadiness of grip. 'Traveller' disapproved of this style.

Another feature of some of the later duelling pistols was the
adoption of a butt which had lost the hockey-stick appearance
and was now cut off square at the end. It was not uncommon to
put a small recess inside the base of the butt closed off by a spring-
operated steel lid. This compartment could be used to hold
certain small items such as caps or a flint. Many of the later
British duelling pistols were only half-stocked, the wood finishing

part of the way along the barrel. The tip of the stock was usually covered by a horn or steel tip. Since the front part of the stock was missing the ramrod was held in place by a metal tube which was secured beneath the barrel.

Although duelling had long been illegal in Britain army officers still indulged in the fatal art. At the accession of Queen Victoria duels were rare but by no means unknown. However, as the social climate changed and more people condemned the practice duelling fell from favour. In 1844 an association which had been formed for the supression of duelling petitioned Queen Victoria to take action. As a result of this social and political pressure Number 98 of the Articles of War, the rule book of the British army, was amended. It now set out quite clearly that in future any officer who took part in a duel would be cashiered and court martialled. This firm order virtually marked the end of duelling in Britain.

On the Continent, with its longer-established and stronger tradition of duelling, the end did not come quite as quickly. French and Belgian gunmakers continued to supply duelling pistols and, unlike the British, they felt that they could legitimately combine efficiency and decoration. Continental duelling pistols tended to be rather florid, with ebony as a favourite wood for the butts and stocks. These were frequently fluted and carved in quite elaborate shapes. Small-bore barrels were also often fluted and the metal butt cap, lock plate and furniture were usually chiselled and blued. Most had the spur trigger guard.

No matter where they were made, in Britain or in Europe, it was customary to supply duelling pistols in pairs which were normally sold in a wooden case complete with all the accessories. British cases were usually of oak with the inside divided into variously shaped compartments, and the whole of the inside, including the lid, was generally covered with green baize. Although there was no standard pattern most of these cases usually held a pair of pistols, a corner compartment for cast bullets, a powder flask and a bullet mould of the correct size. Extra items might include screwdrivers, cleaning rods, spare flints and possibly a few tools.

Some of the powder flasks were of the three-way variety. The main body of the flask contained the powder charge, and was fitted with a pourer which was not usually adjustable, since there was one recommended size of charge for the pistols. Another section held a small number of bullets, normally three or four, and the base could be unscrewed to reveal a compartment large enough to hold two or three flints. Another variety was only two-way—for bullets and powder. Not all cases were equipped with special flasks: some had the more usual copper powder flasks.

Another vital accessory was, of course, the bullet mould. Moulds varied but the earlier ones were of a scissor type, with two curved arms hinged near the top. Each of the prongs ended in a metal hemisphere with the core scooped out, so that when the two sections were pressed together the hollow formed the correct-sized mould for the ball. A small hole enabled the molten lead to be poured in and allowed to set. When the two arms were opened the lead ball fell out. It usually had a small tail, the sprue, still attached, and this had to be cut off. On some moulds a short section on the inside of the two arms was sharpened to give a scissors-like action for trimming the ball.

The piece of flint was of vital importance. The size of the flint varied according to the size of the weapon, a musket flint being very much larger than that required for a duelling pistol. Experience had shown that the best shape for a flint was basically

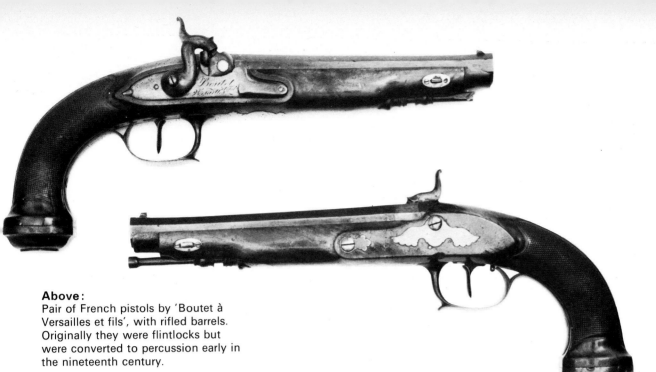

Above:
Pair of French pistols by 'Boutet à Versailles et fils', with rifled barrels. Originally they were flintlocks but were converted to percussion early in the nineteenth century.

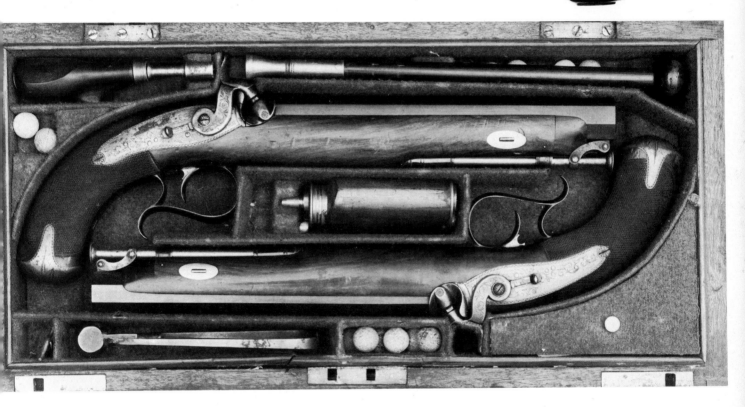

rectangular, with the striking edge thinned down to the form of a wedge. In the military weapon it was reckoned that each flint should be capable of giving a minimum of thirty good strikes. This was, of course not an absolute figure. Some flints were better than others and would go on producing sparks long after their official life was over. Others would strike three or four times and then refuse to function properly. Most of the flints used by the British army were produced at Brandon in Suffolk, and the men whose job it was to shape the flint were known as knappers. The trade has not died out and even today flint knapping is still a useful occupation.

The cases for Continental duelling sets were usually far more elaborate than their British counterparts. Instead of the simple, straight dividers separating the sections, they had carefully

Cased pair of percussion pistols with octagonal barrels and spurred trigger guards. The locks, which are of the back-action variety, are fitted with sliding safety catches. Overall length 14⅞ inches (37·7 cm). The mahogany case bears a brass escutcheon with the name H. Hill Esq.

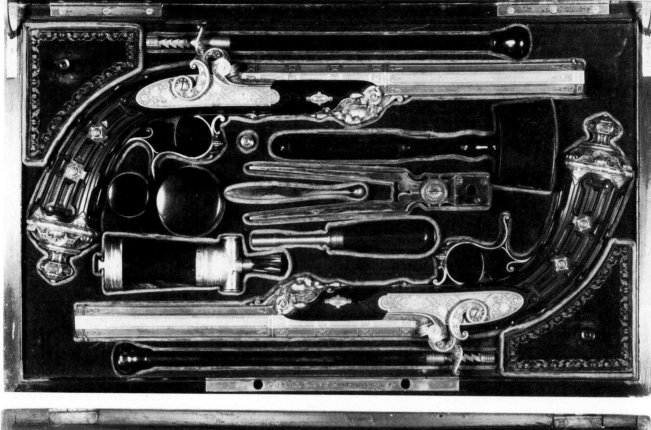

contoured recesses for each item. In place of the green baize the gunsmiths used purple, red or blue linings. The later Continental pistol was often not fitted with its ramrod, and the accessories usually included a ball-headed rod for ramming down the ball. There was often a small mallet for tapping home the ball because many Continental pistols were rifled. The powder flask was sometimes of a fancy patterned variety, with quite elaborate cut offs and measures. With the later percussion pistols the caps were kept in small, often circular, ivory or wooden boxes.

From the late eighteenth century many gunsmiths stuck their trade labels on the inside of the top lid. Some were quite attractive and gave details of the maker's important customers.

In the United States it seems that there was less demand for specially made duelling pistols. The majority of those surviving show very clearly the influence of British makers, although Simeon North, a famous gunmaker of Connecticut, and one or two others, did produce a few. One of the most notorious of American duels was fought with British pistols made by Wogden. It was between Alexander Hamilton a friend of George Washington, and Aaron Burr, the vice-president of the United States. Their quarrel was over the publication of a letter which contained a slanderous reference to Burr. Although the letter had not been published by Hamilton he admitted that he had made the statements contained in it.

The duel, which took place in July 1804, appears to have been fought more or less according to the code practised in Europe. The space measured out was ten full paces, lots were cast for the two positions, and it was agreed that the signal to fire should be a verbal one. The pistols were loaded and on the command both men fired. Hamilton was struck and mortally wounded. There is some doubt about what happened next—some claim that he fired and others that when he was hit he discharged his pistol involuntarily. Although Burr survived the encounter he was forced to leave New York and died in near poverty.

Despite this sad example another duel was fought two years later between two of the leading men of the country, General Andrew Jackson and Charles Dickinson. Jackson claimed that his opponent had slandered his wife and the outcome was viewed with considerable interest by the public, for both men were known to be first-class shots. The event took place on May 30, 1806. Dickinson fired and hit the general in the breast, breaking two ribs but the wound was not fatal. Jackson then presented and, incredibly, the pistol stuck at the half-cock position. Despite his wound Jackson carefully re-cocked the pistol, presented and fired. Dickinson was mortally wounded.

The incidence of duelling in Europe and America decreased steadily during the nineteenth century, but many still felt the need to demonstrate their shooting skill in some way other than at the target. A Dr Devilliers designed some special pistols and bullets for those who wanted to conduct duels in safety. The bullets were of some light material, such as tallow or wax, and the pistols were accurate up to a range of approximately twenty paces. The duellists wore long, loose robes and special fencing masks fitted with a glass visor. The shooter's hand was protected by a shield fitted over the pistol.

As a result of all the great improvements brought about by modern technology, including new propellants which give remarkable accuracy, the duellist today would stand little chance of surviving an 'affair of honour'—not even the author of *The Art of Duelling*!

The genius
of Samuel Colt

One of the limitations of almost all the weapons discussed so far has been that they fired only a single shot. A gun could be reloaded but this took time, and in battle, and even in hunting, a second shot following immediately on the first could be of vital importance. One obvious way of overcoming this difficulty was to carry two pistols. This, however, was not completely satisfactory for it doubled the weight carried and occupied both hands, or at least meant the pistols would have to change hands very quickly. What the gunsmiths, soldiers and hunters wanted was a single weapon which could deliver several shots from one loading.

This idea was as old as firearms themselves. From the very beginning, right up to the early sixteenth century it was not uncommon for a group of barrels, two, three or four in number, to be mounted circularly around a central axis. Each was loaded with powder and ball, and when the uppermost was fired the grip was turned so that the second barrel was presented, and so on. Early in the sixteenth century the idea was developed further and one gun of about 1540 had three barrels which were rotated instead of the weapon itself. The barrels were locked into position by means of a little spring catch.

The same principle was adopted by the makers of wheel-locks, and one such pistol fired steel darts rather than bullets. However, the idea of revolving barrels seems to have gone out of favour, as examples of weapons using this method are seldom found in any quantity again before the middle of the seventeenth century. Another system was the superimposed load, but it was a somewhat hazardous method and accidents were no doubt frequent. A specially made barrel with an appropriate number of touch-holes was loaded. First the powder went in, then the ball, next a tight-fitting wad was pushed in place, and then another charge of powder and ball with another wad. Three such charges seem to have been about the maximum. The lock and touch-hole were brought in conjunction and the last load was the first to be fired. In theory the wad prevented flame or sparks from blowing backwards to the other charges. The lock or barrel was then moved to bring the second touch-hole to the correct position, the second shot was fired and the process repeated. In fact it was not uncommon for all three charges to be fired at the same time, often with disastrous results!

Above:
Rare four-barrelled, ducksfoot
flintlock pistol marked Bass and Co.
All the barrels are discharged
simultaneously. The flat butt has
typical late eighteenth-century silver
inlay decoration.

Right:
Early German snaphaunce revolver
of about 1600. The pan covers were
manually operated. Tøjhusmuseet,
Copenhagen.

An even more elaborate and potentially more hazardous system
was known as the 'Roman Candle gun'. This comparatively rare
weapon was made up of a group of barrels, four in all, united
into a single block. One barrel was loaded in the conventional
way, the second was loaded with powder only, and the other two
were loaded with a series of superimposed charges. The sequence of
events was as follows. The first barrel was fired and the flash from
the powder was transmitted to the powder-filled barrel by a touch-
hole near the muzzle. As the powder burnt down, rather like a
slow-burning fuse, the flame passed through a series of touch-
holes, one after the other, to ignite the superimposed charges, so
that one shot was followed very shortly afterwards by seven more
shots. There were variations on this system, all of which presented
certain difficulties.

Some wheel-locks were made with one butt and two barrels, each with its own lock. In the seventeenth century some flintlocks were made with one lock and two barrels, each with its own pans and frizzen. In the following century the system was modified. Pistols were fitted with two barrels side by side, and each given its own lock and trigger Some makers produced variations on this basic theme, including pistols with a single lock mounted centrally, known as a box lock, working against a single frizzen situated over the two touch-holes. Selection of left or right barrel was made by means of a cover, which could be slid across the pan to cover one of the touch-holes.

One unusual variant of the multi-barrelled weapon was the so-called 'duck's foot', with four or five barrels connected to a single block and lock. The barrels were splayed slightly, hence the name, and the pistols were made for use in confined quarters, where a mob or possibly a mutinous crew on a ship were attacking. Although some such pistols are known to have been used in the seventeenth century, most surviving examples date from the latter part of the eighteenth century.

Another type of multi-barrel weapon was the volley gun, in which the shots, instead of being spread, were concentrated in a single field of fire. The best known of this kind was made by Henry Nock, a London gunmaker, although the idea originated with James Wilson as early as 1779. It was, in effect, a reversion to the basic multi-shot weapon of the late medieval period. Seven barrels were fitted in a single circular block and one single action of the lock fired all seven barrels together.

Probably the commonest multi-barrel weapon was the tap-action pocket pistol, popular during the late eighteenth and early nineteenth century. Two barrels were mounted one above the

Above:
Collier's revolvers were among the most successful of the early repeating weapons. They were originally flintlock but this carbine, No. 121, has been converted to percussion, probably around 1820. Peter Dale, Esq.

Opposite, top left:
The famous address (the arrangement and wording varied on different models). This is from a ·31-inch (7·8-mm) pocket Colt.

Opposite, top right:
The muzzle of a large-calibre, ·45-inch (11·4-mm) percussion pepperbox revolver dating from about 1830. It was effective but awkward to handle since the large barrel block made the weapon very muzzle-heavy. Private Collection.

Opposite, above:
Snaphaunce revolver with the cylinder enclosed in a brass shield, probably made by John Dafte of London. Tower of London Armouries.

Opposite, below:
Superimposed load wheel-lock pistol with three locks, probably made in Nuremberg about 1550. Tower of London Armouries.

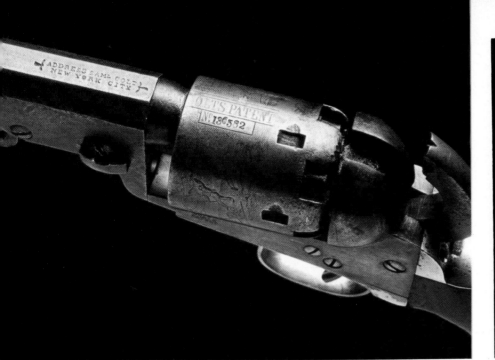
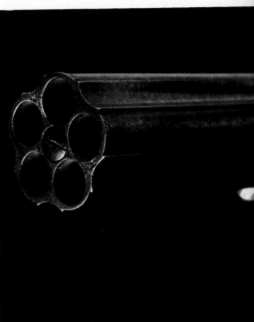

other on a breech fitted with a box-lock. The touch-hole of the top barrel was connected directly to the pan. The touch-hole of the lower barrel was connected to the pan by means of a thick metal disc with a depression at the top which, in effect, formed the second pan.

The two barrels were loaded and the block was turned to bring the hollowed section uppermost, positioned so as to be beneath the pan. A quantity of priming powder was put in and the cylinder was rotated then by means of an external fitting, the so-called tap. As the block rotated it now presented a solid surface at the base of the pan. A quantity of priming powder was put in and the cylinder was the solid wall of the breech section. The pan was now primed, the frizzen closed and the safety catch applied. The weapon could be carried with reasonable safety in the pocket. In case of an attack the pistol was drawn, the safety catch slipped, and the pistol cocked and fired. This discharged the top barrel, which was

127

Top:
Flintlock pistol with three barrels
made by Lorenzoni about 1680 and
carrying the Medici arms. The barrels
had to be rotated by hand but the
design is better than many. Only
one lock is used to ignite (separately)
the chambers through a cylindrical
breech block. Victoria and Albert
Museum, London.

Above:
The chambers of one of the best of
the flintlock revolvers, by John Dafte
of London. Overall length $33\frac{1}{8}$ inches
(84·1 cm) Late seventeenth century.
The Wadsworth Atheneum, Hartford,
Connecticut.

connected directly to the pan. The tap was now turned bringing
into place the second quantity of priming at the base of the pan.
The weapon was recocked and was then ready to fire the second
shot. Although most tap-action pistols had two barrels a limited
number were made with three barrels.

Because of the nature of the mechanism there were many
problems involved in creating a multi-shot flintlock weapon.
Since each barrel had to be served by one cock or frizzen it was
difficult to arrange this without a very cumbersome procedure. The
prospects of a really good multi-shot weapon remained elusive
throughout most of the eighteenth century. There were attempts,
some quite successful, to produce flintlock revolvers, but they were
all somewhat complex and rather expensive. A design by Elisha
Collier, patented in 1818, was probably the most advanced and
satisfactory.

Quite apart from the mechanical problems there were weaknesses inherent in the system itself. Although far less vulnerable to
the elements than the matchlock, the flintlock was still somewhat at
risk and the sportsman out in heavy rain or mist had problems. For
the hunter there was the additional disadvantage of the hangfire.
There was a short but nevertheless appreciable delay between the
time when the trigger was pressed and the moment when the
bullet actually left the muzzle. When the trigger was pressed it

Flintlock revolver by John Tocknell of Brighton with seven hand-rotated barrels. Overall length 8¾ inches (22·2 cm). Art Gallery and Museum, Glasgow.

operated the sear. This released the cock which swung forward to strike sparks which fell into the priming. The priming flashed and the flame passed through the touch-hole to ignite the main charge, which itself had to burn before enough pressure was generated to drive the bullet forward. When the priming fired there was a very noticeable flash of flame and spurt of smoke, and contemporary prints of the period clearly show this. In battle this was of no consequence, but it gave a momentary warning to the bird or deer which the hunter had so carefully stalked and started the creature moving before the bullet had left the muzzle.

Many attempts had been made to overcome the problem of the flash of the priming powder. Some wheel-locks were fitted with a kind of chimney over the pan, which carried the smoke away from the firer's face. Shrewd hunters were able, by instinct and experience, to compensate for this hangfire, but, nevertheless, for the average shooter it remained a serious handicap.

Some sought to overcome the difficulty by trying to find a faster, simpler and more efficient method of ignition. However, by the beginning of the nineteenth century the flintlock had reached its peak of perfection and there was little more that could be done to speed up its action. The solution was found by Alexander John Forsyth, who was the minister at the Manse of Belhelvie, just to the north of Aberdeen. Forsyth, who had graduated at King's College, Aberdeen, had taken over his father's parish. He was a keen shooter, but like so many men of his time he had an interest in a number of subjects including chemistry. He read about substances which had been known of for some time, but were then becoming popular scientific curiosities. These were the fulminates of mercury and silver and their interesting quality was that they would explode upon impact. Forsyth believed that by mixing some of these very unstable materials with gunpowder he could encourage more rapid burning and so reduce the hangfire time.

Percussion pepperbox by W. Parker
of London of about 1830. It is a
fine-quality weapon with engraved
German silver mounts. It has the
common type of bar hammer. Private
Collection.

Tap-action, double-barrelled,
flintlock pistol with top barrel
removed. The tap is visible on the
side of the breech. About 1780.

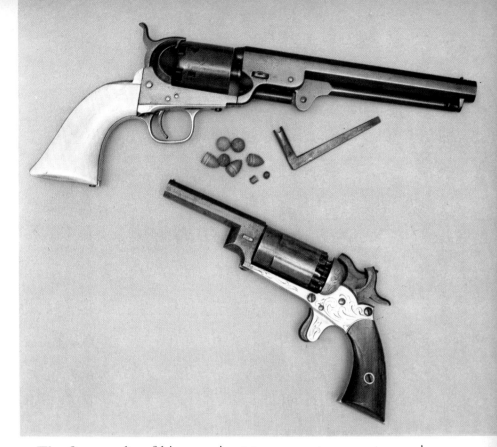

Right:
Above. Colt Navy Percussion
Revolver, ·36-inch (9-mm) calibre
and fitted with ivory grips, together
with bullets, percussion cap and
special key for undoing the nipples.
Below. A Walch revolver which was
most unusual, as it fired ten shots
by means of double-loaded chambers
and two hammers. Private Collection.

The first results of his experiments were not very encouraging, since the fulminates were extremely dangerous to use. He then decided that their qualities might possibly be utilized, not as the main propellant, but as a means of prime ignition. At first he experimented by replacing the priming powder with these special chemicals. Again the results were not very encouraging. The fulminates tended to burn so quickly that they just flashed in the pan and the flame did not pass through the touch-hole to ignite the main charge. With further experiments he found that indeed the explosion of the fulminate was sufficient to ignite the main charge, provided it was carefully positioned.

He tried several methods and in 1805 he adapted a standard flintlock and found that, with his modifications, it was easily primed and far more certain of fire. He used the lock throughout the summer of that year and it proved very satisfactory.

In 1806 Forsyth went to London in the hopes of interesting the Ordnance in his new invention. Lord Moira, the Master General of the Ordnance, considered the possibilities of this new development and agreed that Forsyth should carry out some experiments in the Tower of London. Forsyth was anxious to return to his parish, but was persuaded to stay on and supervise the work, which began in July of that year. It was soon discovered that, although his methods was quite simple in theory, in practice it offered certain difficulties. There were accidents, the detonation was too powerful and sometimes fractured locks, but eventually, after much trial and error, he produced a workable system.

In March 1807 Lord Moira left the Ordnance and the new master-general decided, for reasons of his own, that there was little point in continuing with the experiments. On April 10 Forsyth left the Tower after having claimed his various expenses. He decided that, although he had patriotically refused to do so before, now was the time to take out a patent on his invention, and this was duly enrolled on September 3, 1807. In June 1808 a double-fronted shop in Piccadilly, London, was opened up as the Forsyth Patent Gun Company.

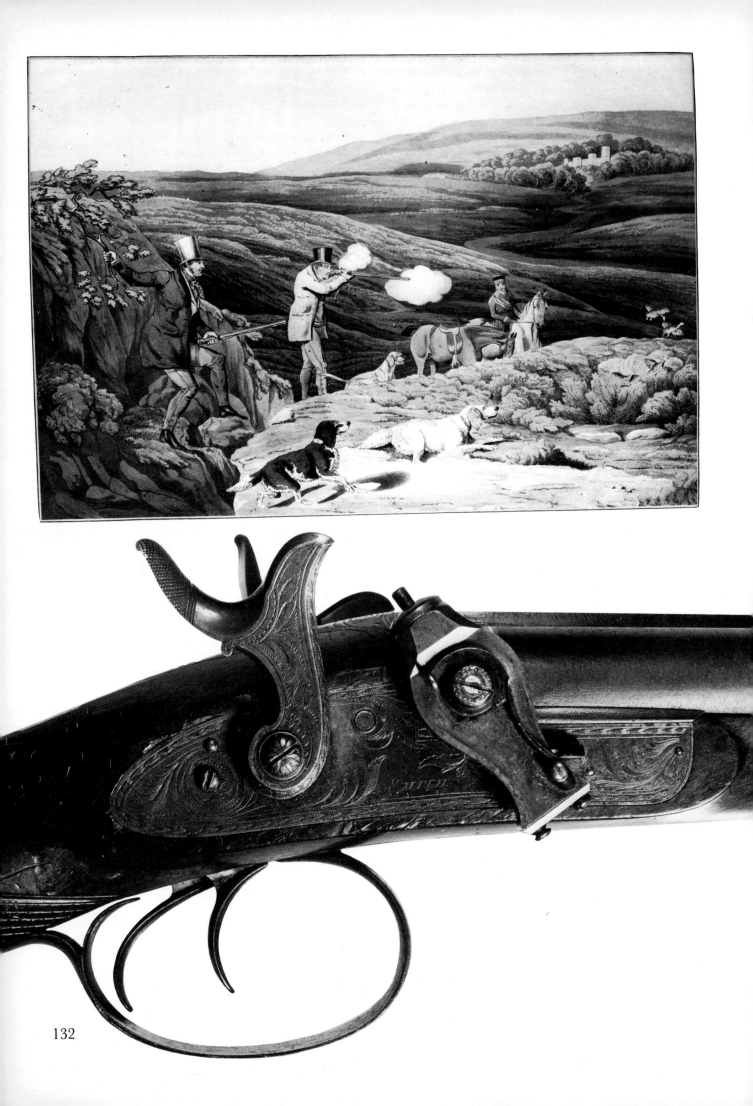

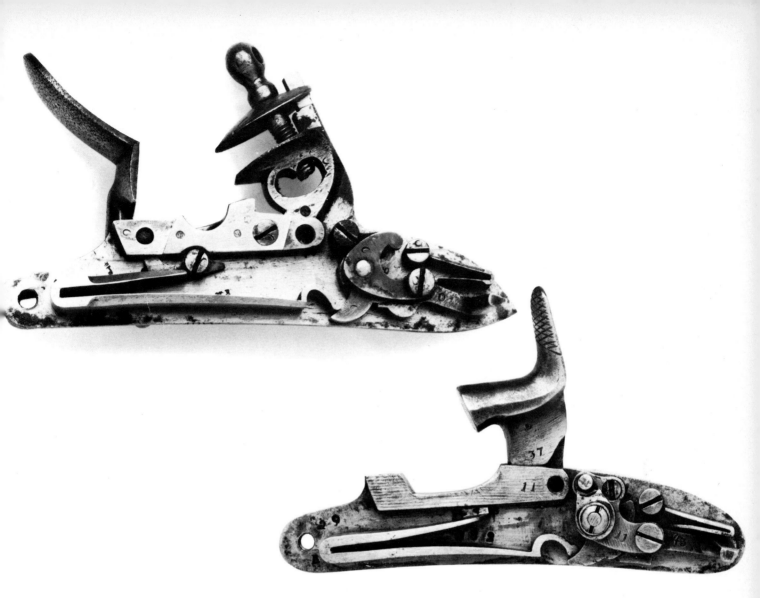

Although there were various modifications and alterations, the basic Forsyth priming mechanism, usually known from its shape as his 'scent bottle,' consisted of a container which held the fulminate. This was attached to a central pillar replacing the old pan. A hole was drilled from the touch-hole, through the cylinder and up to a small depression. The container rotated around this central column. Into the base of the container was loaded the fulminate and in the top section, which was normally above the central pillar, was a spring-loaded plunger.

The method of operation was as follows. After the fulminate had been loaded as described, the container was then turned through 180 degrees and a few grains of fulminate allowed to trickle through a small aperture into the central pillar. The container was then returned to its normal position, so that the spring plunger was again above the fulminate. In place of the old flintlock cock a solid-nosed hammer was fitted. When the trigger was pressed the hammer hit the plunger, forcing it down to strike against the grains of fulminate, which exploded and flashed through the touch-hole to ignite the charge.

The device worked although the degree of tolerance in constructing the container had to be fairly small, and there was an inherent risk that the fulminate in it could be detonated by the flash. However, providing the container was well maintained, greased and oiled, the risk was quite small, and it seems that accidents were rare.

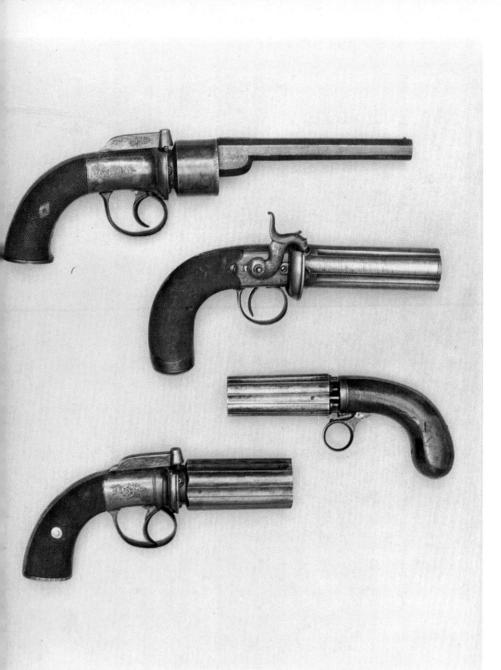

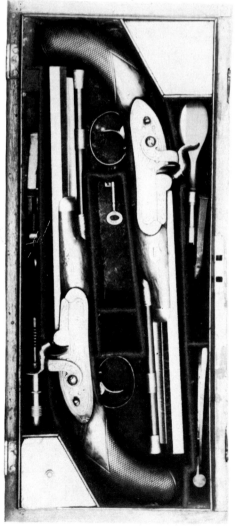

There were attempts to infringe Forsyth's patent, but in general he was successful in preventing people from making similar mechanisms. In 1818 the most important of his lawsuits granted him the patent, not just of his particular mechanism, but of the percussion lock in general. In view of the great step forward that the percussion lock represented it would be pleasant to report that the minister of Belhelvie was able to return and live a life of comfort in his parish, rewarded by a grateful nation. Alas, the reverse was the case. When in 1838 the British army decided to convert their weapons to percussion Forsyth, quite reasonably, suggested that he deserved some recompense for having introduced the system. He was awarded a mere £200.

At first he seems to have been satisfied with this parsimonious reward but on reflection he decided that this was rather ungenerous. Accordingly, with the support and encouragement of many friends and influential people, he applied for some increase. Eventually, in 1843 it was agreed that the sum should be increased to £1,000. However poor Dr Forsyth did not have the opportunity to enjoy his triumph, for he died the same year.

A number of pistols and long arms were produced with the Forsyth 'scent bottle', but it was not a completely satisfactory system and there were many attempts to make it more convenient, safer and easier to use. One great handicap was that the fulminate was in the form of a powder, which meant that it was awkward to handle and liable to accidental detonation. Some safer and simpler system was required. A whole range of devices were tried including quills, small copper tubes filled with the fulminate, pellets and little patches of paper containing the fulminate. The most satisfactory and generally adopted solution was that of the copper percussion cap. This consisted of a small copper cup-shaped device, on the inside base of which was deposited a very small amount of the fulminate. A short metal tube (the nipple) pierced with a small hole which led directly into the breech, was fitted to the barrel. The cap was slipped on to the top of this nipple and was held in place by friction.

The internal mechanism of the lock was unaltered but the cock was replaced by a hammer varying in design, but basically an S-shape and with a hollow nose that fitted over the nipple. As the hammer swung forward it struck the cap against the top of

Below:
Double-barrelled percussion pistol, half-stocked with captive ramrod and back-action lock. The locks have a safety catch bolt behind the hammer. This pistol was made by the gunsmith, J. Purdey, of Oxford Street, London. About 1841.

Bottom:
Percussion overcoat pistol with swivel ramrod by Wm & In. Rigby, Irish gunmakers famous for good-quality weapons. Many of their pistols were made with the butts recessed to hold two or three bullets.

135

English percussion revolvers.
Top. Adams self-cocking revolver,
1851. No. 5976.
Above left. Deane Adams, double-
action revolver. Bore ·45 inches.
No. 194837. About 1860.
Centre right. Daws, double-action
revolver. Bore ·4 inches. No. 1651.
Bottom. Kerr double-action
revolver. Bore ·4 inches. Patented
1858–9.
Pattern Room, Royal Small Arms
Factory, Enfield.

the nipple, caused the fulminate to detonate and so sent the flame directly into the breech. The front of the nose encircled the cap and so prevented any splinters from flying off the nipple.

The copper percussion cap was generally adopted during the 1820s, but there is much controversy about the identity of the original designer and inventor. Several well-known figures of the period laid claim to having designed it but, in fact, there is no conclusive evidence one way or the other as to which of the main contenders—Peter Hawker, James Purdy, Joseph Egg or Joshua Shaw—had the best claim.

One of the problems facing the army authories during the first half of the nineteenth century was the fact that when the percussion lock became available their troops were still largely armed with flintlocks. Most felt that it was impossible to scrap all their existing stocks and replace them with new weapons, and a great deal of time and effort was devoted to finding systems which allowed the flintlock to be converted to percussion. The same applied in the private sector and many sporting guns, pistols, and blunderbusses were changed over to the new system.

Although the procedure varied, most flintlocks were converted by drilling out the touch-hole and inserting a short, drum-like filling with a nipple attached, or fitting a nipple directly to the barrel. Pan, frizzen and spring were removed from the lock plate

Right:
Deane Adams revolvers. It is very unusual to find two cased together. They are fitted with side-rammers for pushing home the bullets into the chambers. Like all Deane Adams they carry numbers: 18048R and 18009R. About 1860. R. Egles.

Below:
Beaumont-Adams percussion revolver by Adams and Company, London, with the British War Department mark W↑D. Probably made between July 1855 and August 1856. J. Howarth, Esq.

An unusual percussion pistol which exhibits many features of a much earlier style of flintlock, but the silver fittings bear the hallmarks of 1863.

Opposite:
Above. Spenser repeating rifle Model 1867. Calibre ·50 inches (12·7 mm). The action was worked by the trigger guard. Overall length 46½ inches (118 cm). Barrel 28 inches (71·1 cm).
Below. Colt percussion rifle with side hammer. Calibre ·58 inches (14·7 mm). Overall length 49 inches (124·5 cm). Barrel 31 inches (78·8 cm). Pattern Room, Royal Small Arms Factory, Enfield.

Opposite, from top to bottom:
1. Double-barrelled over and under percussion pistol by D. Egg, Pall Mall, London, with walnut butt. Overall length 9 inches (22·9 cm).
2. Pepperbox with bar hammer and top safety catch by Hollis and Sheath, London. Overall length 11⅛ inches (28·3 cm). About 1845.
3. Percussion revolver by J. Lang, Cockspur St, London, with special spring-loaded ramrod. Overall length 11 inches (27·9 cm). About 1850.
4 and 5. Pair of percussion pistols with octagonal barrels by Westley Richards of London. Overall length 12¾ inches (32·4 cm).

Belt hooks support the pistols of this coastguard of about 1830. Holsters did not become common before the mid-nineteenth century.

and the cock was replaced by an appropriately shaped hammer. Many of the later Brown Bess muskets were so adapted, and when the Brunswick and Enfield rifles were adopted by the army they too were fitted with the percussion lock.

The percussion system also simplified the construction of the so-called pepperbox pistols which were, in effect, revolvers with clusters of four to six barrels, rotated by hand to bring each one in position by the lock. However, the weapon had been clumsy and rather inconvenient to carry. The percussion pepperbox consisted of a solid cylinder of metal drilled with five to six bores, each fitted with a nipple. Each of the bores, or barrels, was loaded and a cap placed on its nipple. The first shot was fired. Then the barrel assembly was turned to bring the next bore into line ready to fire and there was usually some form of catch to ensure an accurate alignment. This weapon gave the shooter five or six shots but, of course, the great disadvantage was that both hands were required to operate it.

It was fairly obvious that the next step was to produce some form of pepperbox in which the rotation was done mechanically. Tradition, unsubstantiated by hard facts, has it that Henry Humberger, a gunmaker from Ohio, devised a self-cocking pepperbox in 1832. The term self-cocking means that, as the trigger is pulled back, the cylinder is rotated and the hammer raised and allowed to fall, the whole action being started by the movement of the trigger.

The first patented self-cocking pepperbox (1837) appears to be that of another U.S. maker, Ethan Allen, although he is supposed to have made his first in 1834. Also in 1837 another variety of pepperbox was patented in Belgium by Mariette, for which a British patent was granted in 1840. The distinctive feature of these weapons is that the trigger is in the form of a ring and the nipples are situated at the rear of each barrel, horizontal with the axis. In these guns the lower barrel is fired first.

The pepperbox was satisfactory up to a point, but it had its disadvantages, one of the most obvious being the considerable weight of the barrel assembly. The weapon tended to be very

138

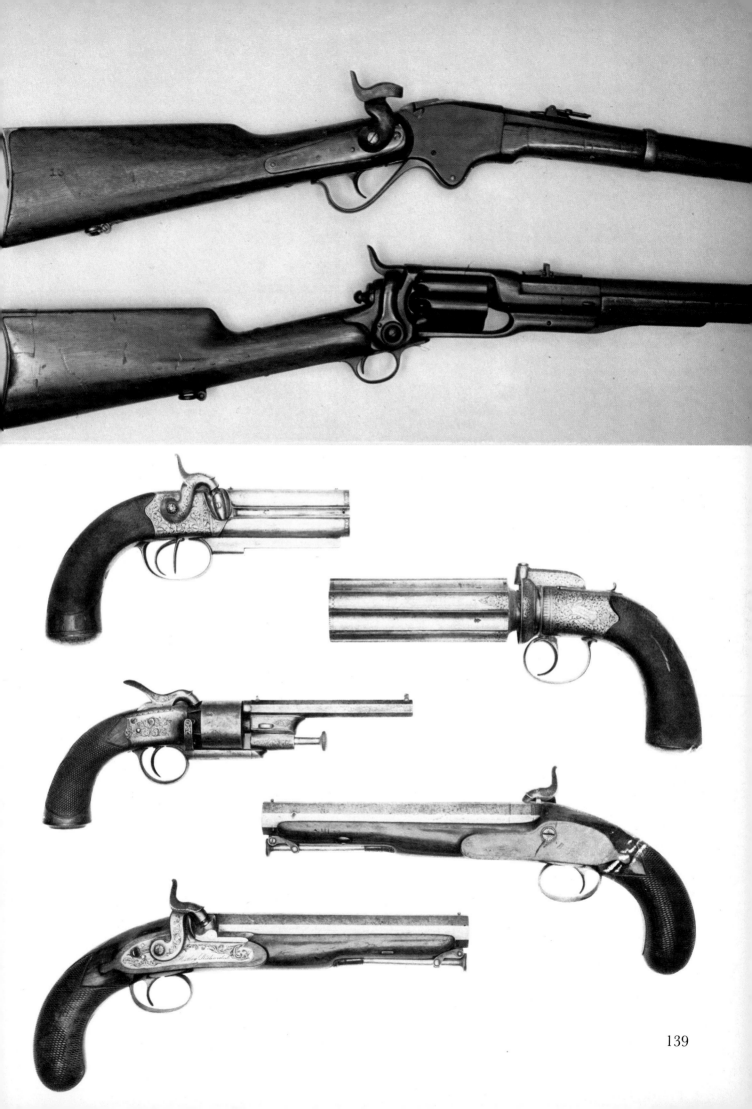

Typical bar-hammer pepperbox revolver made by Thomas Jackson, of Edward Street, London. About 1840. Tower of London Armouries.

Samuel Colt holding one of his very successful percussion revolvers.

muzzle heavy, rather bulky and not very convenient for carrying in a pocket for personal defence. There was also the danger of the chain-fire, that is, of one cap setting off all the others, although this could usually be averted by careful design. These guns were also smooth-bore and inaccurate. An attempt was made to overcome the lack of accuracy by a compromise. The barrel assembly was made much shorter, in effect turning it into a revolver cylinder, and a rifled barrel was fitted to the front of the assembly. These so-called transitional revolvers enjoyed a certain popularity around the middle of the nineteenth century but they were only a rather cheap compromise. By the late 1840s a much more satisfactory revolver was becoming available.

The name of Samuel Colt is probably the best known of all names in the story of firearms. He was undoubtedly a great innovator, a man with vision, enthusiasm and drive, but it is doubtful whether his contribution to the firearms story is quite as great as the legends surrounding him would suggest.

In his youth he was impetuous and tried his hand at many things. According to tradition it was while on a voyage to Calcutta on the *S.S. Savannah* that he is supposed to have occupied himself whittling away at the wooden model of a device that he had been considering for some time. From this was to come the first really sound commercially produced revolver. Basically Colt's system consisted of a little arm which engaged with a projection at the rear of the cylinder and as the hammer was pulled back this arm rose up, pushing the cylinder round. When it was correctly positioned another little arm came up and locked the cylinder in position. This was most important because one of the problems of the early revolvers had been the escape of gas and energy when the chamber and barrel were not accurately lined up.

Colt returned to America in 1831 convinced that his system was practicable and worthwhile developing. He visited England and on October 22, 1835, was granted an English patent. On his return to the United States in the following year he was granted an American patent and now set about establishing a company. He attracted capital from some New Yorkers and formed The Patent

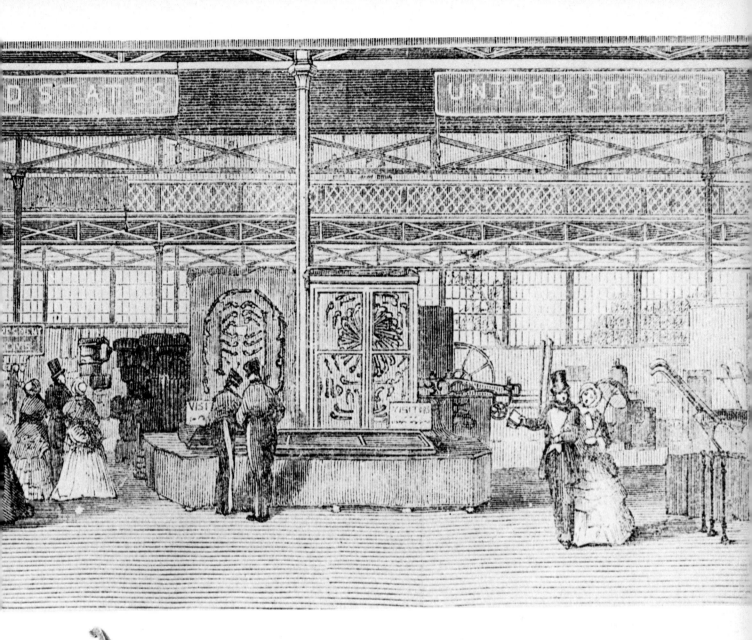

Top:
Detail from an engraving showing part of the American Gallery at the Great Exhibition of 1851. The two soldiers are in front of Samuel Colt's stand.

Above:
Colt's Paterson Belt pistol of 1836. It has a concealed trigger which drops down when the hammer is pulled back. Winchester Gun Museum, New Haven, Connecticut.

141

Pair of Model 1861 Colt Army percussion revolvers in the original mahogany, brass-bound case, with all accessories including one spare cylinder. Both are inscribed on the back strap of the butt 'MARK FIRTH ESQ FROM PRESIDENT COLTS PFA Mfg.CO.' and are numbered 12989 and 12990. Mark Firth was almost certainly one of the family owning the company which supplied Colt with steel for his London factory. Pattern Room, Royal Small Arms Factory, Enfield.

Arms Manufacturing Company of Paterson, New Jersey. Either through anxiety to get into production or possibly carelessness, Colt had not carried out really exhaustive tests and many of his early weapons proved defective. He tried to interest the U.S. army in his revolver but the tests that were carried out unfortunately did not go very well and the weapon received only faint praise in the official report.

If there was one talent that Samuel Colt possessed it was the ability to promote himself and his goods. He missed no opportunity to publicize his weapon at fairs and demonstrations, or with trade cards, and newspaper advertisements. It looked as if Colt was on the road to success. He was awarded the gold medal of the American Institute and he even managed to sell fifty of his rifles to the troops fighting the Seminole Indians in Florida. The weapons proved most satisfactory in the very difficult surroundings of the Everglade Swamps. However, sales were disappointing. In fact, the only really large sale was of 180 Paterson holster pistols, 180 carbines and 100 rifles to the Texas navy. Unsatisfactory reports were received and Colt was at loggerheads with some of his

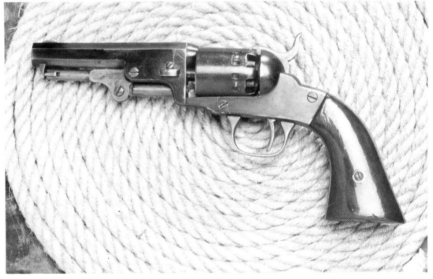

business associates. Finally in 1842, as a result of a court order, the Patent Arms Company was sold up.

Colt was not discouraged from continuing his experiments and in 1844 he tried hard to interest the U.S. navy in a combined knife-type revolver, in which the trigger guard served as a part of the hilt and also as a loading lever.

However, success still eluded Colt until he met the man who was to set him on the path to fame and, if not fortune, at least to a comfortable living. A Captain Samuel H. Walker wrote to Colt on November 30, 1846, telling him how, in the summer of 1844, a group of sixteen men had fought eighty Comanche Indians killing and wounding half of them. According to Captain Walker their success was due entirely to the fact that they were using Colt's pistols. In January 1847 a contract was drawn up for 1,000 pistols with 9-inch barrels to fire a bullet of thirty-two to the pound.

Colt's problem was now to supply the weapons. Fortunately he had already written to another gunmaker, Eli Whitney, asking if he would be prepared to undertake their manufacture and

143

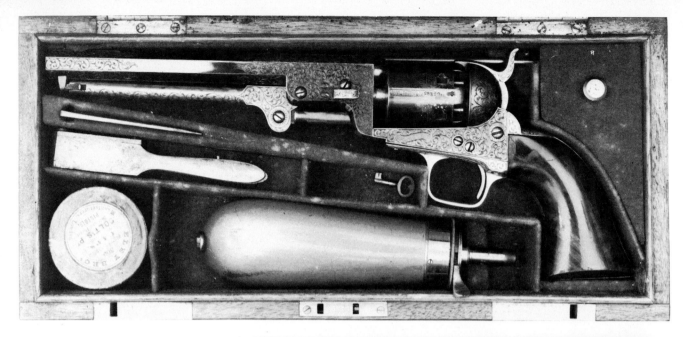

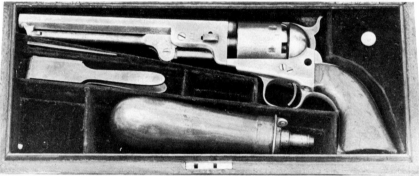

Top:
Cased 1851 Navy Colt No. 28329, with silvered back strap. The revolver is engraved and the case is inscribed 'Edward Micklam R.E.' and belonged to a commandant of the Royal Engineers.

Above right:
Cased 1851 Navy Colt with powder flask, bullet mould and nipple key. The empty section held a tin of percussion caps. This particular example bears Enfield stampings on the butt and may have been part of an official British order.

Whitney had agreed. Captain Walker also suggested improvements on the original design, and the finished revolver was a good solid piece of workmanship. Colt had engraved on the cylinder a representation of a fight between Indians and cowboys, and most of his later percussion revolvers carried an engraved scene on the cylinder.

His pistols now began to sell steadily and Colt set up a factory in Pearl Street in Hartford, Connecticut. New models were developed and by 1849 business was so good that Colt returned to Europe, taking up further patents and exploiting every opportunity to promote his revolvers. He was back again in Britain in 1851, the year of the Great Exhibition. Colt thought this was a fine opportunity to place his firearms before a world market, and he displayed 450 weapons in the American section of the Exhibition. Colt's shrewd exploitation emphasized that his was a good, solid, simple weapon and that all the parts were interchangeable. If the mainspring broke it was possible to order from stock and replace it. If the cylinder was lost a new one which would fit exactly was immediately available. Colt also continued his normal practice of presenting revolvers to anybody he thought might be of assistance in promoting the sale of his weapons.

So encouraged was Colt by his reception that he decided to set up a London factory. Late in 1852 he acquired some premises at Bessborough Place, Pimlico, and sent over machinery from his Hartford factories. He ordered his steel from Thomas Firth and Sons in Sheffield and in 1853 he was ready to supply the British market from his London factory. The outbreak of war with Russia stimulated the demand. On August 2, 1855, some 9,000 revolvers

Engraving of Roberts Adams loading one of his percussion revolvers. During the early 1850s he was Colt's only English rival of any consequence.

Mid-nineteenth-century percussion revolvers. The top three are Colt 1851 Navy pattern. The second from the top carries British ordnance marks and the third has been covered with decoration, probably in India. The lower two are British Beaumont Adams revolvers.

were ordered for the British army. Although factory production ceased in 1857 Colt maintained an agency in London which continued to do quite good business, especially at the time of the Indian Mutiny in 1857.

In the United States business was expanding and Colt created an entirely new factory in South Meadows, just outside Hartford, by the side of the Connecticut River. Colt was now riding on a wave of success, making frequent visits to Europe and extending his range as far as Russia. Honours were heaped upon him and one which he apparently treasured was his appointment as a colonel in the Connecticut state militia. On January 10, 1862, at the comparatively early age of forty-seven and certainly at a peak of his achievement Colt died. However, this was not the end of his work and his company still flourishes.

During his lifetime Colt produced a variety of weapons, mostly handguns, although there were also a number of long arms. One of his first successful revolvers was the Paterson. The barrels were octagonal and, the cylinder had the nipples set well into the rear, so that the raised area in between acted as a very efficient nipple guard. The early Patersons were made with concealed triggers, which were in fact a safety device. No trigger was visible until the weapon was cocked. This action disengaged the trigger, which dropped down into position ready for firing.

All Colt's early weapons were of the single-action variety. The hammer had to be pulled back manually and this rotated the cylinder, lining it up ready for the next shot. When the trigger was pressed the hammer fell forward to fire the shot and stayed in that position until it was again pulled back by hand, rotating the cylinder. Colt's Paterson revolvers were sold with various accessories, including some patent powder flasks.

Most of Colt's pistols were designated by the size of their calibre, ·28 to ·31 inch being usually referred to as pocket revolvers. The ·36 ones were known as belt revolvers and larger calibres were holster revolvers. The early pocket Patersons were five-shot revolvers, firing a bullet between ·28 and ·34 inches. The larger versions, the belt model, were also five-shot and all pistols were produced with a variety of barrel lengths. In addition to the pistols a number of Paterson long arms were made, although later on the Colt Company was rather to neglect the long-arm market and concentrate on pistols.

With the adoption of the Walker pistol the characteristic Colt shape may be said to have arrived. This Walker pistol was a good solid weapon firing a ·44-inch bullet and was a six-shot. The gun itself was quite heavy, weighing 4 lb 6 oz. Beneath the round barrel was fitted an ingenious loading lever. In the old percussion pistols the bullet had been pushed down the barrel by a ramrod. Colt had the loading lever permanently secured to the revolver. Powder was poured into the cylinder and a bullet placed on top. By operating the lever the ball could be forced down until it sat firmly on top of the powder. This system was obviously very convenient and there was no danger of losing the ramrod. The next models from Colt were different versions of the Dragoon revolver, which was basically similar to his earlier Walker. In 1848 Colt began producing the pocket revolver which fired a ·31-inch bullet and was largely a scaled-down version of the Dragoon. It weighed only about 22 oz, had a 5-inch barrel, and the cylinder was engraved with a scene showing Indians fighting a battle.

In 1849 came the ordinary pocket revolver, which was to prove one of the most popular of his pistols. Like the small Dragoon (the 1848 model) it was a ·31-inch calibre, but two models were available – one a five-shot and the other a six-shot. The scene depicted on the cylinder was a stagecoach hold up. Then in 1851 came the Navy or belt revolver. This was a ·36-inch weapon, with a six-shot capacity and a 7½-inch octagonal barrel. It was engraved with a naval battle scene, based on a victory won by the navy of Texas over that of Mexico. It was an extremely accurate weapon and saw service in the hands of many famous shots, including Wild Bill Hickok, the Indian scout and United States marshal.

The shape for the single-action Colt revolver, once established, was to remain largely unchanged. One exception to this general pattern was the one known as the Root's side hammer. It possessed a number of features which were not present in other Colt percussion revolvers. These had all been of the open-frame variety, which meant that the barrel was separate. The Root's model had a solid frame, the cylinder being set within the frame, with a top and a front section holding the barrel. Apart from the solid frame the other big difference was that the hammer, instead of being inserted inside the frame, was attached on the outside right-hand side. The trigger was of the sleeve type, that is, only a very small amount of trigger projected beyond two metal arms placed either side of it and no trigger guard was fitted. Removal of the cylinder was a little more complicated than on other models, and it was not a popular weapon.

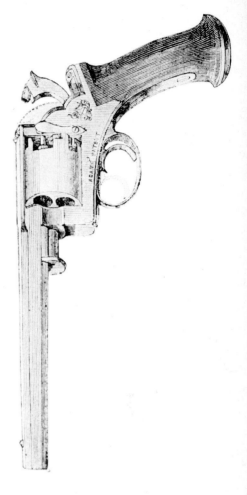

The Deane Adams percussion revolver. Adams' revolvers had some success in the United States.

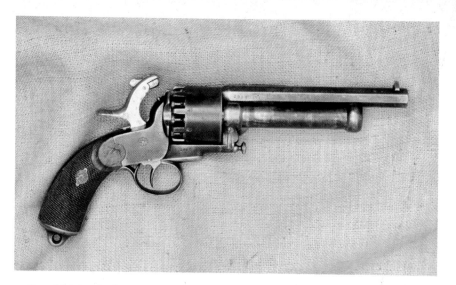

In 1860, feeling perhaps that the ·36-inch calibre did not always meet the requirements of the military, Colt introduced the 1860 Army revolver. This was a six-shot ·44-inch calibre weapon, usually with a 7½-inch or 8-inch barrel. It weighed 2 lb 10 oz and was a very satisfactory weapon, being much used during the American Civil War. Over 200,000 were made between 1860 and 1873, when it was largely replaced by a new model. In 1861 Colt produced another Navy revolver, which incorporated a different style of ramrod and was also fitted with a round barrel in place of the original octagonal one.

Further extensions of the range came in 1862 when a ·36-inch five-shot pocket Police model was produced. It had the general appearance of a scaled-down Army revolver, but it is easily recognized by fluting in the cylinder. In 1862 a pocket version of the Navy was produced with a ·36-inch calibre. Most of Colt's production of long arms were really revolvers with a very long barrel fitted with a shoulder stock. The majority had the Root's side hammer. The cylinders were larger and were engraved with a hunting scene. The calibres of the rifles ranged from ·36-inch up to ·56-inch. Colt also produced carbines and rifled muskets for the Civil War.

When Colt went to London in 1851 and began advertising his revolver the response from the British gunmakers was, naturally, rather hostile. Strangely enough, although many British makers supplied pepperboxes, revolvers were extremely rare on the market. There was, in fact, only one competitor producing anything like Colt's weapon and that was Robert Adams, whose revolver was patented in February 1851, shortly before the Great Exhibition opened. His revolver differed from Colt's in many respects. Colt's was single-action, which meant that the hammer had to be cocked with the thumb. Adams' revolver was self-cocking with no spur on the hammer, so that it could not be operated manually. When the trigger was pressed the hammer was cocked and the cylinder rotated. Colt's revolvers were made in two parts, the barrel and the frame. Robert Adams' revolvers were far more solid, the barrel and frame being all united into a single piece.

An immediate rivalry developed between those who favoured Adams' self-cocking weapon and those who preferred Colt's single-action revolver. In fact a test was carried out in September 1851, between an Adams against an 1848 Dragoon ·44-inch Colt. According to the reports the weapons emerged as roughly equal. Neither had the edge as regards accuracy and neither was worse than the other as regards misfires. The Adams was, if

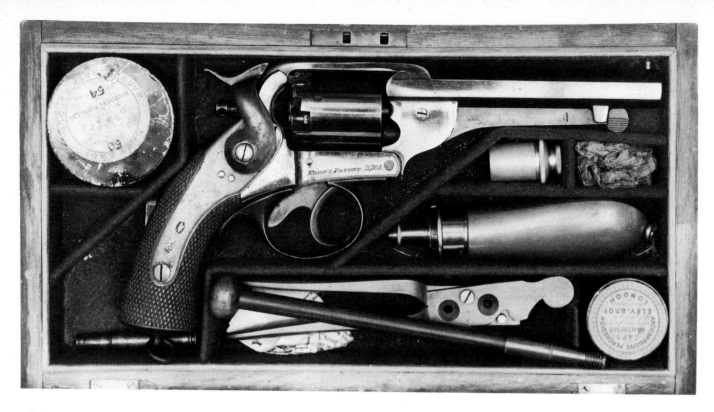

A Kerr patent percussion revolver with five-shot cylinder, made by the London Armoury Company. No. 11305. The oak case is lined with green baize and the accessories include a tin of bullets, powder flask, oil bottle, bullet mould and cleaning rod.

Opposite:
Colt single-action revolver. A very fine example, nickel-plated and engraved overall and numbered 117390, which suggests that it was made in 1886. The grips are of ivory and are carved with a steer's head. The contemporary holster and belt has forty-eight loops to hold ·45-inch (11·4-mm) cartridges. H. Watkins.

anything, a little faster in discharging shots. Ironically the relative positions of Adams and Colt were reversed in 1853, when Adams took his pistol to New York for an international exhibition. It is quite possible that while he was there he made contact with the Massachusetts Arms Company, for they made versions of the Adams' revolver both in ·36-inch and in ·31-inch calibres.

Adams's self-cocking revolver was actually produced in London by the firm of Deane, Adams and Deane, but in August 1856 Adams dissolved his partnership with the two Deanes. In February 1855 Lieutenant Frederick Beaumont of the Royal Engineers had filed a patent application for a lock mechanism which had the great advantage of offering the shooter a choice. The hammer could be activated by the trigger as in the self-cocking revolver, or it could, like Colt's, be cocked by pulling back the hammer with the thumb. With single-action the hammer could be cocked and aim taken, and only a comparatively small pressure was needed to fire the revolver. With double-action much greater pressure was needed to move the trigger, which had to rotate the cylinder and cock the hammer, making accurate shooting a little bit more difficult.

In February 1856 Robert Adams joined the London Armoury Company, in which Beaumont held a small number of shares as did John Deane. The factory was in Tooley Street, which runs parallel with the Thames, near London Bridge. Robert Adams left the London Armoury Company in 1859 and it went into voluntary liquidation in 1866. In the ten years between 1856 and 1866 the company produced three main types of revolver, one of which was patented by the company's superintendent, James Kerr. In some ways this model resembled Colt's Roots, for it had a side hammer and a solid frame. It was so constructed that any gunsmith or designer could easily cope with a breakdown, and the lock mechanism was detachable. It seems certain that a considerable number of these weapons were sold to the Confederate States of America, one cargo of 900 being landed in Wilmington, Virginia, in 1864. The London Armoury Company also produced Beaumont Adams revolvers.

150

Although at the time of the Great Exhibition Adams was Colt's only serious competitor, other British makers did produce revolvers. One by Joseph Lang was, in comparison with the more sophisticated models of Adams and Colt, of a rather primitive style – almost a kind of transition revolver. The cylinder had nipples mounted vertically rather than horizontally and the barrel was secured to the central spigot in much the same way as Colts revolvers.

More elaborate and better-made were the Daws revolvers, another popular weapon of the period. These were single- or double-action and were characterized by the use of a loading

Top. Cheap, five-shot percussion revolver produced in bulk in centres such as Birmingham and Liège. *Above.* Tranter double-trigger percussion revolver marked 'H. Beckwith, London, No. 20024T'. Patented in 1853.

Opposite:
1. Dean Harding percussion revolver. About 1855.
2. So-called transition revolver with pepperbox frame and attached ramrod. About 1850.
3. Percussion pepperbox revolver of common form.
4. Tranter double-trigger revolver with detachable side-rammer.
5. Small travelling flintlock pistol with two barrels side by side. About 1800.
6. Smaller model double-trigger Tranter percussion revolver.

American revolvers (7 to 11).
7. ·22-inch pocket pistol with silvered barrel by T. J. Stafford, New Haven, Connecticut. About 1860.
8. ·30-inch teat fire by the Connecticut Arms Company, Norfolk, Connecticut. About 1865.
9. ·32-inch rim-fire marked 'B.A.Co.'
10. ·41-inch Colt clover-leaf revolver, so called because of the shape of the cylinder. Four-shot only. 1871.
11. 'My Friend' knuckle-duster pistol. About 1865.

lever very similar to that fitted to the Colts and also by the very pronounced guard mounted on the hammer to prevent the possibility of any shattered pieces of a percussion cap coming back to injure the shooter. Another famous name of the period was the Webley firm, which began production in Birmingham.

One of the more interesting of the British revolvers produced at this time was the Tranter double trigger. The object of this patent was to overcome the problem of the hard trigger pull associated with double-action shooting. Tranters were fitted with a very long trigger, which extended through a slot in the base of the trigger guard. Pressure on the lower section, below the trigger guard, merely rotated the cylinder and cocked the hammer. The weapon was fired by pressure on a smaller trigger which was set into the top section of the long arm within the trigger guard. This system enabled the weapon to be brought up to the aim position and the hammer cocked. This position could be firmly held by the lower fingers while the index finger need only touch the top trigger to fire the weapon.

Tranter revolvers were produced in a variety of calibres and like most percussion revolvers of this period could be purchased in a case rather like the duelling pistols. The cases were normally of oak or mahogany and the compartments in both American and British versions were generally formed by straight fences and the whole case lined with baize. Components within the case varied somewhat, but almost every one included a powder flask, usually of copper with a nozzle which was graduated so that it could be adjusted to give two of three different measures of powder. Small paper cartridges, with short lengths of tape to tear them open were also available. Other items included a bullet mould, normally a double one so that two bullets could be cast in it at the same time, and some had a cleaning rod and some form of nipple wrench. This last was a small spanner specially shaped to fit over the head of the nipple, so that it could be unscrewed for cleaning or changed if it had been damaged.

In addition to all this there might well be a tin of percussion caps, boxes of lubricant, a small oil bottle in white metal, and possibly a screwdriver and sundry other items. Many of these percussion revolvers, including Colt's, offered a detachable stock which could be fastened to the butt of the revolver, so converting the weapon into something like a small carbine. It enabled the weapon to be held firmly for more accurate shooting. Some cased sets included the stock as part of their accessories. More rarely pairs of pistols (Colts, Adams and Tranters) were supplied cased together.

One feature which had come into general practice on nearly all these percussion revolvers was the use of numbers. Colt began the custom of marking the main parts of his revolvers with a number. Thus the barrel, frame and cylinder of a new weapon would all bear the same number. In the case of British revolvers, the majority of which were solid-frame with barrel and frame united, the only numbers were on the side of the frame and on the cylinder. In the Colts these numbers are a fair indication of production rate and are extremely useful in dating any particular weapon. With British revolvers the numbers do give some guidance as to date but they are by no means as precise as on the Colts.

Percussion revolvers remained in general use until the end of the nineteenth century, although from the late 1860s an increasing number of cartridge weapons were coming on to the market. Names such as Webley, Tranter and Adams continued to figure in the firearms world but that of Colt has maintained first place.

153

The era of
the Winchester

A breech-loading gun using a Lorenzoni system, made by an English gunmaker, John Cookson, who worked from 1670 to 1680, probably in London. Victoria and Albert Museum, London.

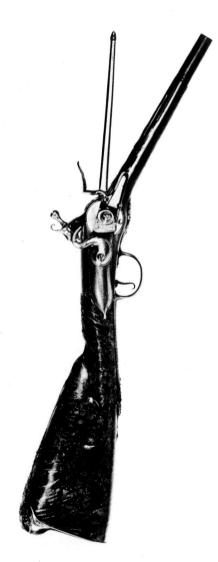

Forsyth's invention of the percussion system opened the way to important developments in the firearms world, but they came about only gradually. Industry, governments and even the shooting public did not immediately go over to the new system. There was, as always, a reluctance to change. In the 1820s the adoption of the percussion cap speeded up the conversion from the flintlock. By the 1840s most governments had re-equipped their military forces with percussion muskets or rifles, either by converting their old flintlock weapons or by adopting entirely new percussion models. By this time the majority of sportsmen, despite a few diehards who still proclaimed the virtues of the flintlock, were using percussion guns. Colt and European makers now offered revolvers with a convenience in handling and rate of fire beyond the imagination of an eighteenth-century shooter.

Despite these great innovations virtually all firearms still suffered from the severe handicap of being muzzle-loading, a slow and potentially dangerous system. Many sporting books of the period stress how important it was to be careful when loading. The danger was greatest for hunters who still used loose powder rather than paper cartridges. If there was a glowing spark left in a barrel when the next charge of powder was poured in the result could be catastrophic. As the hunter inserted the powder his flask was over the barrel and a sudden flash could well ignite the entire contents of the flask.

A number of safety powder flasks were available and they usually consisted of a device which, by one means or another, allowed only one charge of powder to be held over the muzzle when loading. One of the commonest methods was to hinge the nozzle so that it could be filled with powder and swung clear of the body of the flask before pouring the powder down the barrel. In this way, should there be an accidental flare only one charge exploded.

For the soldier and the rifleman there were paper cartridges. These had a long history, and experiments were going on to see how they might be improved. The cartridge paper served as a wad, which was not always consumed in the shot and was blown out of the barrel. A glowing wad, which might travel ten to fifteen feet from the muzzle and then fall to the ground, was an obvious fire hazard. The same was true of wadding in shotguns.

154

Repeating flintlock with the action operated by a side lever. It bears the name Parker, a London maker operating from 1792 to 1842. Overall length $44\frac{1}{2}$ inches (113 cm). Barrel 27 inches (68·6 cm). Bore ·45 inches (11·4 mm).

One way of overcoming the danger was to make the cartridge not of ordinary paper but of some very easily combustible paper or similar material. However, no matter what material was used these paper or skin cartridges were very vulnerable. They were easily torn or damaged and, of course, powder could seep out. They were also susceptible to damp and were always a little awkward to use. The soldier usually tore the end open with his teeth, but this was not easy with small revolver cartridges, and they were fitted with a short length of tape at the end. A sharp tug on the tape tore open the end easily.

There were many attempts to improve on these cartridges. In June 1855 Colt and William Eley, whose name was to become famous in the history of cartridge making, were granted Patent 1324 for a powder case of sheet foil enclosed in an outer case, with a tape attached to the rear end by means of which 'it may be readily torn off'. A box of these paper and skin cartridges was often included in a pistol case.

Closely associated with the problems of cartridges was that of breech loading. If powder and ball could be inserted directly into the breech this would be more convenient, safer and certainly much simpler than muzzle loading. The idea was not new—some of the first firearms had been breech-loaders. The earliest cannon had a separate breech block which was charged with powder and ball and then locked in position at one end of the barrel. When the shot had been discharged the empty block was removed and a fresh, loaded one put in its place.

A variation of this system was used on both wheel-lock and flint-lock weapons until well into the eighteenth century, but in this case the breech stayed put and the barrel was removed. Pistols fitted with this system were said to have 'turn-off' barrels. The barrel was unscrewed and powder poured directly into the breech, normally

Top:
Danish flintlock magazine rifle dated 1670. The stock carries the mark of King Frederick III. Tøjhusmuseet, Copenhagen.

Above:
The earliest-known gun fitted with the Lorenzoni system of breech loading. A heavy breech-lock was rotated by a side-lever to allow powder and ball to fall into the breech. This example is signed Giacomo Berselli. About 1680–85. Musée de l'Armée, Paris.

slightly recessed to assist with the seating of the ball, which was then placed into position. The barrel was screwed back on, the lock cocked and primed, and the pistol was ready without the necessity for a ramrod and the usual complicated loading technique. On seventeenth-century pistols intended for use on horseback, the barrel was attached to the breech by means of a bar and a running ring, so as to prevent accidental loss.

A number of these turn-off barrels were rifled, with the bore made very slightly smaller than the diameter of the bullet. The short barrel was obviously much easier to rifle than that of a long arm. Prince Rupert, who led the cavalry in the army of Charles I was reputedly a dead shot with such pistols. The story is told how, armed with a pair of these 'screw-barrel' pistols, he aimed at and hit the weathercock on the steeple of St Mary's Church at Stafford. When it was suggested that this was more a matter of luck than skill, he repeated the shot with the second pistol.

There were attempts to overcome the inconvenience of having to unscrew the barrel to get at the breech. Numerous systems designed to give direct and easy access to the breech were tried. One British method, which was considered for adoption by the army, was that patented by Frederick Prince in February 1855. The barrel had a large bolt projecting at the base and this was used to unlock and move the entire breech assembly forward. Hans Busk, one of the leading supporters of the British volunteer rifle movement of the mid-nineteenth century was very impressed with Prince's breech-loader. In his book *The Rifle and how to use it*, published in 1859, he illustrated this weapon and stressed that it used the same ammunition as the Enfield rifle, which was by that time the standard British rifle. Busk stated that at a trial at Hythe, one of the main British centres of shooting at that period, Prince 'fired one hundred and twenty rounds in less than 18 minutes, and surely it is not easy to imagine any exigency of modern warfare requiring a soldier to deliver his fire much oftener than once in 9 seconds'. Busk then went on to say that this rifle was certainly a perfect weapon, and he included a rather unusual testimonial from a group of twelve London gunmakers vouching for its efficiency and virtues.

Prince's system was not adopted although an American invention patented in 1854 by a Lt-Col. J. D. Greene, was put to some use. This was a carbine whose heavy, 18-inch barrel was turned, moved forward and pushed sideways to allow access to the breech. The system was cumbersome, even when it was combined with a tape primer invented in 1854 by another American, Dr Edward Maynard. This method of capping was ingenious, with small pellets of fulminate spaced along a thin strip of paper, which was rolled up in the same way as the caps in children's toy guns used to be. As the weapon was cocked the strip was pushed up to place a cap over the nipple.

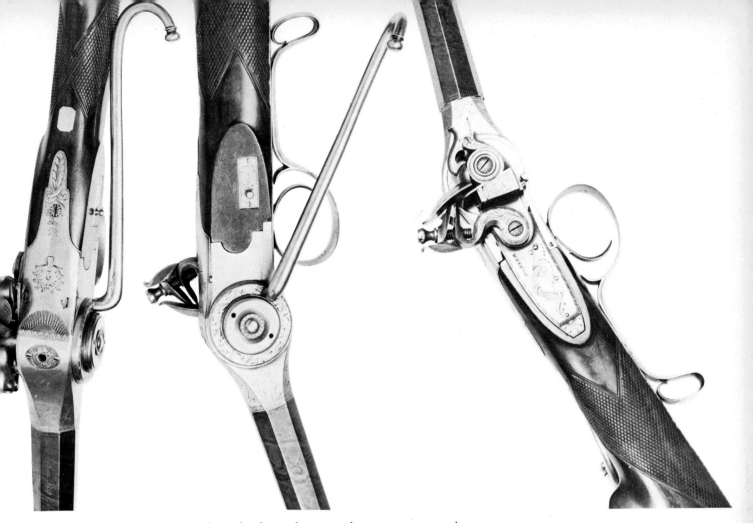

An alternative to moving the barrel was to have some opening which gave direct access to the breech. The Ferguson rifle, already mentioned, had one such device, but it was not the first. As early as 1700 a Frenchman, Isaac de la Chaumette, had used a vertical screw plug very similar to that on the Ferguson. Chaumette went to London and in 1721 took out a British patent for his weapons. Other gunmakers are known to have evolved similar systems.

One great disadvantage of the breech-plug method was that cartridges were not really suitable, so the time saved by loading at the breech was lost by having to use loose powder and bullets. Another method was to use a breech which could be pivoted to allow loading. Designs were numerous and various, but most consisted of a hollow block which was released and then tilted up to receive powder and ball. In the United States one such breech-loader was officially adopted by the U.S. army in 1817. The system, which had been patented in 1811 by John R. Hall and William Thornton, was fitted in both flintlock and percussion weapons. The chamber differed from most earlier systems in that it incorporated not only the breech but also the lock mechanism.

The British military authorities were not inclined to adopt a breech-loader until they were convinced that it was practical. In 1839 a Danish gunmaker, Løbnitz, offered the government a breech-loading musket and pistol, which used a pivoted breech operated by means of a side lever. The weapon was rejected by the British but the Norwegians adopted a very similar one in 1842. This model is of particular interest because it was an underhammer percussion system. The lock was situated beneath the stock of the musket and the hammer swung upwards to strike the cap. One of its virtues was that it left the barrel sight-line uncluttered with nipples. It also removed the risk of any injury to the shooter, which might have been caused by flying pieces of spent cap.

From left to right:
Details of a repeating flintlock carbine. The loading sequence is activated by rotating the lever at the side. Powder, ball and priming are all loaded automatically. The weapon bears the name of a famous London gunmaker, William Parker. Bore ·45 inches (11·4 mm). Overall length 44½ inches (113 cm). Barrel 27 inches (68·6 cm).

Superimposed load rifle made by
W. Mills of London. The system uses
a sliding lock which is moved back
after each of four shots. It was
patented by Jacob Mould in 1825
and presumably transferred to
Captain Ritso, whose name appears
on the lock.

Breech of a modern double-barrelled
shotgun by Boss and Company,
operated by a lever on top of the
small of the butt. The strikers are
concealed and the weapon is
described as hammerless.

Lefaucheux breech-loading pin-fire gun with drop-down barrels. About 1840.

Similar to the pivoted breech, but more prone to problems, was the completely separate breech, which closely resembled that used in the earliest artillery. King Henry VIII had at least two wheel-lock guns fitted in this manner, which offered the advantage of facilitating a high rate of fire by having a supply of loaded cylinders ready at hand.

However, all these systems suffered from one great disadvantage. Unless the joint between the movable breech and the barrel was very secure and tight there was an escape of gas. This was not only potentially dangerous to the shooter, but it meant a loss of power which reduced the speed of the bullet.

Many of the breech-loading weapons used the paper cartridge, but they still had to be capped or primed. The solution which many gunmakers sought was some form of cartridge which contained its own priming, the propellant charge and the projectile. Such a cartridge could be loaded into the gun, fired and either burnt up or withdrawn and perhaps used again. However, until the percussion cap was developed there was still little chance of producing such a cartridge. The percussion cap certainly made it possible but there were many problems to overcome before the cartridge was perfected.

One of the most efficient systems was produced as early as 1812, when a Swiss gunmaker, Samuel Johannes Pauly, took out a patent in Paris. Pauly had seen service as a sergeant-major in the Swiss artillery. He was evidently a man of intelligence and initiative, for he prepared reports on how artillery could be better handled and he also designed a balloon. There was to be an attempt to fly it to London, together with three others, but it never took off. During a period in France he became interested in gunmaking, probably through contacts with St Etienne, an important French gunmaking centre.

Pauly's patent was for a system which, in effect, is the same as a modern shotgun. It had a 'break' action which dropped the barrels to allow direct access to the breech. This was not a new feature, for earlier weapons had used similar systems, but the importance of Pauly's design lay in the cartridge. This had a wooden or brass base with a recess at the centre, into which went a cap or a pellet of detonating material. The base, according to the patent, could be of 'boxwood, papier mâché, lead or 'some plastic or yielding substance'. It was tapered slightly so that it fitted snugly into the breech of the barrel, which had a corresponding taper. This simple idea ensured that when firmly in place the base helped to seal the breech and so reduce the escape of gas. There was also a narrow rim or lip round the base to make it easier to extract the cartridge and this again helped seal the breech.

159

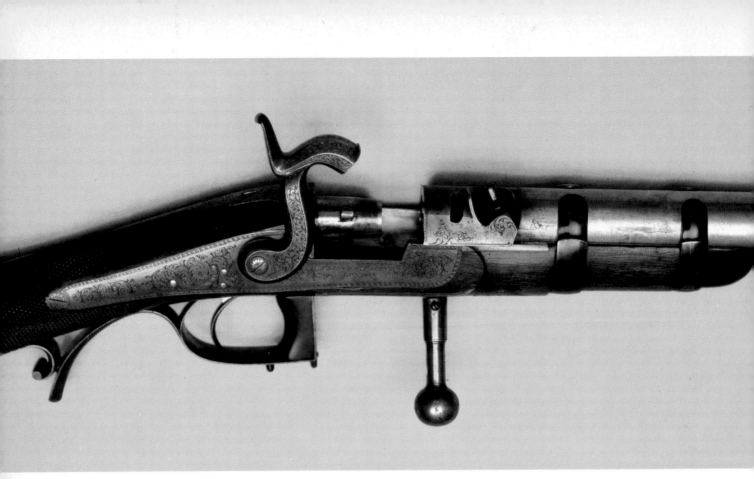

Breech-loading carbine patented by Frederick Prince 1855. The long bolt is used to push forward the barrel and expose the breech. John Jarvis, Esq.

Secured to the base was a paper tube 'glued, tied or fixed', and into this went powder and shot or ball. It appears that the cartridge cases were green or yellow, presumably as a means of identification for shot and ball. Pauly later took out another patent in which he added a flap pierced with a hole to cover the breech and cartridge and yet permit the striker to hit the primer. To load the weapon a lever lying along the top of the breech and butt was raised and this automatically retracted the striker pins for safety. The cartridges were dropped into the breech and the action closed. The strikers, operated by a spring, were housed in the bottom of the breech mechanism and were cocked by an external swan-shaped lever.

The gun was undoubtedly one of the most efficient of its period. It was thoroughly tested and the supervising commission reported that Pauly fired 300 shots without a hangfire or misfire. It was intended primarily for a sporting weapon and one advantage was that it was so easy to unload. The entire action and detonating mechanism were completely enclosed and the trouble caused by dampness, wind and rain was completely eliminated. One of the dangers with both flintlock and percussion weapons, indeed with all non-cartridge firearms, was that the trigger might be pressed and the priming ignited, but not the main charge. The shooter, especially if excited or in danger, might well think that it had fired and that he had missed. He reloaded the weapon, so that, in fact, he now had a double load. After a battle weapons were picked up and found to be, not double loaded, but with triple, quadruple and up to as many as sixteen extra loads. Fortunately for the owner this last one had failed to ignite. Had it done so the result would have been catastrophic. Pauly's gun did away with any possible danger of this happening.

Another great virtue claimed for this weapon was that it could be loaded while its owner was walking along. This was possible with any firearm, but the difficulties of coping with a powder flask when strolling through a forest and trying to measure out an

Three American carbines.
Top. Triplett and Scott carbine which used a ·50-inch (12·7-mm) rim-fire cartridge. Seven cartridges were held in the butt magazine and the barrel was rotated through 180° to let the cartridge enter the breech. Note the unusual positioning of the sling swivels at the rear of the butt. Overall length 38 inches (96·5 cm). Barrel 20 inches (50·8 cm). Patented 1864.
Centre. Ball repeating carbine made by Lamson and Company. Calibre ·5 inches (12·7 mm). The tubular magazine beneath the barrel held seven rounds. The trigger guard operated the loading mechanism. Overall length 37½ inches (95·3 cm). Barrel 20½ inches (52 cm). Patented 1864.
Bottom. George Morse patented a system of converting percussion weapons (one of which is shown here) to breech-loading in 1856. Calibre ·54 inches (13·7 mm). Overall length 40½ inches (102·9 cm). Barrel 20½ inches (52 cm). Pattern Room, Royal Small Arms Factory, Enfield.

exact amount can readily be imagined. In bad weather it was impossible to ensure that the powder stayed dry unless the shooter found a sheltered spot or perhaps held a coat over the piece. Not only did Pauly's gun have these great advantages, but under controlled conditions it was found to shoot much harder than other contemporary weapons.

The commission which examined it gave it unqualified approval and said that it should be placed 'in the front rank of hunting arms known up to the present time'. The Emperor Napoleon himself was interested in the weapon and ordered further tests, However, his verdict was that from a military point of view it did not meet all his requirements and, consequently, although he expressed a pious hope that the 'advance of chemical and mechanical sciences' would lead to success, he was not really interested. Although the weapon in action was ingenious the main interest lies in the cartridge which was, to all intents and purposes, exactly the same as a modern shotgun cartridge.

Cased sets of Pauly's gun included among their accessories a brass former, around which the paper was rolled to make the appropriate-sized cartridge case. The restless mind of Pauly applied itself to a whole host of other problems including the ignition of guns by means of compressed air. He also undertook to give a demonstration of his balloon but his commercial acumen does not seem to have matched his enthusiasm and intelligence. He died a pauper in obscurity. In addition to his double-barrelled sporting gun a number of his pistols are also known, but despite the excellence of his ideas, they did not arouse general interest and breech-loading cartridge weapons were not to become available for many years.

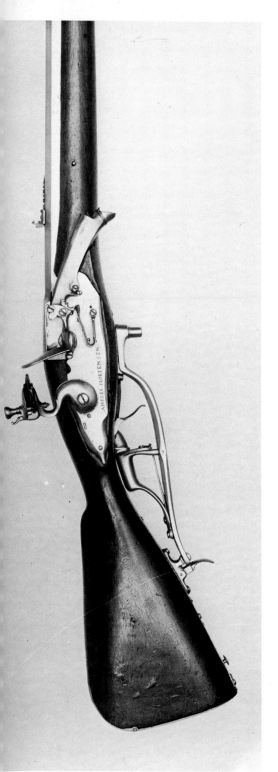

Danish flintlock magazine rifle of about 1680 by Andres Mortensen. The action was operated by means of the trigger guard. Tøjhusmuseet, Copenhagen.

Pauly's invention did not lead to any immediate changes but it pointed the way, and numerous other gunmakers, particularly the French, were working on the problem. One very sophisticated weapon was produced by a Professor Galy-Cazalat in 1824. It used a revolving breech block which was rotated to allow a cartridge to be inserted and then turned back again to its original position in order to place the cartridge in direct contact with the breech. One interesting feature was that the striking mechanism, housed within the stock, was operated by a circular coiled spring, and struck forward. It was, in effect, what was to become known later as a bolt action. In 1829 yet another Frenchman, Clement Pottet, took out a French patent for a cartridge fitted with a removable base, which held a small pocket of detonating material.

Two very significant innovations were made by Casimir Lefaucheux. In 1832 he designed a break action for shotguns which has continued in use until the present. The barrel was locked by means of a lever ending in an eccentric stud, which engaged with a cut-out at the base of the barrel. As the lever was turned the barrels were released and dropped down.

Three years later he produced the first of the pin-fire cartridges, which was to remain in use for many many years. It consisted of a brass cap around which was fitted a paper cartridge holding powder and ball or shot. Detonation was achieved by placing a percussion cap inside the metal base. A pin set at an angle passed through the metal base, with one end resting on top of the percussion cap. The cartridge was loaded into the breech which was cut with a small slot so that, with the cartridge in position, the pin projected slightly above the top of the breech. The hammer on the weapon was solid and, as it fell, it struck the pin which, in turn, hit the percussion cap and so produced ignition.

There were various types of pin-fire cartridge. Some had the primer set at the centre of the base; others had it set into the solid base itself. One patented by an English gunmaker, William Greener, in 1864 had the pin set at an acute angle and the percussion cap was not at the base of the charge but at the centre, the aim being to make the ignition more instantaneous. One French patent of 1859 made the pin serve a double purpose: not only did it ignite the charge, but it was so solidly embedded in the metal base that it could be used to extract the empty cartridge from the breech.

Devices such as this were not ideal, for the cartridge case was fragile and liable to damage. Nevertheless, the fitting of the primer at the centre of the base was a very important development. However from a military point of view it presented problems. With the pin-fire cartridge there was an obvious danger of accidental discharge, since the pin projected above the breech and a knock could easily detonate the cartridge.

Armies were constantly on the watch for new and improved methods of ignition, and in 1840 the Prussian army led the way in adopting a bolt-action cartridge rifle. The system was designed by Johann Nikolaus von Dreyse. This gunmaker was by birth a Prussian but had worked with Pauly in Paris and was therefore well acquainted with the idea of cartridges and breech-loading. In 1827 he devised a bullet with a small charge of fulminate inserted in a base cavity. He intended that the fulminate should be detonated by a needle which passed directly through the breech, and planned to modify the existing flintlock weapons to take the new system. Unfortunately the fulminate was uncertain in action and Dreyse himself was injured in an explosion. Undeterred he continued to experiment and finally produced a modified breech.

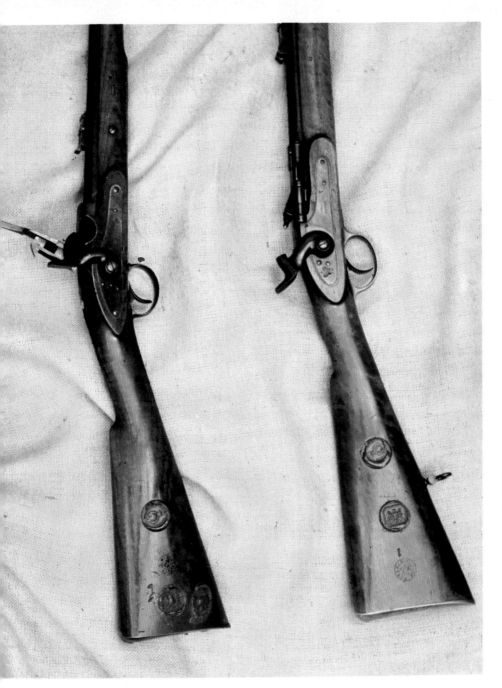

Breech-loading carbines.
Left. Westley Richards ·45-inch (11·4-mm) patent breech-loader. Sealed pattern of 1866. The so-called monkey tail was raised to give access to the breech.
Right. Lancaster Snider ·577-inch (14·6-mm) carbine for the Royal Engineers. Sealed pattern of 1866. Pattern Room, Royal Small Arms Factory, Enfield.

Below left:
Page from the *Illustrated Times*, May 1868, showing the action of the French Chassepot rifle. Pulling back the firing pin was a separate movement from the opening of the bolt.

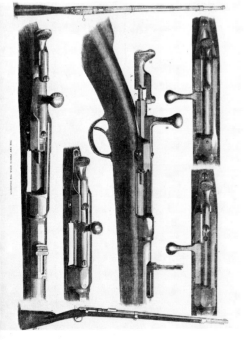

The action was patented in England in 1831 and in 1835 he finally produced his bolt-action, needle-fire rifle. The breech was exposed by means of a bolt which was rotated to the left and drawn backwards. The cartridge was inserted and the bolt pushed forward to close the breech. On later models this action automatically compressed the spring which was to drive the needle forward. On earlier models, however, the needle had to be pulled back before the bolt could be opened. The needle passed through a spigot into the breech where it pierced the thick base of the paper cartridge and the charge of powder and then struck the primer. Ignition was rapid and the paper cartridge was consumed. The bullet was ·66 inches in diameter and roughly egg-shaped.

The weapon suffered from two rather severe handicaps. The needle was in the powder when this was burning, which subjected it to very considerable strain. The explosion heated it up, after which it cooled, altering the temper of the metal and the result was that the needle was deformed or fouled and corroded to such a degree that it broke.

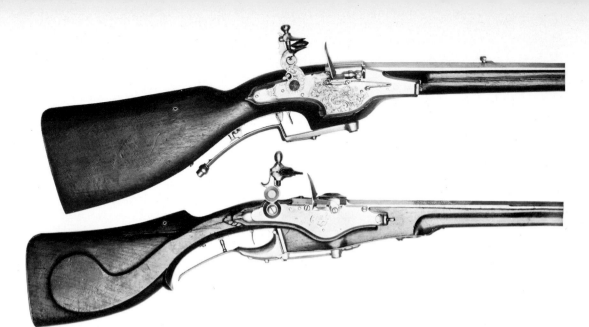

Another problem was that the cartridge did not obdurate, which meant that it did not seal up the breech and so prevent an escape of gas and smoke. Accounts of this rifle speak of very considerable escapes of gas from the breech, although these were somewhat exaggerated and varied from model to model. The Dreyse needle-fire rifle was tested in combat in 1864 and again in 1866 when Prussia carried out two very successful wars against first Denmark and then Austria. Prussia's rapid victories were in no small measure due to the new weapon.

A Frenchman, Antoine Chassepot, who saw the disadvantages of the Dreyse, decided that the first thing to do was to make a much firmer seal at the breech. This he achieved by fitting the face of the bolt with a thick rubber washer. He also reduced the damage to the needle by situating the percussion cap right at the base of the paper cartridge, so that the needle had to make only a slight penetration. The cap was so designed that the flash passed through a series of small holes to ignite the charge. Since the bullet was slightly larger than the bore of the barrel, when driven forward it bit deeply into the rifling. This feature was to be one of the problems of the Chassepot, as a great deal of lead was deposited along the rifling.

To gain access to the breech Chassepot used a very similar system to the Dreyse with a bolt which was opened by turning the stud one quarter of a circle to the left and drawing it back. The Chassepot proved itself to be an efficient weapon and was ahead of many of its rivals in that it fired a much smaller calibre bullet than most— ·434 inches—a trend that was to continue with most military weapons.

The next important evolutionary step towards the modern metal cartridge was taken in 1855 when Clement Pottet took out another patent. His cartridge now had a metal base, in the centre of which was a percussion cap with a little tube leading through the base. In order that the cap should be activated a small anvil in the shape of a tiny shield was fitted into the cavity where the cap was situated. Thus when the striker descended the detonating material was struck against this anvil and so flashed and exploded the charge.

Three years later François Eugène Schneider designed a base with a slightly different anvil which could be fitted to a paper or metal case. Schneider's designs were acquired by a well-known British gunmaker, George Daw, who received a British patent for them in 1861. In 1866 Colonel Edward Boxer of the Royal Laboratory at Woolwich, London, combined the Schneider idea of the metal base with cap and anvil enclosed inside, and an expanding case. When the main charge exploded the brass case was sufficiently flexible to give slightly and expand to make an extremely tight fit in the breech and so reduce gas leakage to an absolute minimum. The modern centre-fire metallic cartridge had finally arrived! It was not yet in its final form, for the first Boxer cartridge was built up from a body of coiled brass wire with an iron base, but in 1867 a cartridge was made from solid drawn brass. Loading was so much simpler, since the shooter could now carry with him cartridges which were completely self-contained. All he had to do was open the breech, insert the cartridge, and close the breech, and the weapon was ready to fire.

Impressed by the success of the breech-loading Dreyse rifles of the Prussians and the Chassepot of the French, other countries began looking for ways of converting their old muzzle-loaders to cartridge breech-loaders. In Britain a special committee was set up in 1864 to consider some fifty designs. The system adopted in 1867 for converting the Enfield rifle was designed by Jacob Snider of New York. It involved removing two inches of barrel at the breech and slightly widening the new breech so that it would accept the Boxer cartridge, which was pushed in by the thumb. The space behind the cartridge was fitted with a breech-block which was hinged on the right. It was held in place by a small spring-loaded pin situated near the base. A striker extended through the breech and was so angled that it could be struck by the hammer and driven down to strike the centre primer. The empty case was extracted by means of a little claw fitting on the breech block assembly, which had to be pulled back by hand for extraction. Unfortunately it only withdrew the case from the breech, and the rifle had to be tipped over to eject it completely. The original cartridge used in the Snider was the composite one with a metal case and a cardboard cylinder, but it was not very satisfactory. It was only with the adoption of Colonel Boxer's brass cartridge that the weapon became a reasonably efficient one.

The Snider, the Dreyse Needle Gun and the Chassepot set the pattern for breech-loading military rifles equipped with metallic cartridges, but they were all still single-shot weapons. What was sought by military designers was a breech-loading rifle which could be loaded with a number of cartridges—in other words a simple repeating or magazine rifle.

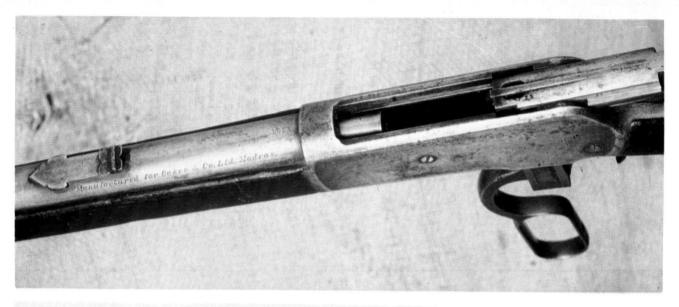

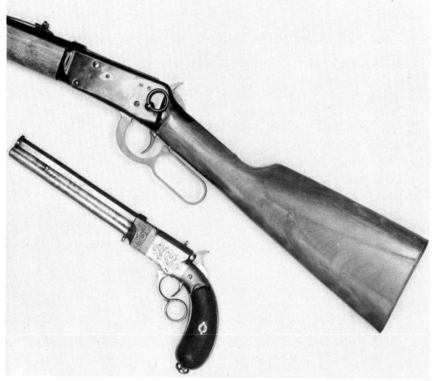

From the seventeenth century onwards there had been attempts
to produce such weapons. In a Chinese book on war published in
1621 reference is made to one which was reputed to have fired a
string of 100 bullets. In France Wilhelm Kalthoff had been producing repeating flintlock guns and others were made in the Netherlands and Denmark. They were all rather complicated, since the
firing mechanism was the flintlock. They had separate magazines
for powder and ball, which were usually fitted into the butt. A
similar mechanism was used by an Italian gunmaker, Michele
Lorenzoni of Florence. However, all these flintlock weapons were of
complex construction, liable to breakdown, and certainly not very
suitable for military use. They were also potentially dangerous–
with a constant risk of explosion.

Probably the first really practical step in the direction of the
modern repeating rifle was made by a Walter Hunt. He was a
prolific inventor and in 1848 he was given a patent for a bullet
which he described as a 'rocket ball'. It was essentially a hollow

The forerunner of the Winchester repeating rifle – the Henry rifle with brass frame and long, under-barrel magazine. The operating lever has a small catch at the rear which holds the lever locked. About 1866. Winchester Gun Museum, New Haven, Connecticut.

bullet with the inside filled with powder and the hole blocked with a wad and a layer of paper. Hunt also designed a rifle which would hold these bullets in a twelve-shot tubular magazine situated beneath the barrel. The bullets were withdrawn and loaded into the breech by means of a mechanism which was operated by moving a little loop situated beneath the barrel. The firing pin was activated by a coiled spring. Hunt called it the Volitional Repeater.

Although in theory it seemed quite sound, there were serious practical problems. The whole mechanism was operated by one finger through the loop. This was, to say the least, uncomfortable and very wearing on the finger. Lewis Jennings took over the design and in 1849 he was granted a patent for his improvements. The action was modified and instead of a straight backward and forward movement which had been the feature of Hunt's rifle, Jennings now had a lever action. The trigger was pivoted and operated the reloading action. However, both mechanisms lacked the simplicity which was so important for a hard-working, reliable weapon. Despite these problems the system had possibilities and two Americans saw the potential.

Daniel Wesson and Horace Smith had joined forces in 1852 and they now held a number of firearms patents. One such patent was for a lever-operated toggle action which they realized could be used to work a breech-loading mechanism. In 1854, backed by Courtland C. Palmer, Smith and Wesson set up the Volcanic Repeating Arms Company at New Haven, Connecticut, to manufacture repeating firearms. The Volcanic pistols that they made looked as though they had two barrels, one above the other, but the lower barrel was in fact a tubular magazine which held the cartridges. The trigger guard ended in a ring, and when the guard was pushed down and raised again a cartridge was drawn out of the magazine, inserted into the breech and the action was cocked. Models with 6-inch, 8-inch and 16-inch barrels were made in a ·38-inch calibre. Some pistols had a detachable shoulder stock which could be fitted to convert them into carbines. Proper carbines were also available with 16-inch, 20-inch and 24-inch barrels, and on these the trigger guards ended in an oval loop rather than a ring. The loop was big enough to accommodate three fingers so that operation was much simpler than when only one finger could be used on the ring guard. The bullets were hollow and held the main charge of powder, while the primer was at the base, held in place by a cork or brass plate.

The Volcanics received some very good publicity, so good, in fact, that it might well have been invented by the company. One account of the results of a shoot by a Colonel Hay of the British army was, one suspects, rather more imaginative than factual. Despite these favourable reviews the Volcanics were not well received by the shooting public. There were problems, including breakdowns, mostly caused by the ammunition, which was very variable in its performance. There were jams caused by the cork or brass base getting stuck in the mechanism or barrel. There were delays in production, sales fell and the company was in financial trouble. Finally in 1857 it went bankrupt.

During the brief history of the firm the name of one man began to figure prominently. He was not primarily a firearms expert, but a well-to-do shirt manufacturer. It seems the Oliver F. Winchester joined Volcanics chiefly as a financial venture, but he saw that firearms offered an exciting and profitable field of commerce. Winchester took over the company when it went bankrupt and formed the New Haven Arms Company. He now held the

patents on the Volcanic as well as shares in the company. His new firm continued to make Volcanic arms but the defects remained and business was no better. However, the means to success were at hand.

Winchester had chosen as his supervisor or plant manager, Benjamin Tyler Henry, who had assisted in the production of a number of firearms and was familiar with Lewis Jenning's rifle. Henry realized that the basic cause of most of the difficulties with the Volcanic arms was the ammunition. He devoted three years' work, research and ingenuity into solving the problem before achieving success.

Henry had worked with Smith and Wesson and had been concerned with the production of their rim-fire cartridge. The basic difference here between the centre-fire cartridge and the pin-fire lay in the siting of the fulminate. Instead of being concentrated into one particular pill or cap it was spread over the whole of the base of the cartridge and was held in place by a thin metal washer. This was later modified and the compound was no longer placed over the whole of the base but in the rim. The fulminate was held between the top and bottom of this rim, which was hollow. When struck with the hammer the top was forced down on to the base, which was usually pressing on something fairly solid, and detonation was simple and direct. Henry developed a ·44-inch cartridge, improved the lubrication and later changed the design of the bullet. Since the cartridges were under some pressure inside the magazine it was just possible that a pointed bullet might bang against the base of the cartridge and cause detonation. Henry flattened the nose of the bullet and so reduced this danger.

Now that Henry had a suitable cartridge the next step was to modify the old Volcanic action to ensure a more reliable firing system. In order to make certain that the hammer would detonate the rim-fire compound Henry split the striking pin. The double blow considerably reduced the chances of a misfire. The fifteen ·44-inch bullets were still housed in a magazine situated beneath the barrel. The section of the magazine near the muzzle could be swung to one side for loading, and a spiral spring kept the ammunition under pressure against the carrier block. The barrels were about 24 inches long and the whole gun weighed around ten pounds.

The early models of the Henry rifle were offered commercially on the market for the first time in 1862, although the action had been patented in October 1860. These models had an iron frame

Sharps carbine New Model of 1859. The patch-box is of brass as is the butt-plate. The action is operated by moving the trigger guard. This particular model is fitted with a disc primer patented by R. Lawrence in 1859. Winchester Gun Museum, New Haven, Connecticut.

Internal mechanism for a Maynard tape primer lock. As the hammer was cocked the levers operated and turned the tape up to bring another capsule of primer into position on the nipple.

168

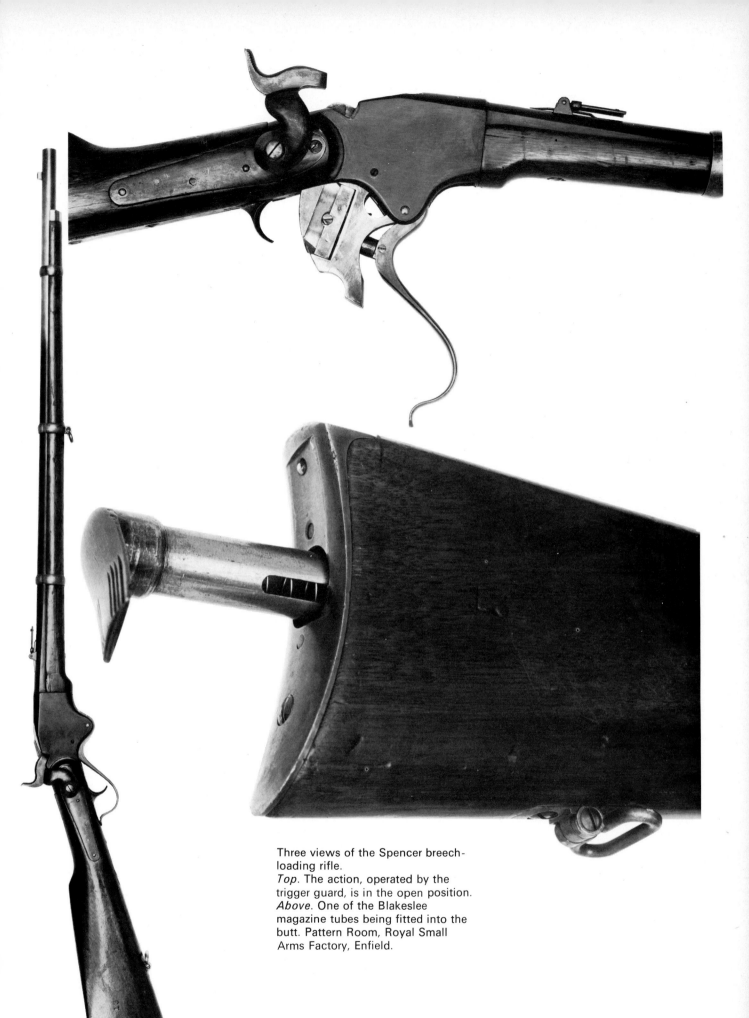

Three views of the Spencer breech-loading rifle.
Top. The action, operated by the trigger guard, is in the open position.
Above. One of the Blakeslee magazine tubes being fitted into the butt. Pattern Room, Royal Small Arms Factory, Enfield.

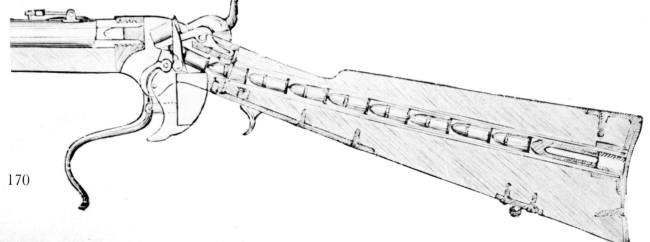

but this was soon discarded in favour of brass and many of the receivers housing the mechanism were engraved. The development of the Henry rifle coincided with the outbreak of the American Civil War (1861–65) and it might have been expected that either party in the conflict would have been happy to acquire them in bulk.

The New Haven Arms Company offered the Henry rifle to the Federal government and in May 1862 a lieutenant in the U.S. navy carried out a whole range of tests on the weapon. It is recorded that 120 rounds were fired in 340 seconds which included reloading time. This averaged out to one shot in just under three seconds, compared with the muzzle-loader which took about twenty seconds per shot and the breech-loader which was down to about ten or twelve seconds per shot. The accuracy proved to be satisfactory and one model was fired over a thousand times without being cleaned. Although the barrel was said to be filthy there were no mechanical difficulties.

Despite this remarkable test result, Brigadier-General James W. Ripley, Chief of Ordnance, was not greatly impressed. He rightly pointed out that the Henry rifle required special ammunition which they did not possess and this would mean a long delay before sufficient stocks could be built up. He also questioned whether the weight of the rifle with the loaded magazine was not excessive. Ripley was also a little concerned, probably unnecessarily, about the danger of crushing or breaking the cartridges and the magazine when the weapon was carried on horseback. The Henry was never purchased in bulk although in 1863, during the course of the Civil War, the Union government ordered 250 rifles.

Many of Winchester's models were produced in two versions – the rifle and the carbine. This ·44 inch (11·17 mm) Model 1894, No. 1390, is the lighter horseman's carbine with its characteristic saddle ring at the breech. This could be fitted with a loop or attached to the belt to prevent accidental loss. E. Kempster, Gunsmiths.

Shortly afterwards Ripley was replaced by a Brigadier-General Ramsey, who said that he thought repeating arms were worth having but that it was difficult to supply then in the quantities required. He also stated that there was a choice between three different weapons: the Colt, which was expensive and dangerous to users; Henry's rifle which was expensive and too delicate for service; and the Spencer, which was at the same time 'the cheapest, most durable and most efficient of any of these arms'.

The Spencer which was obviously a rival to the Henry had been designed by Christopher Spencer and patented in 1860. It used rim-fire cartridges, of which seven were housed in a magazine situated in the butt of the weapon. The trigger guard was, like that on the Henry, the operating lever. As it was pushed down the breech block extracted the fired case. Closing the lever pushed a fresh cartridge into the chamber and the cartridge was fired by the side hammer. Unlike that on the Henry rifle the lever was solely for loading, and the external hammer still had to be cocked before the weapon could be fired.

The rate of fire of the Spencer was speeded up by a cartridge box patented by Blakeslee. This held a number of tubes already full of cartridges and, instead of loading in single cartridges, the empty tube was simply removed and a new, full one dropped into the butt magazine. The weapon was obviously effective and saw considerable service during the American Civil War.

Although the New Haven Arms Company was unsuccessful in obtaining big government contracts for its weapon, accounts show that it supplied extraordinarily large amounts of ammunition, over four million cartridges being purchased. This was due to the fact that a large number of private individual and state companies equipped themselves with Henry's repeating rifle. One of the features of the New Haven Company's advertising campaign was the publication of accounts of the personal experiences of people who had used the weapon. One, a Captain James Wilson, was attacked in his house by a group of seven mounted guerrillas who threatened to shoot him. He persuaded them to take him outside before carrying out their threat and, on his way through the door, he grabbed his Henry rifle. With five shots he killed five men. The sixth shot hit one in the hand and the seventh shot killed him. Wilson then killed the seventh man with his eighth shot.

Some of these accounts deserve to be treated with caution, but one of the best-known and most-often repeated is alleged to have been made by a Confederate soldier confined in a Northern prison. He is reputed to have said: 'Give us anything but that damned Yankee rifle that can be loaded on Sundays and fired all the week'.

Despite such glowing tributes to the Henry rifle two faults soon made themselves apparent. One was that the firing pin was apparently rather fragile and frequently broke. The other was that the metal forming the tube of the magazine was too thin. There were a number of reports about the tube being dented, which prevented both loading and inserting the cartridges into the breech. Trouble in feeding cartridges into the breech had also resulted when the spring-loaded plunger had been allowed to fly back to hit and deform the cartridges.

Below:
The open action of the Winchester Model 62, introduced in 1932 and abandoned in 1958. This is a pump-action rifle chambered to take ·22-Long or ·22-Long Rifle cartridges. Large numbers were used in shooting galleries and ranges. They could be taken down, i.e., easily separated into barrel and butt. No. 15655. E. Kempster, Gunsmiths.

The 'Frontier' played an important part in stimulating the development and production of firearms in the United States. This painting by Charles Schreyvogel shows a dawn skirmish between cavalry and Indians. Two Indians are shown with Winchesters although they did not usually possess these. Thomas Gilcrease Institute of American History and Art, Tulsa, Oklahoma.

173

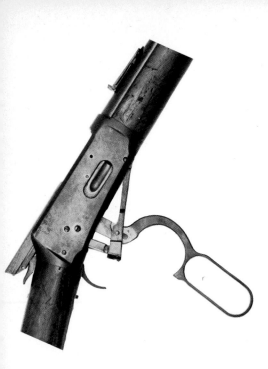

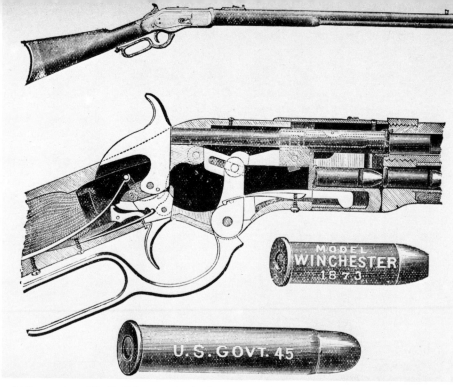

When the Civil War ended the demand for rifles fell off considerably and there was some concern in the company about its poorer prospects. However, there was still one market which offered hope and that was the frontier which was opening out and expanding west. Oliver Winchester was not discouraged and in 1866 he formed the Winchester Repeating Arms Company. The old New Haven Arms Company went into liquidation.

With the creation of the new company Winchester moved his factory to a building in Bridgeport, Connecticut, and in the same year the first of the true Winchester rifles was announced. Every effort had been made to overcome the problems of the fragile firing pin, the extractor and the rather inferior design of the magazine. The prospectus of the Model 1866 rifle declared that the loading and firing mechanism was exactly the same as in the Henry but changes had been made in the magazine which was now stronger and had a greater capacity. The magazine held fifteen cartridges, and an extra one could be inserted directly into the breech, since it could also be used as a single-shot weapon.

One of the main differences was in the method of loading. To avoid having to open the magazine in order to insert the cartridges, a gate with a spring-operated cover was built into the frame on the right-hand side, and the cartridges were pushed through this into the magazine. Model 1866 was a really first-class weapon, and most of the problems inherent in the Henry had been overcome.

Winchester made a special trip to Europe and entered the Henry rifle for a series of tests being carried out by the Swiss Ordnance in their search for a new rifle with which to equip their armies. The Henry received very good reports from the Swiss, but they decided not to accept it and instead adopted a Vetterli bolt-action rifle. One reason for this was possibly that the Vetterli could be built in Switzerland, whereas Winchester had insisted that if his rifle were adopted it would have to be manufactured in the United States. A Henry had been entered for the British army tests in 1867 and when the 1866 model appeared the British Ordnance asked that two samples should be sent for testing. Their conclusion was that the Winchester was undoubtedly the best of the repeating rifles, but they were apprehensive because of the complicated mechanism and the weight. Accordingly they did not recommend that it should be accepted.

Right:
Schutzen ·22-inch (5·58-mm) rifle
made by Hammerli of Switzerland,
with pronounced prongs and thumb
hole in the butt. The front support is
held in the left hand for shooting in
the standing position. Overall
length 44 inches (111·8 cm). Barrel
29 inches (73·7 cm). Pattern Room,
Royal Small Arms Factory, Enfield.

Below:
Finely decorated Model 1894
Winchester rifle. The stock is carved
and the metal chiselled and inlaid.
Winchester Gun Museum, New
Haven, Connecticut.

Winchester was more successful in Mexico with Benito Juarez,
who was leading the revolt against the Emperor Maximilian.
Juarez ordered 1,000 rifles and half a million rounds of ammunition to be delivered at Brownsville in Texas. He then changed
his plans and demanded delivery at Monterrey in Mexico. After
some delays payment was made in silver coin. Addis, the Winchester representative, who had delivered the consignment,
faced the daunting prospect of transporting a very large sum of
money through largely lawless country. He hired a coach, driver
and guards, and to keep himself awake because he trusted nobody,
he used to stick a scarf pin into his thigh. He is supposed to have
taken three days to return.

The Winchester Repeating Arms Company was expanding.
In 1868 it took over the Spencer Rifle Company and in 1869 the
American Repeating Rifle Company. The next year the company
moved back to new premises in New Haven, and signed a contract
to supply 15,000 muskets and 5,000 carbines to the Turkish government. In 1873 the Winchester Company produced another model,
the Model 73, which was designed to use the new centre-fire
cartridge. This cartridge was more powerful than the old rim-
fire and the weapon looked like outshooting any of its previous
competitors. Another big difference between the Model 66 and the
new Model 73 was that the old brass frame was replaced by one of
iron or steel. The Model 73 remained in production until 1919,
the last one being sold in 1924.

In order to ensure continuing interest in his products, in 1875
Winchester announced a special feature. He claimed that although
all his gun barrels were extremely accurate, every now and then
during the test firing that every barrel underwent, one or two
barrels would prove themselves to be exceptionally accurate.
Those barrels were to be marked as 1 of 1,000. Barrels whose
accuracy was very high but not quite as good would be designated
1 of 100. These barrels would be fitted to sporting rifles and each
would be given a hair trigger and a particularly fine finish. Needless to say these special weapons were more expensive than the
standard model.

Despite their very considerable market and their success in the
commercial field the Winchester Company was still unsuccessful
in its attempts to interest the U.S. Ordnance. In September 1872

175

Open action of the Model 1895 Winchester repeating rifle. This model is an unusual example of the Winchester, since it has a fixed box magazine instead of the customary, tubular magazine below the barrel. Pattern Room, Royal Small Arms Factory, Enfield.

tests were begun to select a new breech-loader at the Springfield armouries. The model chosen by Winchester as their entry was a specially built Model 66. The weapon passed all the early tests. It fired 500 rounds without cleaning and coped well with the specially malformed cartridges with which it was also tested. However, when it was subjected to dust it was found that the weapon jammed solid. The official report stated that no matter what exertion was applied it failed to clear the dust. The outcome of the tests was that the U.S. army stayed with its single-shot Springfield Model 73 carbine. The troops who died at the battle of Little Big Horn in 1876 were armed with these weapons. Custer's last stand might perhaps have ended in victory if the U.S. government had adopted the Winchester for general issue.

The 1873 model was produced with ·44, ·38 and ·32-inch calibres and a lighter version, the carbine, was also made. There were special models including a military version adapted to take a bayonet. It was fully stocked, with the magazine enclosed within the wooden stock. For the Spanish market a ·4-inch calibre carbine was made, although this was only supplied in the one order in 1878–9. The carbine, which was intended for use on horseback, was distinguished by a saddle ring fitted on the left-hand side just to the rear of the breech. The Model 1873 was supplied in quantity to countries all over the world. Some 300,000 seem to have gone to Central America; others went to China, Haiti and Morocco.

Not only did the Winchester Company manufacture its own rifles but it was now deeply involved in the cartridge business. In 1872 Winchester obtained a contract to supply the Turks with 200,000 Martini Henry rifles, although Winchester did not actually make them. They sold the contract to the Providence Tool Company, Rhode Island.

The one big limitation of the 1873 model was its range. Because of the size of cartridges used, a ·44-inch calibre bullet with 40 grains of powder, it was only effective up to about 600 feet. What was needed was a weapon capable of firing the much more powerful government ammunition—a ·45-inch cartridge with 70 grains of powder. It was a very impressive cartridge, effective up to a range of 1,800 feet. The difficulty lay in modifying the machinery to produce mechanisms robust enough to withstand the much

William Cody (1845–1917), otherwise known as Buffalo Bill, leaning nonchalantly on a Winchester rifle which he used for his trick shooting. Much of his impressive accuracy was obtained by using shot rather than ball cartridges.

stronger kick and reaction of this heavier cartridge. The outcome was the Model 1876, which proved to be a popular weapon, particularly when it received enthusiastic endorsement from Theodore Roosevelt. It was also adopted in the carbine form by the Royal Canadian North West Mounted Police and remained in service with them until 1914. Oliver Winchester died in 1880 after seeing his faith in the company vindicated.

The firm was now thriving although sensitive to competition and in 1883–4 Colt's Patent Firearms Company began production of a repeating rifle very similar to the Winchester. The company responded by having a number of revolver models created incorporating features which were better than those of Colt's revolvers. A gentleman's agreement was reached and both firms confined themselves to their own particular sphere.

Although the Winchester had made its name as a repeating rifle the firm was well aware of the potential market for good single-shot weapons and in 1885 it announced a new model. It was an excellent weapon and by making appropriate variations in the size of frames and barrels it could be produced almost from stock. It could be adapted to fit 45 different cartridges, from the tiny ·22-inch right up to the ·50 express cartridge. It was popular for target shooting and also for hunting. The company also introduced in 1886 the first of its single-shot Schuetzen rifles. These were specifically target models, with elaborate trigger guards and lever actions. The distinctive feature, however, was the enormous

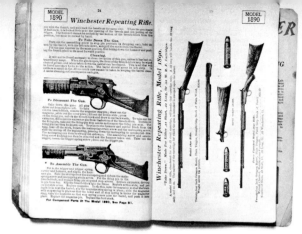

Winchester catalogue of 1911 showing details of the 1890 pump-action rifle.

So well established had the Winchester rifle become that almost every illustrator depicted Indians and cowboys armed with it. Indians are here shown running off cattle. Radio Times.

Opposite:
Winchester firearms are as popular today as ever and new models are in production. On the right is a modern ·30-30 model and on the left a modern, Italian-made copy of the early brass-framed Model 1866, which was in production until 1898. E. Kempster, Gunsmiths.

butt with rear-projecting ears which slipped around the shoulder so ensuring a very stable shooting position. Shuetzen rifles were a Swiss idea and since they were essentially target weapons they were given hair triggers. Another feature on some rifles was the fitting of a hand rest just beneath the breech. A short vertical bar with either a disc- or an ovoid-shaped grip was attached, again primarily for use in target work.

One weakness of which the firm had been well aware but had done nothing about was the actual mechanism of the Winchester. The earlier models used a link and toggle to join their lever to the movement and this was not always as strong or reliable as it might be. The problem was aggravated by the use of the more powerful cartridge. Two new designers, the Browning brothers, who were working with the company, turned their attention to this problem. They completely redesigned the mechanism and, in place of the rather weak link and toggle, they fitted two solid levers. Other changes were made and in 1886 another model was produced incorporating the new design. These solid arms were much more reliable, and had a longer life and the ability to stand up to harder knocks.

In 1887 the company diversified even further and began producing lever-action shot-guns. They had previously handled shot-guns but these had not been Winchester products, merely Winchester imports. The 1887 model held five shots in the magazine and a number were purchased by stage coach companies for use by their guards. A neater version was introduced in 1901.

The company was constantly looking for fresh markets and produced a steady flow of new weapons. In 1892 it offered an updated version of the old 1873 and this was followed by the Models 1894 and 1895. Each new model offered some improvement or a different calibre.

In 1892 Winchester broke new ground to design a pump-action ·22-inch rifle. These still had a magazine under the barrel but the weapon was cocked and loaded by sliding a wooden grip beneath the barrel backwards and forwards. In the following year they applied the same idea to a shotgun.

The company has continued to experiment and their more recent products have included self-loading rifles, pistols and commemorative issues of their rifles and carbines, such as those in honour of Buffalo Bill (1965), the Canadian Centennial (1967) and Theodore Roosevelt (1969).

Other makes of firearms were fitted with lever actions but it is fair to say that in the eyes of the public, rightly or wrongly, if it has a lever action it is a Winchester! During the great days of the western frontier the Winchester was only one weapon of many which saw service, but such was its character that it is still thought of today as 'the gun that won the West'.

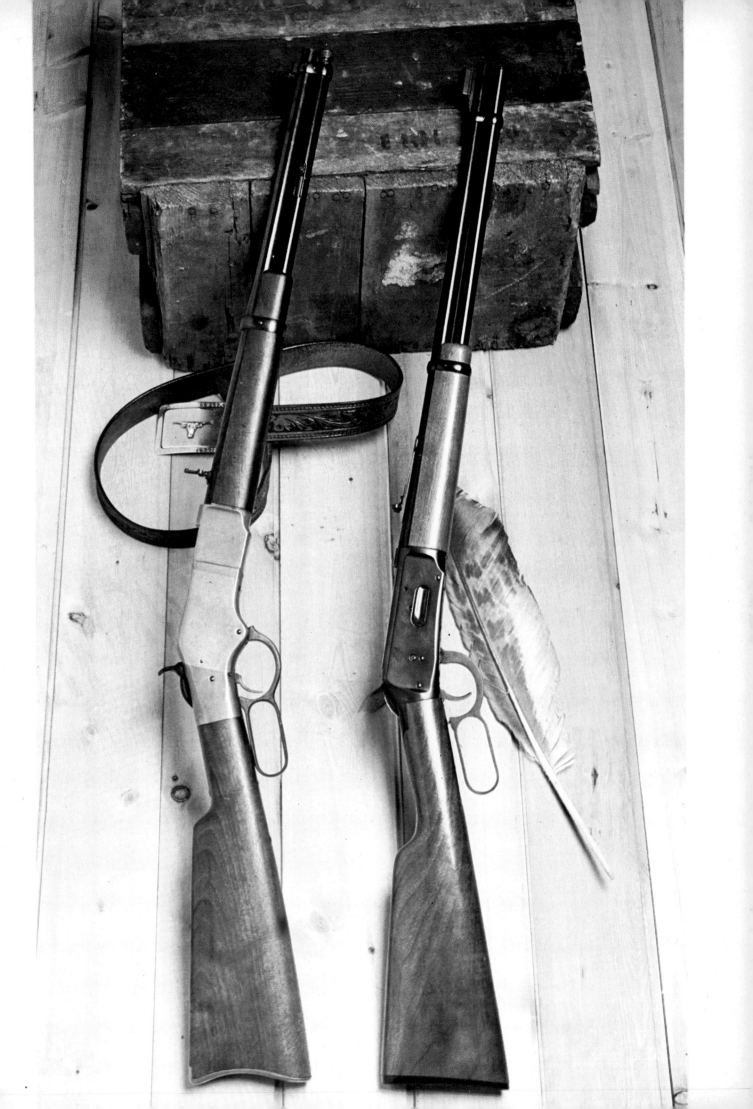

Enfield
and the modern rifle

An Elgin cutlass pistol, patented in 1837 – a combined weapon ordered in limited quantities by the U.S. government. This one is marked 'Elgin's Patent, C. B. Allen Springfield, Mass. 109.'

During the late Middle Ages certain towns became predominant in the manufacture of firearms. Their products exhibited certain characteristics which indicated their place of origin, for they were essentially local in design. The towns were often those which had already specialized in the production of swords and armour. They were usually near to the trade routes, conveniently situated to receive supplies of coal and metal and, most important, close to a source of water power.

In Germany the main production centres were Nuremberg, Augsburg and Suhl, and from these towns came a high proportion of the late-sixteenth century wheel-locks. Although most towns in Britain had some local gunmakers the biggest centre was London and it remained so until the latter part of the eighteenth century when Birmingham began to take over the commercial trade. British firearms production was sufficient to meet normal demands, but in times of war the supply was found to be inadequate. During the Napoleonic Wars the government had tried to obtain extra weapons from Liège, the main Belgian manufacturing centre. However, the standard of workmanship there was considered unsatisfactory and the quality of the muskets was severely criticized. Liège dominated the cheap gun market until Birmingham began to rival it during the latter part of the nineteenth century.

One sure indication that a town was an important centre of arms production was the establishment of a proof-house. Liège gunmakers were proving their barrels as early as 1621. In 1672 they drew up proof rules and agreed that a special mark should be placed on those weapons which passed the tests satisfactorily. The mark was part of the city arms, a tower, but in 1810 when Liège was part of the Napoleonic Empire, a new proof-house was built and a new mark was used. This was an 'E', also used by some French towns, but below it were added the letters 'LG' with a star, all enclosed within an oval. Later there were other changes but the 'E LG' mark is still in use today.

In France the main centre of production was St Etienne, which had a list of proof rules in 1792. In 1810 Napoleon, having re-organized almost every other aspect of French government, turned his attention to the firearms industry. He ordered that, in future, all military weapons purchased by the government should be proved and stamped with the letter 'E', the initial letter of the word *éprouvé*. The letter was sometimes surmounted with a crown or amended slightly, as in the case of weapons made in Paris, which had the letter 'E' with 'P' in an oval.

The Austro-Hungarian empire opened an Imperial Armoury in Vienna in 1842, although there was another centre at Ferlach which also proved weapons. However, no formal rules were drawn up until 1882 and they they were only optional. In 1891 proof-houses were set up at Budapest, Ferlach, Prague, Weihert, and Vienna.

In the United States, although the firearms industry grew to be extremely important, no public proof-houses were ever established. Weapons purchased for the armed forces were inspected and tested and then stamped with the initials or mark of the inspector. The United States differed from European countries in that its gun-making industry was not a gradual development but grew up suddenly after the Revolutionary War. Apart from the Pennsylvanian Long Rifle there were few American-made weapons before the war, most being imported from Europe. When war came supplies were cut off and the Americans were thrown back on their own resources.

In each colony Committees of Safety were set up, their chief task being to establish new sources of supply, to equip the local militia and generally to assist in making the colonies ready for war. Supplies in the hands of gunmakers were purchased or requisitioned and efforts were made to create an arms industry. It was essential to obtain weapons quickly and in 1776, at places such as Springfield, workers were formed into groups making separate parts of the musket. The skilled men produced the more difficult pieces and assembled the weapons, while the unskilled were given the less demanding jobs. Most of the Committee of Safety muskets were virtually copies of the British Brown Bess.

In February 1776 the Continental Congress set up another committee to arrange for the manufacture of muskets and bayonets, and it authorized the expenditure of some $10,000 on contracts. It is of interest to note that it was a man from Lancaster County, Pennsylvania, William Henry, who was appointed Superintendent of Arms and Military Accoutrements.

When peace came in 1785 the colonies had an army equipped with a whole range of muskets—French, British and Committee of Safety models—all of slightly different patterns. It was obvious that standardization was essential and that the new country should have its own arms industry. In April 1794 it was agreed to set up a national armoury at Springfield, Massachusetts. There had been an arsenal and powder magazine there from 1777 and some muskets had been made at this site. It was decided that the French Charleville musket, Model 1763, would be the pattern for the new musket. The first weapons were completed in 1795, a mere 245 in number, which were designated Model 1795.

The Springfield flintlock was very similar to the French musket. Both were of a ·69-inch calibre and the only real difference was that the Springfield was slightly lighter—8 lb 14 oz, compared with around 10 lb for the French one. The lock was stamped with a small spread eagle, the initials 'US' and, behind the hammer,

From top to bottom:
1. U.S. flintlock pistol with lock marked 'U.S., R. Johnson Middn Conn. 1842'.
2. U.S. percussion pistol with lock marked 'U.S., H. Aston, Middn Conn. 1849'.
3. U.S. percussion pistol for naval use, with lock marked 'N. P. Ames Springfield, Mass'.
4. U.S. percussion pistol dated 1853. Lock marked 'Palmetta Armoury S.C. Columbia. S.C.'
5. U.S. pistol with tape primer and shoulder stock fitted to butt.

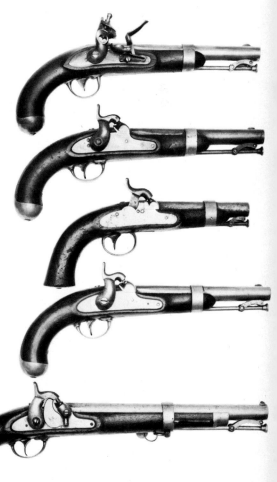

181

Top:

Above. The Greene carbine, patented in 1857, fired a ·53-inch (13·46-mm) bullet. It is fitted with a Maynard tape primer, and also has a movable barrel to permit breech-loading. Some of these weapons were purchased by the British army. Overall length 34¾ inches (88·3 cm). Barrel 18 inches (47·7 cm).
Below. The Starr Carbine, patented in 1858, used a ·52-inch (13·2-mm) rim-fire cartridge. The breech is opened by depressing the trigger guard. The same firm also made percussion revolvers. Overall length 37½ inches (94·3 cm). Barrel 21 inches (53·3 cm). Pattern Room, Royal Small Arms Factory, Enfield.

Right:

Bullet moulds. The large one is for the Enfield rifle of 1853 and casts a ·577-inch (14·65-mm) bullet. The one on the lower right is for the ·36-inch (9-mm) 1851 Navy Colt. The two at the top are for eighteenth-century flintlock pistols.

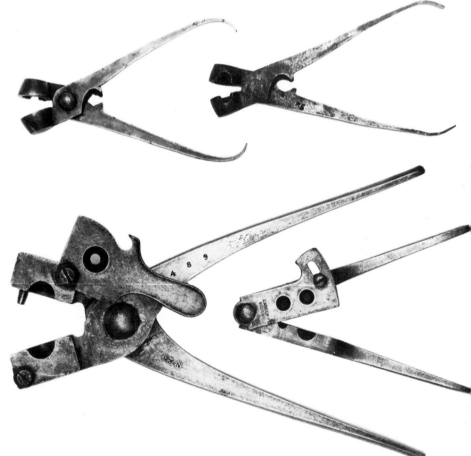

the name Springfield. The stock was of black walnut and the barrel roughly 44½ inches in length. The Springfield musket, like the French model, used bands to secure the barrel to the stock. The furniture, lock and barrel were all of polished iron. In addition to these muskets manufactured at Springfield about 7,000 more were obtained under private contract.

In 1796 another armoury was set up at Harper's Ferry, Virginia, but production did not begin there until 1801. The model 1795

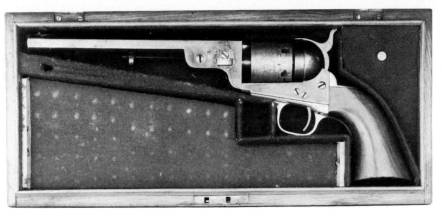

Right:
1851 Percussion Colt revolver converted to take ·38 centre-fire cartridge. The loading lever has been removed and a side ejector fitted in its place. The oak case is of the English pattern.

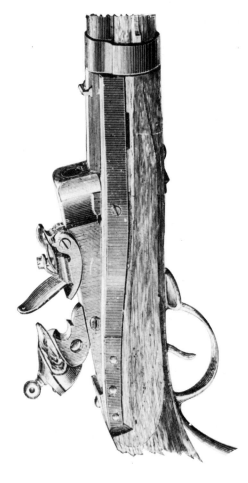

The rising block of the Halls carbine. It was, in effect, a pivoted chamber which was loaded and then locked into position, primed and fired.

continued in production with variations in detail until 1835. A board of officers was set up in 1835 to decide on standard armament and equipment for all the U.S. services. The musket which they chose as a model for the new weapon was the French Model of 1822. It was the last of the smooth-bore flintlock muskets and was produced at both Springfield and Harper's Ferry from 1840 to 1844. The Model 1835 had the same calibre–·69-inch–but the barrel length was reduced to 42 inches.

In 1842 the Ordnance Department decided on the manufacture of a percussion musket but the one produced was really only the Model 1835 fitted with a percussion lock. It was made at the two armouries from 1844 until 1855.

As well as muskets both armouries produced a number of flintlock and percussion rifles and in 1803 the superintendent of the Harper's Ferry armoury was ordered to begin production of 4,000 rifles with 33-inch barrels. In general appearance these recalled the famous American Long Rifles. Experience showed that the Model 1803 was perhaps not as strong as it might be and a new model was introduced in 1814 and modified in 1817.

In 1819 John H. Hall, an assistant armourer at Harper's Ferry, designed a breech-loading flintlock rifle which was adopted by the army. It had ·52-inch calibre bullet and a $32\frac{3}{4}$-inch barrel. The escape of gas between the breech and the end of the barrel was considerable, but it remained in production for some twenty-five years. In 1841 a muzzle-loading percussion rifle with a calibre of ·54-inch and a 33-inch barrel was adopted. It is interesting to note, in view of comments made in the eighteenth century, that originally it was not intended to fit this rifle with a bayonet. However, in 1855 many were given a brass-hilted sabre bayonet $22\frac{1}{2}$ inches long.

Under the impetus of the Civil War, the armies on both sides experimented with a whole range of breech-loading weapons. Many proved very satisfactory although all suffered to varying degrees from the problem of gas leakage at the breech.

Cartridges were undergoing further development since the first metal cartridge designed by Flobert in Paris in 1847. His cartridge was satisfactory for pistols, but it had serious limitations. It was difficult to construct a case soft enough to permit rim-fire ignition, yet strong enough to withstand the greater pressures generated by the bigger charge of powder used in rifles and carbines. Eventually these problems were overcome and soon, like the British, the Americans were faced with the big task of converting their percussion weapons into breech-loaders. Their final choice, in 1865, was a system devised by Erskine Allins, Master Armourer of the Springfield Armoury. It used a breech block hinged at the front and secured in position by a spring catch. A striker pierced the block and was struck by the ordinary percussion hammer. The

This Second Empire Gendarme d'Élite, has a well-made percussion musket, produced by an efficiently organized French firearms industry.

copper case of the ·58-inch cartridge was extracted by a device fitted in the chamber. In 1868 a new model was approved and the Springfield Rifle, with modifications, was to remain in service for many years.

In 1872 a Board of Officers was set up to consider the whole question of breech-loading. They tested over 100 weapons, but decided to retain the old Springfield system. They recommended that the calibre should be reduced to ·5 inches and that this should be made the standard calibre for revolvers, rifles and carbines. The rifle used a centre-fire cartridge with an extremely heavy bullet of 405 grains weight, using 70 grains of powder.

In 1892 it was finally decided that a magazine rifle should be issued to all U.S. forces and, after many tests, the Krag-Jorgensen was chosen. It had been developed by two Norwegians at the Kingsberg Arms Factory in Norway and the first examples were produced in 1894. This weapon was a ·30-calibre bolt-action with a magazine for five rounds. The Krag-Jorgensen was not a great success. It was very slow in loading and its ballistics were relatively poor.

In 1896 the U.S. navy adopted a magazine rifle which had been patented by James P. Lee, a Scotsman who had emigrated to the United States. He was the first man to place the box magazine below the breech. His rifle used a much smaller calibre than most military weapons of that period, only ·236 inches. The bullet was light, weighing 112 grains but it achieved a very high muzzle velocity of 2,550 feet per second.

In 1900 another Board of Officers was convened to consider the adoption of an improved rifle and they chose a modified Mauser, which was designated U.S. Magazine Rifle Model 1903. It fired a ·30-inch, 200-grain, round-nosed bullet, which developed a muzzle velocity of 2,300 feet per second. The magazine held five cartridges. In 1906 different ammunition was introduced which gave a muzzle velocity of 2,700 feet per second, with a bullet weighing only 150 grains. This rifle was produced at Springfield between 1904 and 1922, as well as at another arsenal which had been established at Rock Island, Illinois.

When the United States entered World War I in 1917 it was found that the two U.S. arsenals were unable to supply weapons in the quantities required. To cope with the emergency it was agreed that a British rifle should be used since it had been produced in the United States from 1914, and the machinery, gauges, and the necessary skills were all available. It was not a

Enfield percussion rifle, ·577-inch (14·6-mm) calibre. This was a fine weapon and continued in use with the militia and volunteers long after the regular army had received more modern rifles. The wooden water bottle bears the date 1851. Private Collection.

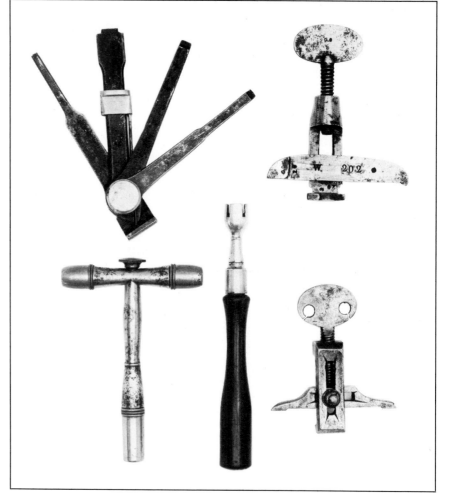

Right:
Example of gun tools.
Above left. A composite tool with several sizes of screwdriver, and nipple pin for clearing any deposit.
Below left. This is intended for a percussion pistol or revolver and consists of a screwdriver and nipple key.
Right. Clamps for securing a mainspring when stripping a lock.

Below:
Left. Adjustable brass shot measure with an ebony handle.
Centre. Steel, double-ended shot container. Each section held one correct charge of shot.
Right. Brass tubular measure.
The central slide is graduated on both sides – one for shot and one for powder.

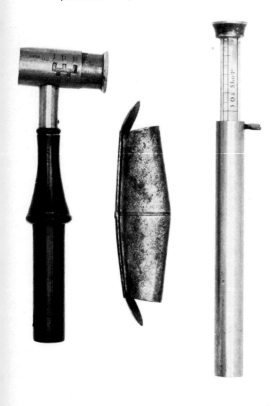

direct copy of the British rifle. The calibre was reduced to ·30 inches so that American ammunition could be used. The weapon was made by the Winchester Arms Company, the Remington Arms Company, and the U.M.C. Company, and was known as the U.S. Model 1917. Ironically the two nations which had shared the Brown Bess, were now, after 130 years both using the same weapon again.

The United States was well ahead of Britain in planned fire-arm production. Until the nineteenth century Britain possessed no national armoury or arsenal. The centre for manufacture was the Tower of London, which was also the headquarters of the Ordnance, the residence of the Master Gunner and the site of the government proof-house. The right to prove arms does not seem to have been taken over by the Ordnance for the Tower before about 1600. Prior to this date two of the London city companies, the Blacksmiths and the Armourers, had proved weapons. It was not until 1638 that a charter was granted to the London Gunmakers Company. The new company claimed the right to prove weapons and adopted two marks: a view mark (a crowned 'V') for the first inspection, and a crowned 'GP' for the final proof.

Following the Restoration in 1660 attempts were made to remedy the confused conditions governing the supply of military arms. First of all the odd buildings scattered around London which were used by the Ordnance were gradually abandoned and a storehouse was built inside the Tower. It was complete with a viewing room, where weapons could be checked, and some work-shops. In 1682 a new proof-house was built on the Tower Wharf. When Birmingham was developing as a centre of the gun trade

Above. Snider conversion to change muzzle-loading rifle to breech-loading.
Below. The Martini-Henry rifle, adopted by the British army in 1871. Imperial War Museum, London.

weapons made there could not be accepted by the Ordnance before they had been proved. The only people authorized to prove them were in the Tower of London and this meant that representatives had to travel to Birmingham with the powder and shot to carry out their work.

The royal proof mark was originally a crowned rose, but from the time of Queen Anne it was replaced by a crown over crossed sceptres, the wand of royal office, the royal cypher and a broad arrow. Two marks were struck on barrels: the crown and crossed sceptres as a proof mark; and the royal cypher and broad arrow as a view mark, and a sign that the weapon was an official government issue one. In 1813 the Birmingham gun makers were given authority by an Act of Parliament to set up their own proof-house. They decided to use as their mark the crossed sceptres and letters 'B C P' within the spaces formed by the arms, and a 'V' for the view mark.

As the demand for weapons increased during the American Revolutionary War and the Napoleonic Wars it was found that the old proof system was being stretched beyond its capacity. In 1804 it was decided that, in future, weapons could be completely assembled in Birmingham. Barrels and metal work had previously been fashioned, proved and viewed, and then sent to London for assembly.

The manner in which the weapons were to be checked was laid down in detail. The barrels were viewed to ensure correct dimensions and the bore was examined. If they passed this test they were taken to the proof-house where they were loaded and fired. They were then left for forty-eight hours and checked again.

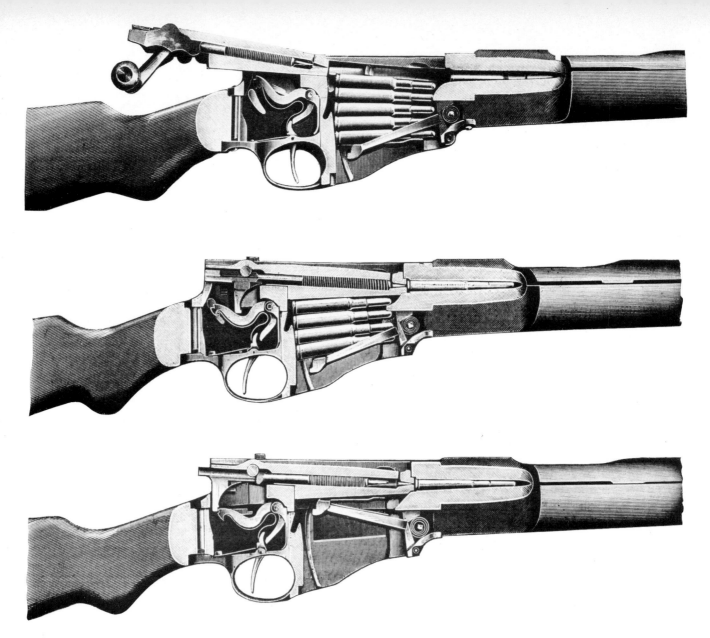

If satisfactory the barrels were now stamped with the proof marks. Ramrods were tested by being bent and then checked to see that they could be straightened again. Locks were examined and marked with a broad arrow on the outside and the viewer's mark on the inside. In some cases the lock was completely disassembled and the parts checked, but sometimes only some parts were individually checked. The musket was then assembled, barrel and furniture were fitted to the wooden stock and it was delivered to the Ordnance Stores for the contractors to finish off the job.

Even with these improvements production was still haphazard and contractors often failed to deliver on time. As early as July 1794 the Board of Ordnance agreed that the only solution was to establish a factory which would be responsible for the production of government weapons. Nothing happened until 1805 when the Tower took on its own permanent staff and began to assemble weapons. Barrels were to be produced at the Armoury Mills at Lewisham, just outside London. These mills dated back to the late sixteenth century but their potential had never been realized. A famous London barrel-maker was made superintendent of the lock and barrel department, but it was not until January 1808 that the factory at Lewisham was ready.

It was expected that the mills would be capable of producing some 50,000 barrels, locks, rammers and bayonets a year. The

Diagrams showing the action of the Lee rifle adopted by the United States Navy.

Opposite, far right:
The model 1861 Springfield rifle produced in bulk during the American Civil War. It was ·58-inch (14·7-mm) calibre and measured 56 inches (142·2 cm) overall. The barrel was secured to the stock by bands. The bayonet was a socket one, 18 inches (45·7 cm) long. Winchester Gun Museum, New Haven, Connecticut.

Opposite, above:
Bolt mechanisms of the Lee-Speed rifle which was at one time considered for adoption by the British army. It was originally an American design but was modified by a Mr Speed of Enfield.

Opposite, below:
American troops at a beachhead on Rendova Island in the Pacific, during World War II. They are armed with Calibre ·30 MI Rifles, the standard issue from 1936 to 1957.

188

machines were mostly water-powered and additional power was supplied by a very expensive steam engine. A proof-house was built and it was decided that the departments at the Tower should also be moved out to Lewisham. In 1815 the Napoleonic Wars ended and, to save money, the number of staff was reduced. In 1818 the Birmingham factory was closed completely.

Even the very limited scope of the Lewisham venture had convinced the authorities that the system of centralized production offered considerable advantages. It was suggested that the Board of Ordnance should build an entirely new arms factory. The site chosen was at Enfield Lock in Middlesex, some twelve miles north of London. The factory was to stand on an island formed by the conjunction of a river and a canal, which meant that there was no problem over the supply of water power. In 1816 George Lovell, a man who had long played an important part in British firearm production, was appointed its storekeeper. In 1817 the proof-house at Lewisham was dismantled and then re-erected at Enfield. Weapons made at Enfield were stamped with the date and the name 'ENFIELD' on the lock and occasionally on the barrel. Proof was indicated by the royal cyphers of William IV and Victoria.

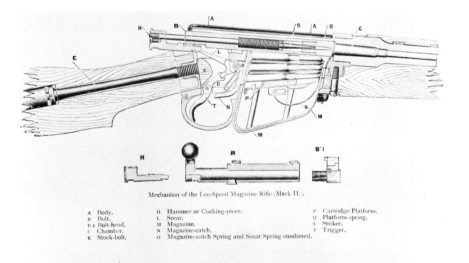

Mechanism of the Lee-Speed Magazine Rifle (Mark II.).

A	Body.	H	Hammer or Cocking-piece.	P	Cartridge Platform.
B	Bolt.	L	Sear.	Q	Platform-spring.
B 1	Bolt-head.	M	Magazine.	S	Striker.
C	Chamber.	N	Magazine-catch.	T	Trigger.
E	Stock-bolt.	O	Magazine-catch Spring and Sear Spring combined.		

When it was resolved that the British army was to adopt percussion weapons the method of production was re-examined. It was decided that the old system of contract work would probably give the best results and in 1839 the Ordnance premises at Birmingham were reopened and partly rebuilt. By 1848 the old system had been re-established. Enfield was still only producing comparatively small numbers of weapons but matters were improving. Under the guidance of George Lovell more machinery was gradually introduced to speed up production. Drillers, steam hammers and even a machine for rifling were in place by the 1850s. Cutting the wooden stocks presented a problem but the new system used at the American arsenal at Springfield was, for some reason, turned down.

In 1854, concerned at the situation in the Crimea, where a disastrous war was in progress, Parliament conducted an enquiry to consider the 'cheapest and most expeditious way of providing small arms'. The Ordnance now suggested that the production should be made independent of contractors. Evidence was given to the Parliamentary committee about the fine results achieved by Colt in his factory. Colonel Colt himself appeared before the committee and was very scathing about the antiquated hand-operated systems used by the British.

The outcome of the enquiry was a compromise. It was agreed that the contract system would be continued, but that new methods of production using machinery should be tested at the Enfield factory. A group of three investigators was sent out to visit the American arsenals at Springfield and Harper's Ferry. There they

Above:
Setting out gun barrels ready for testing in the Birmingham Proof House in 1851. When all the barrels were loaded and in position the room was sealed off and the charges fired by means of a fuse.

Right:
Nineteenth-century view of the Royal Small Arms Factory at Enfield where the work was still largely manual, although many machines were in use.

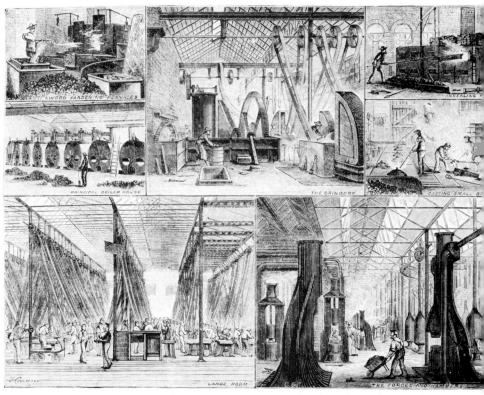

bought machinery for stock- and lock-making and persuaded James Burton, a former master armourer from Harper's Ferry, to go to England in order to supervise production at Enfield. Burton got rid of much of the old-fashioned equipment. In place of the old water wheels he installed a new steam engine and by 1856 the Enfield factory was in full production.

With the development of the metal cartridge in the 1860s Enfield became increasingly concerned with the production of breech-loading weapons. In October 1866 it was decided that the old Snider had served its purpose as a stopgap weapon and that it was now time to consider a replacement. The new weapon had to use a metallic, self-contained cartridge and be capable of a rate of fire not less than twelve shots a minute. About 120 weapons were offered for consideration, as well as nearly 50 different types of ammunition.

After long tests, discussions and experiments, a modified form of a breech action invented by a Swiss, Frederick von Martini, and a barrel with a form of rifling designed by Alexander Henry of Edinburgh, were chosen. The breech action consisted of a block hinged at the rear and activated by a long extension of the trigger guard. When this lever was depressed it tipped the block down at the front allowing direct access to the breech. The cartridge was pushed into position guided by the shaped top of the breech block. The lever was closed and this movement cocked the action and locked the block in position. When the weapon had been fired the lever was depressed and the falling block knocked against a small hook-shaped lever which engaged with the rim at the base of the cartridge. The movement activated this lever, which withdrew the cartridge case. The Martini-Henry rifle was officially adopted in April 1871. It was just over $49\frac{1}{2}$ inches long, weighed 9 lb, and was sighted up to 1,450 yards. The carbines had a shortened barrel and a lesser range, around 1,180 yards. Bayonets were provided for both models—a sword bayonet with a long, straight blade for the artillery and a socket bayonet for line regiments. The Martini-Henry continued in service with the British army until 1891. During its lifetime it was used in Africa, India, Egypt, the Sudan, Canada, Burma and on sundry other expeditions in other parts of the world.

It was not a completely satisfactory weapon and there were many complaints from the troops about its unreliability. One of the problems was not so much the rifle itself as the cartridge. At the Battle of Isandhlwana, Natal, in January 1897 one of the many factors which led to the defeat of the British by Zulu tribesmen was shortage of ammunition. The wooden crates of bullets were secured by copper bands, each of which was kept in place by nine large screws. A shortage of screwdrivers, rusty screws and the sheer physical effort involved in undoing the screws slowed down the supply of ammunition to such an extent that troops were unable to maintain a heavy fire.

Snider breech. The block, traversed by a striker pin, is in the open position for loading. The aperture on the left is threaded to take the barrel and on the right is the tang, by which the barrel is fixed to the butt.

Mechanization came only gradually to the arms industry and as late as 1862 the Enfield rifle cartridge was being rolled by hand.

Despite great courage in resisting their charges, men of the 24th Regiment, unable to maintain a high rate of fire, were overwhelmed and killed by the brave Zulu Impis at the disastrous battle of Isandhlwana in 1879. National Army Museum, London.

When the British army was involved in Egypt in 1882 and the Sudan campaign in 1884–6 the Martini-Henry came in for a great deal of criticism. The army commander, Field Marshal Wolseley, took up the complaints and made himself quite un-unpopular. Questions were raised in Parliament and the correspondence columns of both military and non-military magazines were filled with letters on this topic. The *Illustrated Naval and Military Magazine* claimed that the Martini-Henry 'in its mechanical construction and in other important elements is inferior to most of the arms in use by foreign powers'. It went on to say: 'There was a committee appointed to go into the question of a rifle for the British troops, whose ignorance of the essential and mechanical elements of a thorough soldier's arm had been absolutely proved by the recommendation of a rifle which could not extract the wretched cartridge that failed in the Soudan with the sacrifice of many a valuable life, and of the present bayonet, which is unreliable at the critical moment of single combat.'

In February 1883 a new Parliamentary Small Arms Committee had been formed and one of its tasks was to consider the possibility of improving the Martini-Henry. In 1886 it recommended a reduction in calibre to ·402 inches and an improved cartridge of 85 grains of black powder, firing a bullet of 380 grains. The rifling

British Martini-Henry rifle bearing Enfield markings for 1879. Some of these rifles had longer trigger guard/levers than the earlier models. The greater length gave increased leverage and was introduced in an attempt to facilitate the extraction of the cartridge cases. Pattern Room, Royal Small Arms Factory, Enfield.

194

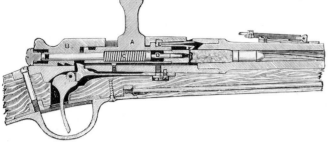

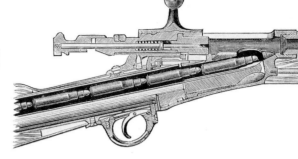

Above:
Engraving of 1892 showing the
main military small arms in service
at that period. All except the
Martini-Henry (bottom left) used a
bolt action.

Left:
Above. Martini-Henry rifle. About
1870.
Below. Lee-Metford rifle of 1889.
Tower of London Armouries.

Below left:
Above. Lee-Enfield carbine with a
six-round magazine, first adopted in
1900. Shown here with the bolt
open.
Below. The SMLE – Short Magazine
Lee-Enfield rifle – which saw service
in both World Wars. This particular
example has a special backsight
fitted – probably for target shooting.
Pattern Room, Royal Small Arms
Factory, Enfield.

195

was also altered and in the same year 70,000 rifles incorporating a
new type of barrel were manufactured at Enfield. They were
known as Enfield-Martini rifles, although they were, in fact,
never issued, and were afterwards made into a special pattern of
the Martini-Henry with the old calibre of ·45 inches.

The Parliamentary Committee had the additional task of report-
ing on the desirability of introducing a magazine rifle. The repeating magazine rifle had been receiving a great deal of attention. As
early as 1866 the Swiss had decided to issue one, and two years
later they approved the Vetterli rifle. It fired a ·41-inch cartridge
and had a tube magazine holding eleven cartridges but the rifle
could be adapted to take as many as thirteen. Another early
magazine rifle was that used by the Austro-Hungarian gendarm-
erie, a Fruhwith pattern of 1870 which was a ·433-inch calibre
weapon holding eight cartridges.

In 1884 Germany was the first of the major powers to equip its
troops with a magazine rifle, when it converted the 1871 Mauser
into a rifle with eight cartridges in a tube magazine.

If the British Parliamentary Committee could agree that a
magazine weapon was desirable, they were to recommend which
particular model would be best. They conducted a poll among
serving officers, and the verdict was that any magazine rifle should
have as simple a mechanism as possible. It should not be too heavy,
the magazine should hold at least five rounds, and it should be
capable of being used as a single-loader. Moreover, its performance
should be at least equal to that of the Martini-Henry. A large
number of weapons were submitted for the trials which were to be
conducted, but after extensive tests only three were left. After a
further stage the choice lay between two. In August 1885 the
committee recommended that an improved Lee rifle with a special
magazine and an Owen Jones rifle should be given further trials.
These resulted in the wholesale condemnation of the Owen Jones
rifle.

Enfield revolvers.
From top to bottom.
1. Adams cartridge revolver Mark II.
·45 inch (11·4 mm) with a side
ejector.

2. Enfield cartridge revolver Mark I of
1880. Calibre ·476 inches (12 mm).
Overall length 11 inches (27·9 cm).
3. Enfield cartridge revolver Mark I of
1880, No. 10. The cylinders are
rifled.

4. Enfield cartridge revolver Mark III
of 1882. Calibre ·476 inches
(12 mm). Pattern Room, Royal
Small Arms Factory, Enfield.

British troops of Loyal North Lancashire Regiment entering Cambrai in October 1918. The short magazine Lee-Enfield rifles are slung. Attached to their bayonet scabbards are the handles for their entrenching tool, the blade being carried in a case at the belt.

In February 1887 further tests were carried out and at the same time there was discussion on the best calibre. In June of that year the Committee reported that, in their opinion, a small-calibre bullet should be adopted by the British army. In January 1888 a ·303-inch calibre rifle, with the Metford rifling and the Lee bolt and magazine was approved. About 350 rifles were made up and sent out to various parts of the world for testing, and the committee sat back to await the reports. Nearly all the replies were favourable. In December 1888 the Lee Metford Magazine Rifle Mark I was approved and put into production.

The introduction of smokeless powder affected the design of repeating rifles. Black powder was not a very efficient explosive, since it left a residue in the barrel and the smoke produced was, of course, a serious handicap. Paul Vieille, a chemist working for the French government, produced a powder which gave a much higher velocity, left far less residue and was virtually smokeless. France, not surprisingly, was the first nation to use this new propellant and produced the Lebel rifle of 1886, which had a tube magazine with eight cartridges and a bore of only ·315 inches. This small calibre was to set the pattern for the rest of Europe. Matchlock muskets had had a calibre of around ·75 inches and the size of bullets was gradually reduced over the centuries.

In July 1890 another British Parliamentary Committee was convened to consider the reports now to hand. As a result several changes were made. It was agreed that ten cartridges were more satisfactory than eight. There were some modifications to the bolt, and the pattern was approved in 1891. The cartridge used black powder, but in 1892 the new explosive, cordite, was introduced and several minor alterations in the design were made.

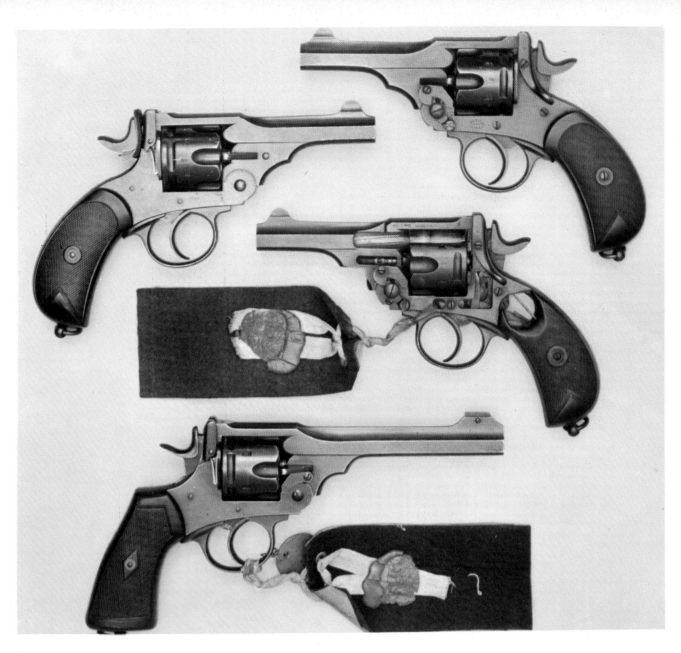

Above:
British army Webley revolvers.
Top right. Mark III introduced in 1897.
Top left. Mark I, introduced in 1887.
Centre right. Mark III – skeleton
specimen and marked 'Approved
24/7/1900.'
Bottom left. Mark VI approved
pattern 5.5.1915. Pattern Room,
Royal Small Arms Factory, Enfield.

Right:
Above. American Springfield rifle
Model 1903A3. Calibre ·30 inches
(7·62 mm). Overall length 37½ inches
(89·9 cm). Barrel 25½ inches
(69·9 cm). Made during World War
II by Remington. No. 3397620.
Below. American Krag-Jorgensen
rifle Model 1898. Calibre ·30 inches
(7·62 mm). Overall length 49 inches
(124·5 cm). Barrel 30 inches
(76·2 cm). Made at Springfield
Arsenal between 1899 and 1904.
Pattern Room, Royal Small Arms
Factory, Enfield.

Above:
Two views of the Mark IV Short Magazine Lee-Enfield rifle made between 1918 and 1929. This was the principal British infantry weapon of World War II. Imperial War Museum, London.

Top:
The EM2, a British automatic rifle developed by a research team at Enfield. It has a twenty-shot magazine of 7-mm cartridges and develops a muzzle velocity of 2,530 feet per second (770 m/sec.), with a rate of fire of 120 rounds a minute. Pattern Room, Royal Small Arms Factory, Enfield.

Another weapon, the Lee Metford Mark II*, was approved in 1895, and this had a safety catch fitted. Further tests were carried out and in November of that year the famous Lee-Enfield rifle was adopted. The main change was in the use of the Enfield rifling in place of the Metford, for it was found that the cordite-propelled projectiles soon wore down the Metford rifling. In 1894 a smaller version of the Lee Metford had been introduced as a carbine, and this was followed two years later by a Lee Enfield carbine, with a barrel 9½ inches shorter than the rifle.

Events were now moving quickly in the armaments world and in 1900 a new Parliamentary Committee was set up to report upon the whole question of small arms for the British forces. After a year's deliberation they recommended the testing of a shortened Lee-Enfield. One thousand rifles with barrels 5 inches shorter were made and tested, and were issued in June 1902. A compromise between the long infantry barrel and the short carbine one, these rifles had a new system of loading. Across the top of the breech was a metal bridge cut to take the new rifle clip which held five cartridges. With the bolt open a full clip was dropped into place over the magazine, and steady pressure with the thumb forced the cartridges out of the clip and down into the magazine. The empty clip was then discarded. The magazine held two full clips, ten cartridges in all, and it had the advantage that it could be re-filled at any time. Some minor alterations were made and the final pattern was approved on December 23, 1902, as the S.M.L.E. (the Short Magazine Lee-Enfield) Mark I. The British system of designating military weapons was by describing the first model as

200

Mark I, the second Mark II and so on. The mark number was altered only if the modifications were extensive. If changes were small the new model was given a star, e.g., MkII*. The Enfield part of the name was derived from the rifling, which had been developed by the Royal Small Arms Factory at Enfield Lock. This rifle had five grooves and was found to withstand the effects of wear much better than the old Metford, which wore out after a mere 4,000 rounds.

The British soldier was well drilled in musketry and a strong emphasis was placed on rapid fire. In 1893 it was calculated that each infantryman in the field was to be supplied with 185 rounds. Of these 100 rounds were carried by the individual soldier, 65 rounds in carts or on mules, and 20 rounds in battalion baggage wagons.

During World War I the S.M.L.E. proved itself both adaptable and reliable. In the hands of trained troops the rate of fire was so high that the enemy thought they were opposed by machine-guns. With some minor changes, such as a little extra strengthening, the rifle could be adapted to hold a special cup on the muzzle. By firing a blank cartridge a hand grenade placed in the cup could be hurled a very considerable distance away.

There were few modifications in the S.M.L.E. during the war years but afterwards considerable thought was devoted to the possibility of change. In 1923 a Mark V rifle was introduced and subjected to tests, but it did not meet with much approval and the project was dropped.

The British, self-loading rifle, SLR L1A1, at present in general service use. It fires a 7·62-mm cartridge at a rate of about 80 rounds a minute and has an effective range of 800 metres. The box magazine holds 20 rounds.

Zig Zag revolvers.
From top to bottom.
1. Webley Fosberry ·455-inch
(11·55-mm) automatic revolver, for
target. Model 3462. Barrel 7½ inches
(19 cm).
2. Webley Fosberry ·455-inch
(11·55-mm) automatic revolver.
No. 2969. Barrel 6 inches (15·2 cm).
3. Webley Fosberry ·455-inch
(11·55-mm) automatic revolver.
No. 739. Barrel 4 inches (10·2 cm).
4. Mauser 9-mm revolver patented
in 1878. The zig-zag grooves are to
rotate the cylinder but, unlike the
Webley Fosberry, the action is not
automatic. The loop at the base of
the frame is to unlock the frame to
permit loading. Pattern Room, Royal
Small Arms Factory, Enfield.

When the various committees sat, the rifle could not be considered in isolation. It will be remembered that one of the weaknesses of the riflemen in the American Revolutionary War was their inability to defend themselves without a bayonet. It was still felt as late as the 1930s that a bayonet was an essential weapon for an infantryman. It had long been known that when the bayonet was fixed it affected the shooting of the rifle and so the question of the best type of bayonet had to be considered at the same time.

The need for a bayonet was accepted by the authorities but it is doubtful whether the troops would have agreed. The bayonet had its uses: for digging, poking the fire, opening tin cans and for suspending things. On its merits as a fighting weapon opinion was less certain. However, the committees considering the matter thought that the current length, around 22 inches, was perhaps excessive. They suggested that for the new rifle a much shorter bayonet would be satisfactory.

They chose a spike bayonet with a rather useless hilt. In 1925 the Mark VI rifle was fitted with these short, spike bayonets. The method of attachment on the rifle was very simple and did away with the old lug and slot arrangement. Some rather gruesome experiments were carried out on the carcass of a newly dead sheep and they showed that, for its purpose, the spike bayonet was quite satisfactory. However, the new-style bayonet was not officially issued for some years.

Short Magazine Lee-Enfield with its bayonet. This particular weapon is one of those manufactured at Lithgow in Australia and differs slightly in detail from the British-made version. The cartridges are dummy rounds for practice and, for easy recognition, the cases are grooved and marked in red.

German troops on the march in Russia during World War II. They carry the standard infantry rifle, the Mauser 7·92-mm Gewehr 98/40, first issued in 1941.

The next point was to consider the rifle that was to go with the new bayonet. In 1926 half a dozen specimens of the Mark VI rifle were produced. Experiments had shown that there was a great deal of 'whip' or vibration in any rifle barrel when the bullet left the muzzle. This affected the accuracy of the weapon and the new model was to have a stiffer barrel. In addition, the nose cap had been removed since it was no longer required to hold the bayonet.

At the same time as the trials were being conducted the system of naming the rifles was altered. The old S.M.L.E. Mark III now became officially the Rifle No.I, Mark III, and the new Mark VI which was currently being tested became Rifle No. 4. It came through its trials very well and in 1930 the Royal Small Arms Factory at Enfield began production. It was decided that 500 of these rifles should be issued to one infantry battalion and 500 to a cavalry regiment for testing throughout the summer. Various modifications were suggested but there was no doubt that the No.4 rifle was far more accurate than its predecessors. After its tests, which had now lasted many years, official approval for the manufacture of the new No.4 Rifle Mark I, together with all its accessories, was given in November 1939 soon after the outbreak of World War II.

Production of the new model did not begin on a large scale until 1941 and was carried on in Canada and the United States. Over a million were manufactured at Long Branch, near Toronto in Canada, and a million more were made by the Savage Arms Company in the United States. Production of the No.4 rifle had to be diverted overseas because Enfield had gone over to the production of the Bren machine-gun which had been adopted in 1935. Other ordnance factories for manufacturing the rifle were set up in Yorkshire, Lancashire, and near Birmingham.

Combat experience during World War II soon made clear the varied nature of the terrain over which the battles were being fought. Desert, jungle, arctic snow—all presented their own particular problems. In the Far East it was seen that if troops were to move through jungle they needed to travel light. It was decided that one very useful step would be to reduce the weight of the rifle. It had also been found that in jungle warfare the flash from the muzzle of the Lee-Enfield was to bright that concealment was difficult and steps were taken to reduce the flash.

The outcome was the No. 5 rifle, with several distinctive features. The rear sling fitting was at the base of the butt, less of the barrel was covered by the wooden stock, and the foresight was protected by two vertical wings. A flash-eliminator, like a slightly tapering funnel, was attached at the muzzle. A special bayonet was adapted to fit over the flash-eliminator and locked on to a lug situated just beneath the foresight.

Top:
Specially scaled-down version of a Ballita rifle used by the Fascist Youth movement in Italy. It is a 6-mm calibre with a 10½-inch (26·6-cm) folding bayonet. Overall length 29½ inches (74·9 cm).

Centre:
This new 4·85-mm light support weapon is the latest product of the Enfield Royal Small Arms Factory. The system can be modified to serve as a personal, self-loading rifle or as a general-purpose machine-gun. It is fitted with an optical sight. Pattern Room, Royal Small Arms Factory, Enfield.

Below:
A modern hunting rifle by Lang of London, fitted with a telescopic sight. It has a pistol-grip butt and a cheek rest.

205

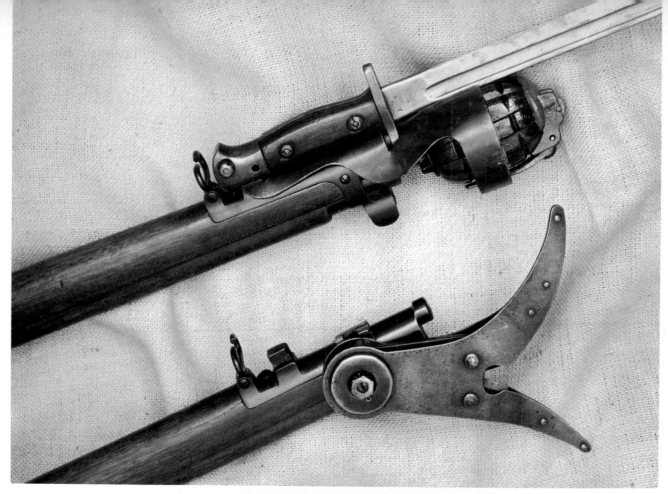

Short Magazine Lee-Enfield rifles
fitted with two devices for trench
warfare.
Above. Grenade discharger 1916. A
long plunger fitted to the base of the
grenade goes down the barrel. The
stock of the rifle is fitted with a
special angled sight.
Below. Cutters for barbed wire—
pattern dated 31.1.17. Seven inches
(24 cm) long, they were fitted to the
No. 1. Mark II rifle. Pattern Room,
Royal Small Arms Factory, Enfield.

Russian partisans during World War II
are briefed by their commander who
is armed with a PPSL 41 submachine-
gun. The rifles stacked in the
foreground are the Moisin-Nagant
M.1891/30 7·6-mm model.

Above:
A page from a popular educational book of the latter part of the nineteenth century, showing the Enfield rifle, the Martini-Henry rifle and sundry artillery accessories.

Above right:
Smokeless powder led to the development of many powerful cartridges including a number designed for big-game hunting. This intrepid hunter of the 1890s is holding a double-barrelled express rifle popular for elephant and rhino shooting.

A group of nineteenth-century cast lead bullets. The very big one is for the Jacob's rifle—a large-bore, double-action weapon.

The Mark V rifle, usually referred to as the Jungle Carbine, was officially introduced in September 1944. It proved to be a very efficient weapon for its purpose, although it suffered from certain sighting problems.

The trend towards smaller-calibre ammunition could not be developed during the war because factories were geared to the manufacture of one particular calibre and changes would have had a disastrous effect upon production. However, in 1945 it was decided that not only would a smaller calibre be useful but a self-loading rifle, with an increased rate of fire, was also to be desired. The new calibre was agreed by a committee to be ·276 inches. Much research went on at the Royal Small Arms Factory and the first design was the Enfield Model I or E.M.I. It was not very successful and there were considerable problems. It was an unusual 'bull-pup' design, in which the wooden shoulder butt was discarded and replaced with a simple shoulder rest and a pistol grip substituted. A wooden section covered the barrel where the left hand gripped and a box magazine was situated behind the pistol grip. E.M.II Model was produced at the end of 1948 and in 1950 it was taken to the United States. It was very accurate and worked well. However, it was felt that the cartridge lacked power.

In May 1957 Britain adopted the Nato cartridge and once again the question of a suitable rifle arose. It was decided to adopt the Fabrique Nationale Fusil Automatique Légère. This rifle had first been tested in 1955 and, after some modifications, was finally accepted as the L.I. A1 rifle. It has a box magazine of twenty rounds with a maximum effective range of about 2,400 feet.

The Royal Small Arms Factory at Enfield gave its name to two of the best of British Service weapons—the 1853 Enfield Rifle and the Lee-Enfield ·303. It is still in operation and very much to the fore in weapon design. In June 1976 it displayed for the public its latest weapon system—the 485. This automatic rifle has a calibre of ·191 inches, one of the smallest yet, with a cyclic rate of fire of 700 to 850 rounds a minute. It is a versatile and accurate weapon, but in today's world of impersonal initials, it is unlikely to bear the illustrious name of Enfield.

Automatic pistols

The adoption of repeating rifles equipped with cartridges and magazines in the latter part of the nineteenth century made warfare more dependent on technology than ever before. The individual soldier now had available a rate of fire beyond the belief of his eighteenth-century counterpart. He carried some 60 rounds, which could be discharged in a few minutes. This fact in itself created problems, since a constant supply of ammunition was essential, and in prolonged battles it was vital to have a commissariat which could maintain the flow.

Cavalry were often equipped with a carbine, although there was some dispute about whether this was the best weapon for them. Cavalry in general and many officers still retained the sword. Committees from armies all over the world met at various times to consider which sword was most satisfactory, but its day was over. Colt had made the revolver a practicable weapon and from the mid-nineteenth century it had become the custom for officers to equip themselves with percussion revolvers. The loading was a little awkward. The most common method was to use the small paper or skin cartridge with a ribbon attached, which could be pulled to break it open. The hammer was set at half-cock and the revolver held with the muzzle pointing upwards. The cartridge was torn open, the powder poured into the chamber and the bullet and paper rammed home with the loading lever. Then each nipple was capped and the weapon was ready to discharge its five or six shots.

The development of the revolver was somewhat slower than that of long arms. The problem was that it was difficult to load a revolver in any way other than that already described. There was no space on the conventional frame for the accommodation of complex systems. The answer when it came was so obvious that it seems surprising that it had not been thought of before. In 1855 Rollin White was granted a master patent in the United States, which included a system whereby the revolver cylinder was drilled right through. This meant that, provided it could be retained in place, a cartridge could be loaded in from the back of the cylinder.

Two other gunmakers, Daniel Wesson and Horace Smith, had designed a revolver which would use a small rim-fire cartridge. The first cartridges had the priming spread across the base but later the case was spun while the priming was fluid so that it was deposited inside a small lip or rim running around the base.

American revolvers.
From top to bottom.
1. Remington Army revolver New Model 1874. Centre-fire ·44-inch (11·4-mm) calibre. Overall length $12\frac{7}{8}$ inches (32·7 cm).
2. Colt Root percussion revolver.
3. Colt 1861 percussion Navy pistol converted to centre-fire by fitting ejector rod, loading gate bored through cylinder, and a firing pin.
4. London-made ·31-inch (7·87-mm) Pocket Colt No. 239. 1857.
5. Colt ·22-inch (5·58-mm) New Line revolver with mother-of-pearl grips. 1875. Pattern Room, Royal Small Arms Factory, Enfield.

A collection of cartridges. Two are pin-fire. Second on the left is a Colt ·45 ACP and in the centre is a ·357-inch Magnum.

In 1856 the Smith and Wesson Company acquired a monopoly of White's patent, and in 1857 they offered the first practical breech-loading revolver with metal cartridges. The hammer was made with a forward-projecting ridge which slammed down on the primed rim and crushed it against the face of the cylinder, so detonating the cartridge. There were early problems, but soon the ammunition was improved and large-calibre cartridges became available.

The first of the Smith and Wesson pistols, Model 1, was in production during 1857–60 and used a short ·22-inch cartridge. It had a sleeved trigger similar to that on the Colt Root's revolver. Empty cases were ejected by 'breaking' the revolver, removing the cylinder and pushing out the individual empty cases by means of the rod fitted to the frame beneath the barrel.

In 1861 improved design and construction permitted the use of a ·32-inch cartridge, and by 1876 the firm was offering a ·38-inch revolver, the so-called Baby Russian. Cartridge design had also improved, and many revolvers were, by the late 1860s, using centre-fire cartridges. Edward Boxer was granted an English patent in 1866 and in America Colonel Hiram Berdan patented amother with a different type of primer.

Smith and Wesson also designed an automatic ejection system. The barrel and cylinder assembly were hinged at the front of the butt and trigger frame and the two units were locked together by a spring catch. To eject the empty cases the catch was undone and the barrel pivoted downwards. This activated a central arm which moved backwards and lifted out the empty cases. It was first fitted on the Model No. 3 ·44-inch, made in 1870.

White's patent expired in 1869, when all other American gun-makers were then free to use the idea. There was a great deal of experimentation and revolvers with and without hammers, single-action, double-action, five-shot, six-shot and even up to twelve-shot weapons were manufactured. Various devices, some ingenious, some quite unrealistic, were produced to allow the revolver to maintain a steady rate of fire—by having second, third, fourth, or, in the case of the Treeby chain gun, a whole series of cylinders, which could be dropped into place as the first one was emptied.

Revolvers can be loosely divided into three main groups: those with swing-out cylinders; those which break open; and those with rod ejectors. The basic difference lies in the means of emptying and loading the cylinder. Swing-out weapons have solid frames and by the operation of a catch the cylinder is unlocked and swings to one side, usually to the left, giving direct access to the chambers. Empty cases are ejected by a hand-operated rod which is pushed backwards. When reloaded with fresh cartridges the cylinder clicks back into the frame. In the second group the revolver breaks and uses a Smith and Wesson ejector system. In the third group the cylinder remains in position in the frame and the cartridges are loaded through a gate giving access to the chambers. Cases are ejected by operating a spring-loaded rod which pushes out each case.

Opposite:
From top to bottom.
1. German service revolver M. 1880, 11-mm calibre. Overall length 13 inches (33 cm). Barrel 7 inches (17·8 cm).
2. German service revolver M. 1880. Short version, blued overall.
3. French revolver Model 1874, 11-mm calibre. Made at St Etienne. Overall length 9½ inches (24·1 cm).
4. Unusual German revolver using a rotary clip of cartridges which fitted inside the breech. Designed by Gustav Bittner of Austria and retailed from about 1893. Calibre 7·7 mm. Overall length 10½ inches (26·7 cm). Pattern Room, Royal Small Arms Factory, Enfield.

Three versions of the Colt single-action Army revolver.
Top. Designed primarily for target shooting, this form, known as the Bisley, was introduced in 1894.
Centre. Shorter-barrelled version with the hard rubber grip bearing the eagle. Introduced in 1882.
Bottom. Wooden grip of walnut, as on the earlier models.
Tower of London Armouries.

These competitors at Bisley, July 1910, are using a number of revolvers including Webley and Colt Army single-action. A range of 200 yards would be unusual today.

The Colt Company had long been interested in breech-loading weapons and they had, like most other manufacturers, made efforts to circumvent the Rollin White patent. Colt's most successful was the method patented in 1868 by F. Alexander Thuer, which involved a plate fitted to the cylinder and a forward-ejecting system. In 1871 a new system was introduced which replaced the flat nose of the hammer with a pointed firing pin. An ejector rod was fitted by the barrel and a bored-through cylinder replaced the old percussion one.

In 1872 research and development into a new centre-fire Colt revolver were well in hand, and in November of that year the new Colt was tested. The Colt single-action army revolver, probably the most famous revolver ever produced, was in production by 1873. The cylinder held six shots and essentially the action was the same as on the percussion revolver, with the cylinder turned and the hammer being cocked by the thumb. To load the weapon the hammer was set at the half-cock position, the loading gate on the right opened and the cartridges dropped in one at a time as the cylinder was turned by hand to line up the chambers.

When all the shots had been fired the hammer was again set at half-cock, the loading gate opened and a long, spring-loaded ejector rod fitted to the lower right side of the barrel was used to knock out each case in turn. To remove the cylinder on the earlier models it was necessary to undo a small screw situated at the front of the frame to release the cylinder pin, which could then be withdrawn, thus permitting the cylinder to be taken out. On later models the screw was replaced by a spring-operated locking device which passed through the front part of the frame.

The original Colt single-action was chambered for the ·45-inch cartridge and had a barrel 7½ inches long. It was an immediate success and was produced in a variety of calibres from ·22-inch rim-fire to ·476-inch Eley. Barrel lengths ranged from 2 inches up to as much as 16 inches on the so-called Buntline, which took its name from Ned Buntline, the famous writer of lurid Western adventure stories. The grips were originally of stained walnut, but in 1882 hard rubber grips bearing an eagle with widespread wings were introduced. In 1896 the eagle was dropped from the grips leaving them simply cross-hatched. This Colt was given several other names apart from its correct one, including 'The Frontier' and 'The Peacemaker'. Models were produced with stocks, long barrels, double-action trigger and so on, but so popular was the original weapon that it has remained virtually in continuous production since 1873.

The famous Mark VI ·455-inch (11·56-mm) Webley revolver used by the British army for many years as its standard handgun. Imperial War Museum, London.

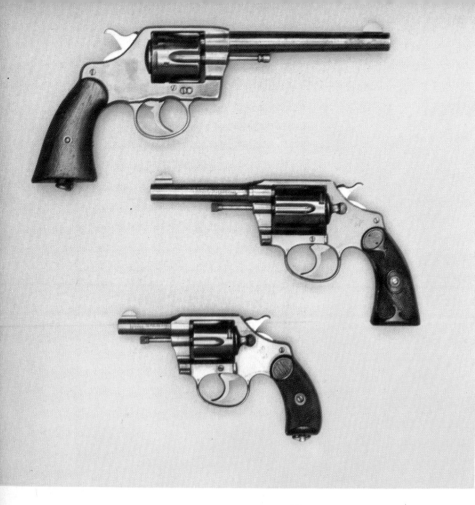

Colt revolvers with swing-out cylinders.
Top. Army Model of 1894. Calibre ·38 inches (9·6 mm).
Centre. Police Positive ·38-inch Special. Model of 1908.
Bottom. New Pocket ·32-inch (8·12-mm) Colt introduced in 1893. Pattern Room, Royal Small Arms Factory, Enfield.

The U.S. army adopted the Colt with a 7½-inch barrel, nickel-plated to give extra wear. It was by no means the only revolver in the West but it was certainly very popular and was carried and used by such people as Pancho Villa, the Mexican patriot, Judge Roy Bean, and even as recently as World War II, General Patton carried a pair into action with him.

Smith and Wesson's monopoly had not been effective in Europe and the gunmakers there had been able to manufacture breech-loading revolvers. In 1870 Austro-Hungarian forces were armed with the Gasser revolver, a large, double-action 11-mm six-shot weapon, with a side rod ejector.

British makers produced a range of dual-purpose revolvers which, by changing cylinders, could be used as cartridge or percussion weapons. Famous makers such as William Tranter produced good-quality rim-fire, and later centre-fire revolvers, as did Daw, Deane and Son, and Webley.

In 1868 the British army adopted a ·45-inch centre-fire Beaumont-Adams revolver which, like the Colt and the Gasser, had a rod ejector. In 1880 a hinged-frame, break-action revolver, designed by the Royal Small Arms Factory at Enfield, was adopted by the British army and remained in service, with modifications, until 1889. In 1890 the first of the Webley revolvers was adopted by the British army.

The firm of Webley had been founded in 1838 by Philip Webley. From 1890 onwards it was primarily responsible for supplying the British army with official-pattern revolvers. These had a short 4-inch barrel and fired the ·450/·476-inch cartridge. The six-shot Webley was to remain the official service revolver for many years. It was a good weapon with a lanyard ring, a top-break action and a general solidity which recommended it for rough use in the field. It was self-extracting, so that when the weapon was broken the empty cases were automatically ejected. Most of the early models,

Right:

Left. Luger carbine with shoulder stock and grip safety, first produced in 1903. The barrel is 11¾ inches (29·8 cm) long.

Centre. Artillery Model Luger pistol with 8-inch (20·3-cm) barrel, complete with its snail drum magazine and (right) leather holster carrying strap and stock. 9-mm calibre. Overall length (with stock) 26 inches (66 cm).

Below right. The Borchardt, the forerunner of the Luger, with (right) its stock and holster. 7·63-mm calibre. No. 75837. Overall length of pistol 14 inches (35·6 cm). Pattern Room, Royal Small Arms Factory, Enfield.

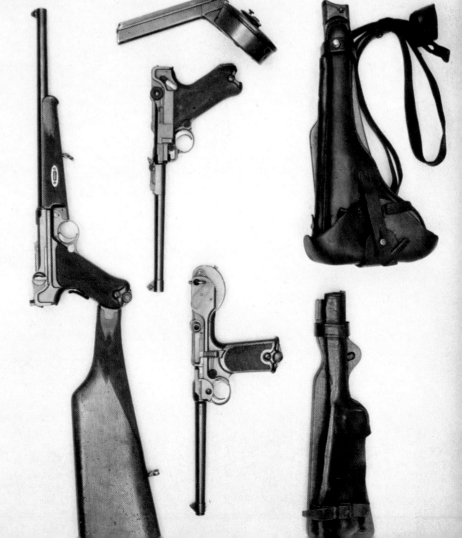

from 1887 to 1905, had 4-inch barrels. The Mark III and subsequent weapons had 6-inch barrels. From June 1915 any pistols of the early marks with the shorter barrels were automatically fitted with the longer ones when they were repaired. Mark VI was introduced in 1915, but in 1927 its title was altered to the Pistol No. 1, Mark VI, and it continued in service until 1947.

In 1926 it was decided to issue a lighter weapon (the Mark VI weighed 2 lb 6 oz). The new model was a ·38-inch calibre, and was designated Pistol No. 2, Mark I. It came into service in 1932 and was officially made obsolete in 1938. In June of that year the Mark I*, a self-cocking model, was issued to tank crews. It was felt that in the confined quarters of the tank it was easy to catch the hammer of an ordinary revolver and cause an accidental shot. A ·38-inch with a conventional double-action hammer was issued in 1943 and remained in service until 1963. It had a 5-inch barrel and it is still produced in quantity for the use of target shooters today.

Webley's produced a whole range of revolvers including the Royal Irish Constabulary revolver of 1867, with which General George Custer was armed when he died at the battle of Little Big Horn. Another Webley, the British Bulldog, figured in American history, for it was a copy of this weapon that Charles Guiteau used to assassinate President Garfield in July 1881.

The revolver had now virtually reached its peak of perfection, although there were to be improvements in design and in use of materials (stainless steel has become very popular over the last few years). There were experiments using different cartridges with varying sizes of bullet, charges and cases. In 1902 the famous ·38-inch special cartridge was introduced by Smith and Wesson, and it proved very satisfactory for most purposes. In 1935 the ·357-inch magnum was brought out. It was designed to produce very much higher muzzle velocity than the ·38-inch special.

The old controversy about single- and double-action shooting remains. Most revolvers today are made in the double-action form, although target shooters prefer single-action since it requires only a light touch on the trigger. However, for combat or practical shooting, when the pistol is being used as an offensive or defensive weapon rather than for sport, double-action is the preferred system.

One field which was explored but not exploited was that of automatic self-cocking revolvers. The idea was that it would make for more rapid fire, without requiring the heavy pressure needed for double-action shooting. The most popular system was that patented by George Fosbery, an officer who served with distinction in India throughout the Indian Mutiny and was awarded the Victoria Cross. He had a strong interest in firearms and held several patents, but the one for which he is best remembered is the Webley-Fosbery revolver. This was first patented in 1895 and the drawing which accompanied the specification for the patent suggests that he had in mind using something resembling the famous Colt single-action army revolver.

Peter Paul Mauser (1838–1914), whose automatic pistols became so famous. His firm has produced a wide range of first-class firearms.

Basically his system consisted of a split frame, one part housing both the cylinder and the hammer, which was free to slide back and forth on the second part of the frame, which consisted of the butt, the trigger and the lower section of the cylinder housing. As the first shot was fired the recoil drove the top section back and, by means of a lug which engaged with a series of zig-zags cut into the shape of the cylinder, rotated it and cocked the hammer before moving back into the firing position. Once it was back in this position pressure on the trigger released the hammer and the process could be repeated until all six shots had been discharged. A small device built into the mechanism prevented it from firing all six shots at once. The trigger had to be pressed for each single shot. The idea was taken up by the Webley and Scott Revolver and Arms Company, and the revolver was produced mostly in ·455-inch and ·38-inch calibres, with barrel lengths of 4 inches, 6 inches or, for target shooting, 7½ inches. A small eight-shot version was also produced.

These weapons do not appear to have come into use before 1900, and they were displayed at the famous shooting centre of Bisley, near London, in 1901. A variation was produced in 1902 and further changes were carried out in 1906. They were included in the list of this famous firm for many years and they saw service during the South African Wars and the First World War. The heavy throw of chamber and barrel could be disconcerting for the target shooter, but not in the hand of an expert such as the world famous Walter Winans. He fired twelve shots in ten seconds and obtained a grouping of some five to six inches in diameter.

One problem with all revolvers was that they took time to load. Cartridges had to be picked up one at a time and dropped into the chamber. Even if some quick-loading device, such as a half-moon clip, was used the time saved was not very great. Another slight disadvantage was their size and weight. Cylinders had to be big enough to hold five or six shots and they had to be circular. Consequently they were rather heavy and bulky, and in fact larger-calibre revolvers were difficult to tuck away anywhere except in a holster.

Rapid fire required the use of the double-action mechanism and this meant a heavy trigger pull which did not make for very accurate shooting. In the hands of an expert very rapid and accurate fire could certainly be achieved with a revolver. In the hands of the merely competent the effort required was considerable and either accuracy or the rate of fire suffered.

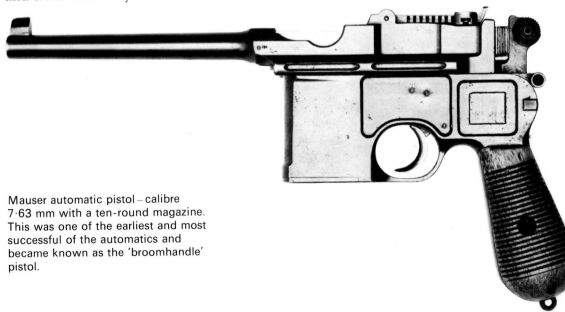

Mauser automatic pistol – calibre
7·63 mm with a ten-round magazine.
This was one of the earliest and most
successful of the automatics and
became known as the 'broomhandle'
pistol.

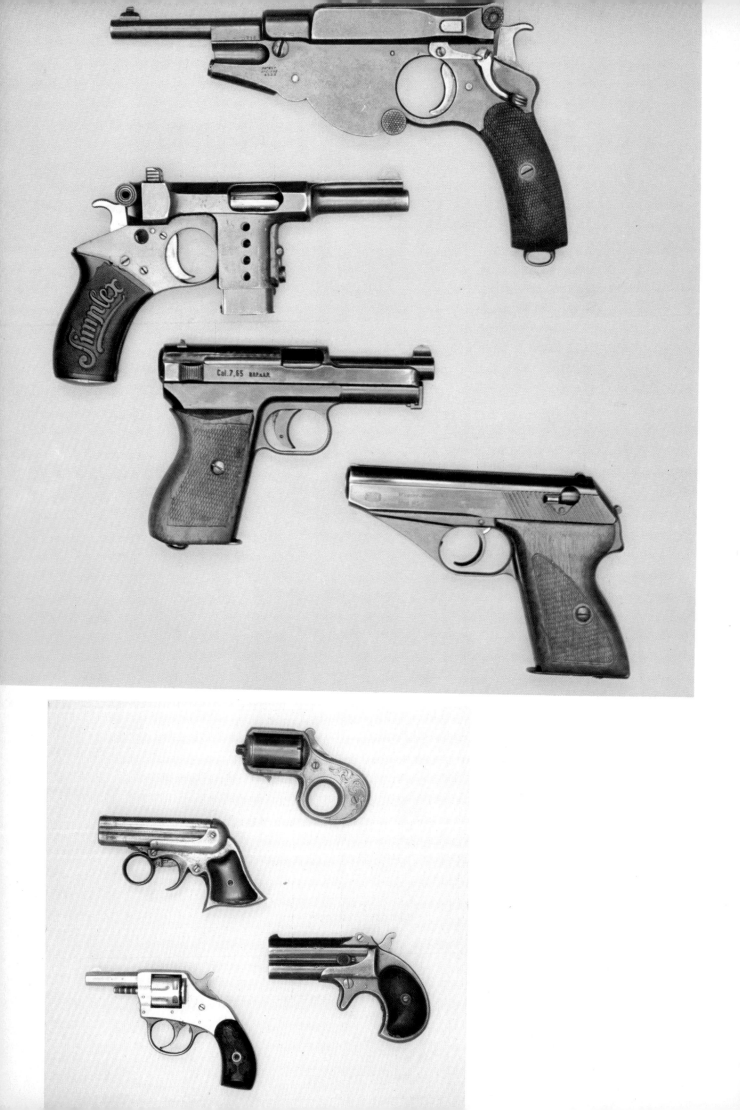

Recruits of the German army in the 1890s carrying their Mauser magazine rifles while being taught how to march.

Opposite, above:
Top. 6·5-mm Bergman automatic pistol with a magazine capacity of five rounds.
Above left. 8-mm Simplex Bergman, available with either six-or eight-round magazines.
Below left. 7·65-mm, 1934, Pocket Mauser Automatic as used for Austrian Naval issue pistol.
Below right. 7·65-mm Mauser H.Sc pistol with eight-round magazine. This weapon can be cocked and fired by pressing the trigger. Pattern Room, Royal Small Arms Factory, Enfield.

Opposite, below:
Top. A 'My Friend' brass knuckle-duster pistol. Only 4 inches (10·2 cm) long, it held seven shots and could be concealed in a clenched fist. No. 5167
Above left. Remington four-shot ·31-inch (7·87-mm) pocket pistol or derringer. Overall length 5 inches (12·7 cm).
Below right. Double-barrelled Remington ·41 inches (10·4 mm). Overall length 5 inches (12·7 cm). Barrel 3 inches (7·6 cm).
Below left. Harrington and Richardson ·22-inch (5·58-mm) 'Young America' revolver made in Worcester, Massachusetts. Overall length 5 inches (12·7 cm). Barrel 2 inches (5·1 cm). Pattern Room, Royal Small Arms Factory, Enfield.

Designers looked for ways in which these problems might be overcome. What was required was an alternative method of making ready the next cartridge. With the revolver the cylinder had to be turned in order to bring a fresh cartridge into position. However, with the lever or bolt action rifles the movement was basically a backward and forward one. Some mechanism or other moved and ejected the empty case, collected a new one from a magazine, and pushed it into the breech. With handguns this movement was extremely difficult to achieve. It had been done with the Volcanic but the weapon had not been well received.

Firearms designers now sought some method of achieving a backward and forward movement which did not require any physical effort on the part of the shooter. They wanted the action to be automatic and the search for the automatic pistol had begun. Most of the weapons so described are not really automatics. They should really be known as self-loading pistols. A truly automatic weapon is one that will continue firing as long as the trigger is pressed and ammunition is available.

Development of the self-loading pistol was virtually impossible before the advent of the metallic cartridge. Moving paper cartridges mechanically presented problems which the technology of the period was unable to solve. They tore easily; they deformed; they would not have fed into a breech easily and any system which might have been devised would have been very prone to breakdowns.

The introduction of the metallic cartridge simplified the whole problem. When a force is applied there is an action in one direction and a reaction in the opposite direction. When a bullet leaves the breech there is a backward kick equal in force in the opposite direction – the recoil. This is present in every firearm, although clever design can minimize or eliminate its effects. It is this backward reaction which is used to operate many types of automatic pistol.

An account of a meeting of the Royal Society in 1664 in London mentions that Prince Rupert had been shown such a weapon that, from the description, must have been an automatic. It is not known exactly what the weapon was and the idea did not become of practical value for many years.

219

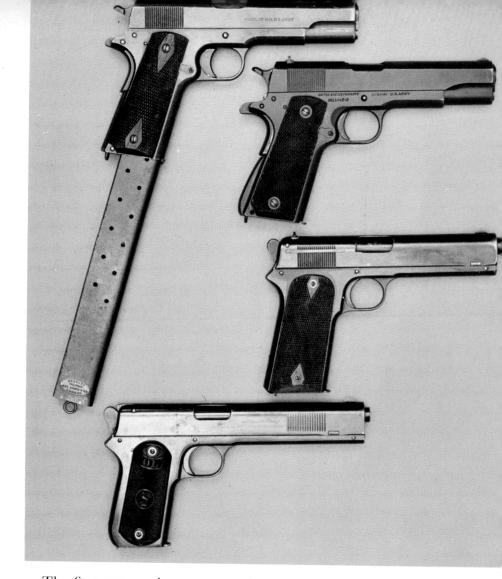

Colt automatic pistols.
Left. U.S. Army 1911 model
·45 inches (11·4 mm) fitted with
special, long 13-inch (33-cm)
magazine by Beesley, St. James's
St., London.
Above right. 1911 A1 ·45-inches
(11·4-mm), No. 1104792.
Below right. 1905 ·45-inch
(11·4-mm) model.
Bottom. 1897 ·38-inch (9·6-mm)
model. Pattern Room, Royal Small
Arms Factory, Enfield.

The first automatic appears to have been one designed by the Spanish firm of Orbea. This was a pistol which was operated, not by the recoil, but by means of gas pressure. This system of operation uses gases formed as a result of the explosion which pushes the bullet forward out of the barrel. A small amount of the gas is tapped off, generally through a little hole drilled at a point along the barrel, to a side chamber where the force is used to operate some form of mechanism which, in turn, activates the reloading and recocking mechanism. The Spanish example is said to have been produced in 1863. It was a revolver which in some ways resembles a Webley-Fosbery, for the gas rotated the cylinder.

The first really practical automatic pistol, and certainly the first to be available on a commercial scale, was that devised by an Austrian, Anton Schonberger, which was produced at Steyr in 1892. The weapon had a 5-inch barrel and fired an 8-mm bullet. It was loaded by means of a clip. The Schonberger was not only the first, but it was also one of the most unusual, since it operated on neither of the main principles, but by the quite small movement of the primer.

The primer was seated well down in the base of the cartridge and when the charge exploded the expanding gases passed back through the connecting tube. The gas pushed back the primer some three-sixteenths of an inch but, small though it was, the movement was sufficient to operate the mechanism.

In 1893 a naturalized American, Hugo Borchardt of Connecticut, patented a self-loading pistol, but being unable to find backing in the United States he returned to his native Germany.

220

Top. Finish Lahti 9 mm (VKT) with eight-round magazine.
Above left. Browning Hi Power 9 mm with a large-capacity thirteen-round magazine. M. 1935 No. E. 0000Z.
Below right. Steyr-Hahn 9 mm M. 1913 made in Austria. No. 17756.
Bottom. Mannlicher 7·65 mm M. 1903 No. 28. Six-round magazine. Pattern Room, Royal Small Arms Factory, Enfield.

The first models were made by the firm of Ludwig Lowe in Berlin. The Borchardt pistol had a rather unusual appearance, as the grip was set centrally and not, as is normal in a pistol, at the rear. This rather awkward design was made necessary by the mechanical loading system. A toggle arm was pushed back by the recoil and returned by a spring, and the only place in which Borchardt could accommodate the spring was behind the butt.

The overall length of the pistol was some 14 inches and it took a ·30-inch calibre bullet. The pistol was sold in a case which held a wooden shoulder stock, a leather holster and spare magazines. There was also a wooden box which looked like a magazine but in fact contained tools, a ramrod and oilcans. The shoulder stock, about 14 inches long, could be secured to the butt by a screw. With the stock the weapon was accurate, but if used without it its unusual shape made it rather awkward to shoot.

The Borchardt pistol was remarkable on two counts. It was the first automatic pistol to become available commercially and it was the first to use a box magazine. This was a metal box with a spring-loaded base-plate. The cartridges were inserted one at a time, usually through some slightly overlapping lip which prevented them from slipping out. Borchardt ammunition was also different, for it was rimless. Rifle and revolver cartridges had a rim which held them in the chamber of the weapon. The rim was also used by the extractor mechanism which, by some means or other, slipped round the rim to pull the cartridge backwards. In a box magazine the rounds had to be able to slip out easily and a rim would have made this very difficult. The rim was removed and a

221

Common type of Luger '08 pattern with short barrel. The milled circular projections were used when gripping the toggle arm. Tower of London Armouries.

deep groove was cut near the base so that the extractor could still grip the case. The Borchardt magazine had a series of holes drilled in the side which lightened it, but this was not their main purpose. The holes enabled the owner to see at a glance whether there were any cartridges in the magazine and if so how many. The magazine held eight rounds.

A year later, in 1894, the firm of Mannlicher entered the market with a pistol which was one of the very few to use rimmed cartridges. The Mannlicher was also different in other respects. The breech stayed still and the barrel moved forward to extract, eject and re-cock. To load the weapon the barrel had to be pushed forward and locked, a clip engaged with a guide and the cartridges pushed down. The problem of the rim was overcome by the way that the cartridges took up their position. They were at an angle, so that the rim of the top one was positioned in front of the one beneath and so on all the way down the magazine.

Another pistol which appeared about the same time was the Bergman, in which the cartridge case was blown clear of the weapon by the gases. It also had a rather unusual method of loading the magazine, which was situated in front of the trigger. The side plate was opened by swinging it clear and a clip of cartridges was inserted into the magazine. The plate was closed and this action locked the bottom cartridge in place. A ring at the base of the clip was then pulled and this removed the clip but left the cartridges in position. The Bergman was comparatively small and fired a 6·5-mm cartridge. In 1897 one of the smallest automatic pistols was produced, the Charola-Anitu. It fired a 5-mm cartridge and it was made in Spain, although proved in Belgium.

All these early automatic pistols were subject to malfunctions, but they were the forerunners of one of the most successful and striking weapons ever to be produced, the famous Mauser. Peter Paul Mauser was born in Württemberg in 1838 where his father and brothers worked at the Royal Arms Factory. He showed himself to be an intelligent and inventive gunmaker. In 1871 Prussia adopted the Mauser-designed single-shot, bolt-action rifle with an 11-mm cartridge.

The success of their firearms brought the Mauser family full circle. After a fire at their own factory they bought the Royal Arms Factory in which they had once worked as employees. In 1880 Mauser produced a tubular magazine for the rifle and it was adopted by many countries including Prussia, Belgium, Spain and

Snail drum fitted to a Luger Parabellum pistol. The pistol is an Artillery model with an 8-inch (20·3-cm) long barrel and is also fitted with a shoulder stock. Pattern Room, Royal Small Arms Factory, Enfield.

Above:
Mauser automatic pistol No. 294902,
together with its wooden holster/
shoulder stock. The leather carrying
harness is dated 1915.

Right:
The common versions of the Luger
'08 pistol.
Top. The Artillery Model with a
7½-inch (19-cm) barrel.
Centre. The Naval Model with a
5½-inch (14-cm) barrel.
Bottom. The standard 4-inch (10-cm)
barrel model. Imperial War Museum,
London.

Germany. In Germany it became the famous Model 1898, essentially the same weapon which saw service throughout both World Wars.

However, it was not so much for the rifle as for the automatic pistol that the firm of Mauser is best remembered. Patents for it were filed in 1896, but it did not appear on the market until 1898. It fired a 7·63-mm cartridge, although it was later adapted for other calibres. It has been argued that Paul Mauser was not the true originator of the system, but that it was conceived and developed by the superintendent of his factory, a man called Feederlee, in 1893–4. By March 1895, with or without the assistance of Feederlee, Mauser had a prototype of his famous 'broomhandle' automatic, and in January 1896 Mauser decided to go into commercial production.

The automatic was a heavy weapon, which was one of the reasons why it was not adopted by more military forces. Most of these weapons were chambered for the 7·63-mm cartridge, but during World War I all commercial production was stopped and Mauser was given a contract to produce 9-mm versions, the standard calibre used by all German pistols. Since externally there is no difference the 9-mm Mausers were branded on the wooden grips with a large figure '9', which was filled in with red paint.

Following Germany's defeat in World War I restrictions were placed on arms production and no Mauser pistols were made for some two years. However the country was subsequently given permission to manufacture weapons to arm its police and in 1920 Mauser went into production once again. The Treaty of Versailles forbad the manufacture of 9-mm weapons and pistols with more than 4-inch barrels. A new Mauser pistol was produced with a barrel of only 3·88 inches. The entire output was intended for the Russian market and consequently this particular model is usually referred to as the 'Bolo' (short for Bolshevik). In 1922 the name of the firm was changed from Waffenfabrik Mauser to Mauser-Verkehr.

In 1932 the *schnellfeuer* or rapid-fire model was produced. This was so constructed that once the trigger was pressed the pistol continued firing until its ammunition was exhausted. A selector was fitted to the left-hand side with two markings 'N' and 'R'. 'N' was for 'normal' and, with the selector in this position, the pistol was single-shot. When set for 'R' ('repetition'), once the trigger was pressed the weapon would continue firing. The floor of the normal fixed magazine in front of the trigger was removed and a long box magazine holding ten or twenty rounds could be simply pushed into position. With the selector set at 'R' the rate of fire was some 850 rounds a minute. For a hand-held weapon this was far too high to be effectively controlled. The shooting, although spectacular, was hardly accurate. Production of this famous Mauser automatic pistol finally ceased in 1939.

The rather unusual shape of the Mauser made it difficult to fit into a conventional leather holster. It was normally supplied in a wooden holster shaped so that the pistol sat in it with just the tip of the butt protruding. The holster served a double purpose. At its tip was a metal catch which engaged with a slot cut into the back strap of the pistol butt. When clipped into position it converted the weapon into a carbine. The wooden holster had to be carried in some way, and it was often suspended with a strap arrangement which also held a spare magazine and a cleaning rod. Some leather holsters were produced but very few seem to have survived. A number of Mauser-type automatics under the name Astra were produced in Spain by Unceta and Company.

Above:
Browning Baby standard (6·35-mm) automatic pistol, designed as a short-range personal protection weapon.

Above right:
Webley and Scott ·32-inch (8-mm) automatic pistol which was adopted by the London Metropolitan police in 1911 as their official firearm.

John M. Browning (1855–1926), a prolific inventor of firearms. He is holding one of his automatic shotguns.

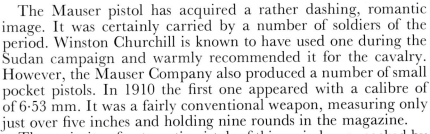

The Mauser pistol has acquired a rather dashing, romantic image. It was certainly carried by a number of soldiers of the period. Winston Churchill is known to have used one during the Sudan campaign and warmly recommended it for the cavalry. However, the Mauser Company also produced a number of small pocket pistols. In 1910 the first one appeared with a calibre of of 6·53 mm. It was a fairly conventional weapon, measuring only just over five inches and holding nine rounds in the magazine.

The majority of automatic pistols of this period were cocked by pulling back the movable top section, usually known as the slide, which was then allowed to fly forward to feed the first round from the magazine into the breech. In 1938 Mauser produced a double-action pistol in which pressure on the trigger automatically fed in the first round, cocked the action and fired the pistol. It was known as the Mauser HSc from the initials of the German words meaning 'hammer, self-cocking'.

One other automatic which is as well known as the Mauser is that commonly called the Luger. It was a development of the awkwardly shaped Borchardt. George Luger was an engineer acting as a salesman and one of his jobs was to demonstrate the Borchardt pistol made by his firm. With his practical experience and his interest in firearms, he realized only too well that the Borchardt had severe limitations. The toggle mechanism it used was rather like the human arm which, when held out straight, is very rigid indeed, but can be easily bent at the elbow.

The big problem was to find a home for the return spring which pushed the toggle back, and the rather peculiar shape of the Borchardt was due to the housing for this spring. Luger, with the assistance of Borchardt, claimed a new patent in March 1900. The basic system was the same but the return spring was now fitted inside the butt, so eliminating the rear projection which had been one of the features of the Borchardt. In order to make the pistol easier to aim Luger redesigned the butt. It now sloped back at an angle of some forty-five degrees, so that when the arm was raised the pistol came almost automatically into the aiming position.

In 1898 the Swiss were carrying out a series of pistol trials at Berne and the Borchardt/Luger with an eight-shot magazine was entered. It came out extraordinarily well, and in April 1901 the Luger was officially adopted by the Swiss government. The first

Left:
Japanese automatic pistols.
From top to bottom.
1. Model 14 1925 Nambu 8 mm
with wooden butt. Overall length
9 inches (22·9 cm). Barrel 4·7 inches
(11·9 cm).
2. Model 1904 Nambu 8 mm No.
6615, known as Papa Nambu.
Overall length 9 inches (22·9 cm).
3. Finely finished 7-mm Baby
Nambu. A scaled-down version of
the Model 1904. Overall length
6¾ inches (17·1 cm).
4. Type 94 Model 34 (1934); 8 mm.
Overall length 7⅕ inches (18·3 cm).
Pattern Room, Royal Small Arms
Factory, Enfield.

Opposite, above:
Mauser automatic pistols with the
wooden holster/shoulder stock.
Above. Schnellfeuer model, with
selector for single shot or automatic
fire, patented in 1931. A box
magazine was loaded in from the
base.
Below. Conventional model, 1898,
with 4¾-inch (12-cm) barrel.
Overall length 24 inches (61 cm).
Pattern Room, Royal Small Arms
Factory, Enfield.

Right:
From top to bottom.
1. Walther P38 9-mm pistol with
wartime finish. Adopted as a German
army weapon in 1938. Overall length
8½ inches (21·5 cm).
2. Italian Beretta Model 51 pistol;
9 mm. Overall length 8 inches
(20·3 cm).
3. Italian Beretta Model 34 pistol;
7·65 mm. An early model used by the
Italian Airforce. Overall length
6 inches (15·2 cm).
4. German Heckler and Koch P9s
9-mm pistol. Double-action, it uses
modern plastics in its construction.
Overall length 7½ inches (19 cm).
Pattern Room, Royal Small Arms
Factory, Enfield.

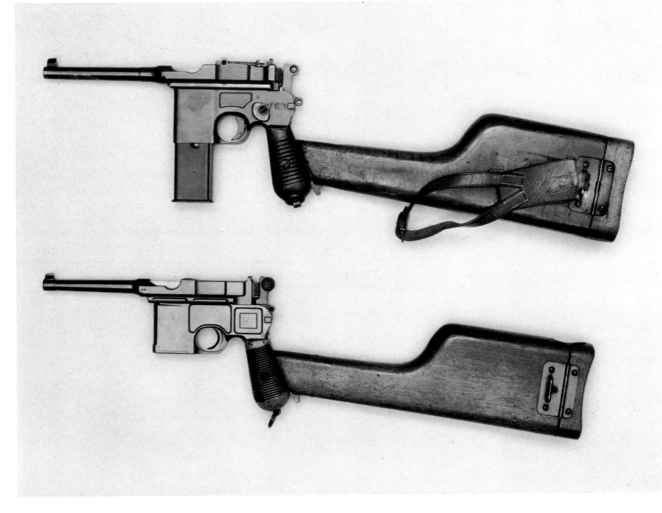

of the real Luger pistols was patented in Germany in March 1900 (as mentioned above) and in the United States in March 1904. Luger drew up an extremely detailed patent, so that every single aspect of his design, now officially called the Pistole Parabellum, was covered. The early model Parabellum retained the characteristic shape, but the distinguishing feature of this model was a butt safety catch. Only when the butt was firmly gripped and the safety catch, situated on the back strap, was pressed home would the weapon fire. It was produced as a commercial weapon with a 4¾-inch barrel, firing a 7·65-mm cartridge. Those pistols for the Swiss forces were engraved with the Swiss cross in a sunburst on the top of the breech.

In 1899 the United States appointed a committee to report on any inventions or devices that might be placed before it and in 1901 the Luger pistol was considered. It was tested thoroughly and although there were a number of minor mishaps, the weapon performed extremely well. The committee recommended that a number should be purchased for trials by troops in the field. Those 1900 Parabellums purchased were engraved with the American Eagle crest on the breech. The U.S. models were used in the field until 1905, when they were withdrawn and placed in store.

In 1902 alterations were made in the design of the Parabellum and the standard length of the barrel was reduced from 4¾ inches to 4 inches, but of much greater importance was the change to the 9-mm Luger cartridge. In 1904 a new model with a 6-inch barrel was officially adopted by the German navy. At the lower end of the butt strap was a lug which accepted a stock to convert the weapon into a carbine.

Above:
The long-barrelled Artillery Luger pistol with adjustable rear sight, introduced in 1917. The loaded magazine was inserted into the base of the butt as shown. Imperial War Museum, London.

In 1906 a new model was produced for tests by the U.S. army, but it was chambered for a ·45-inch calibre bullet. Only a small number were produced and this is now an extremely rare model.

The Parabellums were mostly made in Germany, although some 10,000 or so were produced in 1915–17 by Vickers Ltd of England for a military contract sale to the Netherlands. In 1908 the Luger was adopted by Germany and was to remain the official military sidearm for the next thirty years. In 1908 the grip safety was dropped and in 1914 a new model was manufactured with an 8-inch barrel and an adjustable rear sight. This weapon was issued to the German artillery.

After World War I the length of the barrel was limited to 4 inches, but in 1920 a commercial model was supplied that was not intended for official army use. This had barrels ranging from 10 inches up to 24 inches, available in either 7·65 mm or 9 mm. A new carbine was also introduced in the same year. Some models of this period readopted the grip safety. A circular magazine holding thirty-two rounds, known as a snail drum, was produced. The cartridges had to be loaded with a special device and the magazine wound up at the same time. The magazine could be carried in a special holster. The standard Parabellum holster was quite remarkable, but those for the navy and artillery models had to be extra long to accommodate the barrels. For the longer barrels the wooden stock, in the form of a flat board, was secured to the back of the holster so that it was always to hand. A few Luger holsters were made in a similar style to those for the Mauser, as a hollow wooden box.

Inside the flap of many of the normal Luger leather holsters there is a small pocket which holds a multipurpose tool. It has a screwdriver blade at one end and a small hole in the centre with a right-angled bend at the bottom. This is used to slip over the button which operates the slide in the magazine for ease of handling. Pressing on the button can be rather hard on the finger, particularly when the magazine is nearly full and the spring is exerting maximum pressure.

The automatic pistol began to develop in the last decade of the nineteenth century and it is reasonable to say that it was essentially a European concept, with Germany and Austria predominating. In England it was the firm of Webley that led the way, although Gabbet Fairfax did design one weapon, the Mars. It was produced in ·45-inch and ·38-inch calibres. It was large and clumsy but very powerful, producing the muzzle energy almost equal to that of a sporting rifle. Webley and Scott produced an automatic in a ·455-inch which was adopted by the Royal Navy in 1914. Some were also issued to the Royal Horse Artillery for trial and to the Royal Flying Corps, but they were not generally accepted by the British army.

In America there had been less interest in the automatic pistol but John N. Browning, one of three brothers, gave the world of firearms another of the best known automatics—the Colt ·45. The brothers John, Jonathan and Matthew were all very good gunsmiths, possessing both initiative and ingenuity, and had already made a great contribution in design to the Winchester Company. John Browning became interested in automatic weapons about 1889 and by 1897 he had patented a ·32-inch automatic pistol which was made at Liège in Belgium.

Colt acquired this first patent although the firm never produced any weapons from this model. In 1900 the Browning/Colt automatic pistol was submitted to the U.S. Board of Ordnance for tests. It competed with the Mauser and the Mannlicher, and the

Browning Hi Power 9-mm pistol with the large box magazine holding thirteen cartridges. This is the standard side-arm of the British army and of many other forces. Crown Copyright.

A page from the armourer's official handbook of the Indian army (1916) showing details of the Webley centre-fire revolver, the standard service revolver.

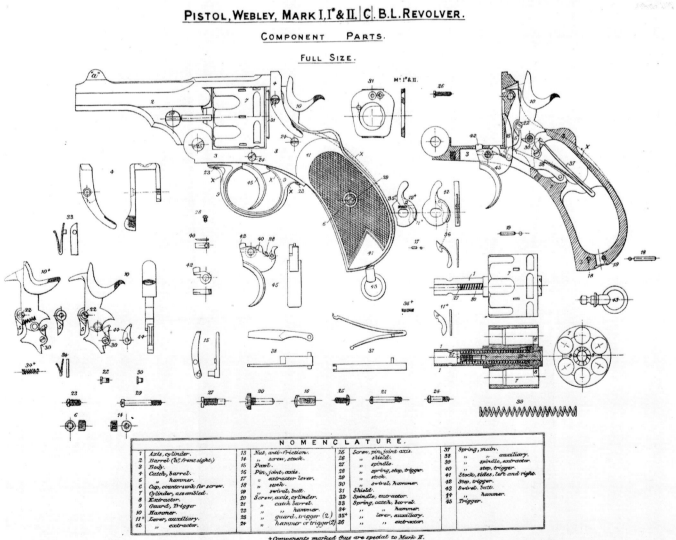

PISTOL, WEBLEY, MARK I, I* & II. C.B.L. REVOLVER.

COMPONENT PARTS.

FULL SIZE.

NOMENCLATURE.

1	Axis, cylinder.	13	Nut, anti-friction.	26	Screw, pin, joint axis.	37	Spring, main.
2	Barrel (w. front sight.)	14	„ screw, stock.	26	„ shield.	38	„ auxiliary.
3	Body.	15	Pawl.	27	„ spindle.	39	„ spindle, extractor.
4	Catch, barrel.	16	Pin, joint, axis.	28	„ spring, stop, trigger.	40	Stock, sides, left and right.
5	„ hammer.	17	„ extractor lever.	29	„ stock.	41	Stop, trigger.
6	Cap, countersunk for screw.	18	„ stock.	30	„ swivel, hammer.	42	„ trigger.
7	Cylinder, assembled.	19	„ swivel, butt.	31	Shield.	43	Swivel, butt.
8	Extractor.	20	Screw, axis, cylinder.	32	Spindle, extractor.	44	„ hammer.
9	Guard, Trigger.	21	„ catch barrel.	33	Spring, catch, barrel.	45	Trigger.
10	Hammer.	22	„ hammer.	34	„ hammer.		
11*	Lever, auxiliary.	23	„ guard, trigger (2)	35*	„ lever, auxiliary.		
12	„ extractor.	24	„ hammer or trigger(2)	36	„ extractor.		

+Components marked thus are special to Mark II.
x Dotted lines....·.------·.. show form of Mark II.

Assault Rifles.
Above. Modern Swiss SIG 7·62-mm self-loading rifle with folding bipod. One of the latest models. Overall length 24¾ inches (63 cm).
Below. World War II German assault rifle MKb 42(H). In service from 1942, this was one of the first of the so-called assault rifles. Calibre 9 mm. Barrel 27½ inches (70 cm). Pattern Room, Royal Small Arms Factory, Enfield.

tests ended with an extremely favourable report on the Colt. It was said to be easy to operate and not prone to malfunction. It had a high rate of fire, was easy to load and, strangely enough, was claimed to be more accurate than the revolver.

Despite this glowing testimonial it was decided that the U.S. armed forces would not necessarily adopt the weapon and that further field trials should be carried out. The great uncertainty was whether the calibre ·38-inch was large enough for military use. The weapon had a magazine capacity of seven rounds, a 6-inch barrel and weighed 2 lbs 4 oz. A number were ordered for testing and some modifications were carried out, a new model ·38-inch being brought out in 1902. In 1903 a smaller pocket version of the military model was produced for commercial sales. Work had begun as early as 1894 on a larger ·45-inch automatic pistol with a much stronger mechanism and a bigger, sturdier frame to cope with the larger cartridge. Some of these models were cut for a shoulder stock, which was secured to the back strap of the butt in much the same way as in the Lugers and Mausers.

In 1907 American gunmakers were again invited to submit their wares for tests by the Chief of Ordnance, with the one stipulation that they had to be ·45-inch calibre. By October 1906 eighteen firms had agreed to submit samples of their weapons, but only eight finally presented their models at Springfield Armoury for the tests. The committee which examined the weapons came out wholeheartedly in favour of adopting an automatic pistol as a standard sidearm of the U.S. forces. It recommended that either the one produced by the Savage Arms Company of New York or else the Colt should be selected. The committee also asked for certain minor modifications to be made.

The outcome was an order for the 1907 Colt ·45 automatic with a grip safety. They were issued to three cavalry units and some were handed out to other units for tests. The results of field service testing were not good. The weapon jammed, it broke and it was not well received. In fact, one report stated categorically that it was 'totally unfit for use by troops'. On some the mechanism was defective and soldiers had the unpleasant experience of pressing the trigger for one shot and having the whole magazine blazing away, without being able to stop it.

Colt devoted some two years more of research and experiment to their ·45 automatic and by September of 1910 the company was convinced that the new weapon would be superior in every respect to the 1907 model. In March 1911 the tests began, its competitor being another Savage automatic. Both were stripped and examined, accuracy was checked and for endurance 6,000 rounds were fired in groups of 100. The Savage had 31 malfunctions of various kinds. The Colt continued to function perfectly throughout. As a result the Colt automatic pistol was recommended for adoption by the U.S. army. It weighed 2 lb 7 oz, had a barrel length of just over 5 inches, and a magazine capacity of seven rounds. It now became known as the Model 1911.

In 1914 a number of Colts were produced with the ·455-inch calibre suitable for British service ammunition, and 1,500 of these were sent to the British Admiralty. The majority of those ordered by Britain throughout World War I seem to have been primarily for the army and the Royal Marines. They were, in fact, withdrawn from these two bodies in the 1920s. In 1923 they were designated as the official service weapon for the R.A.F. and a number are so marked. The pistol saw service throughout World War I, proving itself to be an exceptionally reliable weapon. In 1920 the U.S. Cavalry asked the Chief of Ordnance for some modifications to be made and, as a result, the width of the trigger was reduced, the comb (the curving part at the back of the butt near the top) was extended to give greater protection to the hand, and the lower section at the rear of the butt was curved and arched slightly to give a more comfortable and firmer grip. Some other changes were made as well and the new model was designated the 1911 A1. Over the years it was produced in varying forms and was even used during the war in Korea in the early 1950s. It has proved to be one of the best combat weapons–rugged, reliable and a good shooter.

In addition to the big ·45-inch Colt produced smaller pocket pistols, mostly of ·32-inch calibre. In 1908 a very tiny one firing a ·25-inch bullet was introduced, with only a 2-inch barrel and a six-shot magazine. Versions of the government military model were also produced for competition shooting. In addition to the large-calibre defence weapons a number of target pistols using ·22-inch bullets have also been produced by Colt, beginning with the Woodsman type, which was first so named in 1927 although the series began in 1915.

During World War II a cheap, mass-produced, near copy of the Colt ·45 automatic was manufactured as a single-shot pistol. Known as the Liberator, it was supplied in bulk to the resistance forces in Europe.

Automatics are used for both target-shooting and combat, but controversy about whether they are better than revolvers continues. The movement of the slide does not help accurate shooting and the mechanism can jam, making the pistol useless. A misfire will stop it functioning and unless the weapon is double-action it requires the use of the other hand to re-cock it. Automatics are favoured when concealment is important, because generally they can be carried inconspicuously. However some guards prefer to put up with a slightly more bulky revolver rather than risk a jamming. (When Princess Anne was attacked in 1975 her police bodyguard found that his Walther PPK failed to function.) For fast shooting the automatic probably has a slight advantage and reloading is generally faster than with revolvers. There is, however, no final answer and for most shooters it is a matter of preference.

Maxim and the machine-gun

Most authorities would probably accept that there are at least three distinct evolutionary patterns to be seen in the history of firearms. The first is a gradual decrease in bullet size. Matchlock musket balls were around ·75 inches in diameter, but by the eighteenth century the Brown Bess was using a ball about ·6 inches. The decrease in size speeded up during the nineteenth century and the 1853 Enfield rifles fired a bullet of ·577 inches. Then came the Martini-Henry with a calibre of ·45 inches, and Lee-Enfield bullets were ·303 inches. The latest British weapon is a minute 4·85 mm.

The second trend has been towards an increase in muzzle velocity–the speed at which the bullet leaves the barrel. This has been achieved by a combination of several developments. The design of bullets has improved, their size has been reduced, and propellants have been made more powerful.

The third and most obvious change has been in the rate of fire. Matchlock muskets could probably manage two or three shots a minute. Brown Bess raised the rate to five or six a minute. In competitions the Martini-Henry achieved an average of around sixteen shots a minute, and the Lee-Enfield was noted for its rapid fire. Similar figures could be quoted for most armies at that period. However, the search to achieve a greater volume of fire continued.

By the 1870s very few soldiers and sportsmen did not have access to breech-loading repeating weapons with magazines and metal cartridges. Even with repeating rifles the volume of fire–the number of shots a minute–was obviously limited by the number of men available. Military planners were constantly on the look-out for means of increasing unit firepower. If their troops had a weapon with a potential firepower of ten rounds a minute per man, they would be happy to exchange it for a weapon with a firepower of fifty rounds a minute. Obviously with the new weapon the number of troops could be reduced or the same number made more effective.

The search for maximum firepower can be traced back to the very beginning of firearms. Mention has already been made of multi-barrel weapons, and there were also the *ribaudquin*, which were really no more than a collection of barrels fastened to a frame and fired, either simultaneously or consecutively. They worked but were haphazard and, with most of them, once the sequence of firing started it was impossible to halt it. Designers sought to produce weapons which could provide many shots and could be stopped or started at will.

One of the earliest was the Puckle gun, a form of flintlock revolver patented in 1714 by William Puckle of London. It consisted of a series of chambers, each loaded with powder and ball. These were rotated by a large handle which brought each chamber in line with the barrel, so that it could be discharged. Puckle apparently insisted that the normal ammunition was acceptable for Christians, but for Turks he preferred a square bullet!

The first practical, controllable repeating weapon was the Gatling gun produced in America in the 1860s. It was the invention of Dr Richard Gatling who patented his idea in 1862. It was not dissimilar to the Puckle gun, in that it was operated by turning a handle. It was demonstrated and indeed used during the American Civil War, but the original design suffered from the handicap of poor ammunition. With the metal-cased cartridge the system worked much better. The weapon consisted of a number of barrels which were rotated, activating a series of cams. As each chamber lined up with the barrel its firing pin struck the cartridge and discharged the weapon. Each barrel continued to revolve, and the case was extracted and finally ejected. The cartridges were gravity-fed from a magazine fitted above the breech of the weapon.

In 1869 a technical committee of the British army considered the idea of adopting some form of repeating weapon. Two years later it proposed that a number of Gatling guns should be purchased for trials by both army and navy. The navy took a ·65-inch cartridge weapon, but the army preferred the slightly lighter version using a ·45-inch cartridge – the same as the Martini-Henry ammunition. Gatling guns were also acquired by China, Egypt, Japan, Morocco, Tunis, Turkey and Russia. The Russians made great use of these weapons during some of their campaigns in Central Asia in 1864–76 and they proved terribly effective against the tribal cavalry of the Turkomans.

Picture postcard showing the early wheeled mounting for the Maxim machine-gun as used by the British army at the end of the nineteenth century.

Sir Hiram Maxim seated behind an early model of his heavy machine-gun, fitted with a shield for the gunner.

In British service the Gatling saw action in Egypt and the Sudan, but it was not wholly successful, one of the biggest problems being the extraction of the spent cases which tended to deform, break or jam. Although its theoretical rate of fire was in the region of 600 shots a minute, it was found in practice that the average was only about 280.

During the 1860s and 1870s a number of other weapons besides the Gatling used the multi-barrel system–some more effectively than others. One which proved disastrous was the French mitrailleuse. It has been invented by a Belgian officer, a Captain Fafschamps, about 1850, helped by a man called Montigny. Some were produced in 1851 but it was not until 1869 that Napoleon III was persuaded to adopt it for the French army. In the best tradition of spy stories it was a secret weapon put together at the arsenal of Meudon in 1869–70. When in 1870 French manoeuvres took place, the weapon was sent under wraps to the troops and kept under constant guard to prevent any unauthorized person from seeing it. Vastly exaggerated reports were circulated about its efficiency.

The mitrailleuse consisted of a group of barrels inside a wrought-iron tube, giving it very much the appearance of an ordinary field gun. A plate of cartridges was inserted, the gunner depressed a lever and each cartridge was fed into its barrel. The thirty-seven barrels could be fired separately or, by turning the handle quickly, a volley could be loosed off. When the gun was empty the lever was lifted and a fresh plate of cartridges inserted. It was possible to load and fire the mitrailleuse twelve times a minute, the equivalent of about 450 rifle shots. A wagon which accompanied each gun carried some 6,000 cartridges, and the French were confident that this weapon would permit them to win the war against Prussia which Napoleon, if not actively planning, was at least preparing for. It first saw action in August 1870 at the battle of Saarburck, but only on a small scale. The first big battle was at Wissembург later the same month. The mitrailleuses were positioned and used as if they were artillery, and the Prussian artillery disposed of them with only a few shells.

A contemporary of the Gatling was the Billinghurst Requa battery gun, which had twenty-five barrels mounted side by side on a flat metal platform, and was operated by means of two levers. It was not a true machine-gun, for the cartridges were in

234

German version of the Mexican-designed Mondragon automatic rifle, patented in 1907. It is fitted with a thirty-round magazine. Pattern Room, Royal Small Arms Factory, Enfield.

special clips. When they were dropped into position all twenty-five barrels were fired by a single percussion cap. Another repeater used by the Union forces in the American Civil War was the Ager. The metal hopper through which the cartridges were fed gave it the name of the 'Coffee-mill gun'. It used a revolver system with a single barrel, operated by a crank, and it fired ·58-inch bullets, which were loaded in steel containers. It could fire up to 120 shots a minute, but its big problem was the overheating of the barrel.

The Confederates used an enormous device known as the Vandenberg volley gun, which was actually made in England although it was invented by an American, General O. Vandenberg. It was rather like the mitrailleuse and it fired a ·45-inch calibre cartridge. It could be fitted with any number of barrels, from 85 to an incredible 451. The breech was removable and it was in fact no more than an extension of the old volley gun, for one cap set off a whole group of barrels.

The Gardner machine-gun was invented in 1874 by a William Gardner of Toledo, Ohio, who sold the American patent rights to the gunmaking firm of Pratt and Whitney, at Hartford, Connecticut. It consisted of two breech-loading barrels placed parallel to each other and $1\frac{1}{4}$ inches apart. One man loaded the ammunition into the feed guide while another turned the crank. Tests were carried out by the U.S. navy in 1875 and the gun was highly commended.

The Nordenfelt gun was the invention of Heldge Palmcrantz, a Swedish engineer, who was unable to develop it by himself. He obtained the financial support of Thorsten Nordenfelt of London. It was not unlike the Gardner, with a group of parallel barrels fed by gravity and worked by a lever mechanism.

The British government's Machine-Gun Committee of 1880 drew up a set of requirements considered essential before they would consider the adoption of any particular repeating weapon. They stipulated that it should have a rate of fire of 400 rounds a minute and be able to fire 1,000 rounds rapidly without unduly heating the barrel. They wanted the breech to remain closed for at least one-third of a second to obviate the danger of the cartridge exploding when not fully in the breech. The weapon might have any number of barrels from one to twelve. Nordenfelt submitted his gun, since it was capable of meeting all the requirements of the committee. In July 1882 a ten-barrel Nordenfelt model fired 3,000 rounds of ammunition in three minutes three seconds without a single failure. The weapon was produced in a range of calibres from rifle right up to those firing $1\frac{1}{2}$-inch shells.

A well-used Vickers machine-gun mounted as an anti-aircraft weapon in the North African desert during World War II. The canvas belt carrying the cartridges can clearly be seen.

One of Nordenfelt's more promising projects was a single-barrel, lever-operated machine-gun. It had quite a simple mechanism which could be easily removed. The gun weighed 13 lb, only 4 lb more than the service rifle. It could be fired at a rate of about 180 shots a minute and was, in effect, a forerunner of the later assault rifles or submachine-guns. Although Nordenfelt's machine-gun had its limitations he also produced an armour-piercing bullet, a line of development which was subsequently abandoned and did not come back into use for at least another forty years. His bullet was a hardened steel centre sharpened to a point, and could develop a speed of well over 2,000 feet a second and penetrate two inches of solid iron plate at a range of 300 yards.

The great limitation of all these early machine-guns was that they were hand-operated. If for any reason the soldier was unable to move the lever or turn the handle, the weapon was useless. Most needed two hands to operate them and obviously the rate of fire was limited by the speed at which the weapon could be manually activated. The turning point in machine-gun design came at the end of the century and was due to a very remarkable man, Hiram Stevens Maxim.

The Maxim family were originally of French stock and emigrated first to England and then to Massachusetts. The family later settled on a farm in Maine and there Hiram was born in February 1840. His education was sketchy, but his curiosity and mechanical ability were, even at an early age, remarkable. He was apprenticed to a carriage-maker, but eventually set up on his own with a gristmill. It was there that he produced his first invention which was, of all things, an automatic mousetrap. Most mousetraps of the period operated once and were useless until reset. Maxim devised a clockwork mechanism which reset the mousetrap again and again. He did not patent it, probably he had never heard of the process, and was later to see his design copied by somebody else and selling on a large scale. When the Civil War broke out in 1861 Maxim was working as a wood turner. For a variety of reasons he took no direct part in the war and lived for a while in Canada. While there he produced his second invention, a blackboard paint, for which again he received not a penny in payment or royalties.

After wandering around the country he took a job with his uncle in an engineering shop and gained valuable experience with materials and in technical drawing, in which he soon excelled, although he had no formal training. He produced some original designs for various machines and then left his uncle's employment to move to Boston where he joined an instrument maker. He invented various contrivances, including an automatic sprinkler system for fire prevention, which also notified the fire station of the location of the fire! Eventually he set himself up on his own, dealing with gas machines, but was shrewd enough to see that electricity was soon going to take over as the chief means of illumination and designed an electric light bulb. Most of the generators of that period had permanent magnets and users soon found that their watches had become magnetized. Maxim designed a profitable little machine which he sold to watchmakers for demagnetizing watches.

In August 1881 Maxim, now a reasonably successful and wealthy man, earning $5,000 a year, went to Europe to visit the Paris Electrical Exhibition. His employers, the United States Electrical Lighting Company, now sent him to London to re-organize their branch there. It was at this juncture that he began his experiments in a field totally removed from his other interests. According to Maxim his reasons for turning to firearms were purely commercial. He had been told by a friend in Paris not to waste his time with useful things like electricity. If he could produce a weapon which would enable men to kill one another more efficiently, more quickly and at lower cost then he would make his fortune! Again, according to Maxim, the idea for his new and efficient killer was generated by a sore shoulder he received after firing a rifle.

Recoil had been generally considered simply as a nuisance, but Maxim, with his clear-sighted approach uncluttered by any preconceived ideas, saw it as energy which he might use to operate his new mechanism. In 1883 he produced his first drawing, which was for an automatic rifle. He planned that the recoil of a standard Winchester rifle should, by a series of levers, be used to operate the loading lever.

For various reasons Maxim now decided to apply himself full-time to this new and exciting prospect. He set up a small work-

British ·303-inch (7·69-mm) Vickers heavy machine-gun mounted on an experimental, light-pattern MK 4 tripod. Pattern Room, Royal Small Arms Factory, Enfield.

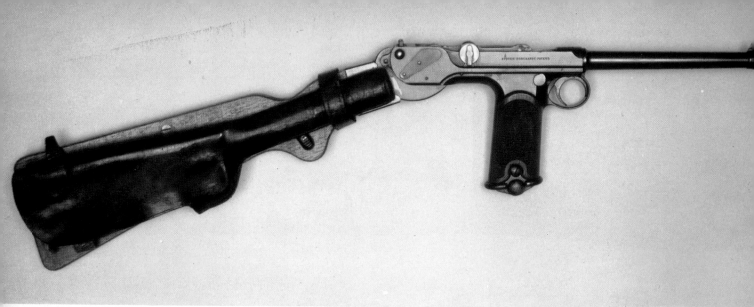

The Borchardt was one of the first self-loading weapons to be fitted with a shoulder stock to convert it to a carbine. The separate board was attached to the back of the holster. Although clumsy when fired in the hand, the Borchardt with a stock was a reliable weapon. Pattern Room, Royal Small Arms Factory, Enfield.

shop in the home of London's jewellery trade, Hatton Garden, purchased machines and began work. All the parts were made by him except for the barrels which he bought from the government. They were manufactured by the Henry Rifle Barrel Company and the superintendent of this firm in London advised Maxim not to waste his time, since hundreds of people had tried to make an automatic gun without success.

The basic concept on which he was working was that as the shot was fired the barrel would recoil, so stretching a spring which, when the recoil stopped, would bring the barrel back to the firing position. This backward and forward movement would be used to operate auxiliary devices which would, in turn, extract, load and fire a fresh cartridge. Maxim saw the need to improve the loading system which in most cases had consisted of a gravity feed. The cartridges were loaded into a box or hopper and simply dropped down one after the other into the position where they were fired. Obviously this system was limited. Maxim devised a procedure which used a belt of cartridges fed in through the weapon from right to left, bringing one cartridge into position each time it moved.

One vital factor in this mechanism was obviously the length of recoil. How far did it need to move before the action would operate? Maxim devised a piece of apparatus which would allow him to control the length of recoil. Then a practical test would soon indicate the optimum length. According to his autobiography, at the very first test he loaded in six cartridges, pressed the trigger and the mechanism operated perfectly. By intuition or good luck he had chosen just the correct length of recoil. In no time at all he had constructed a complete weapon and found that it fired more than ten rounds a second.

When the first news of Maxim's weapon reached the general public it was received with scepticism. However, one of the jewellers from Hatton Garden brought the Duke of Cambridge to see it and he expressed his delight. This seal of approval was sufficient and soon many people of note had been to inspect this fabulous new weapon. Among them was a leading British soldier, Lord Wolseley, who was greatly impressed and told Maxim that there seemed to be no limit to what he was able to do. During the many demonstrations he gave Maxim fired something like 200,000 rounds.

Maxim received some very good advice from another soldier, Lt.-General Sir Andrew Clark, who pointed out to the inventor that although his designs were wonderful they would have to be used by comparatively unskilled troops. Maxim should, therefore,

The Thompson submachine-gun with top bolt, drum magazine and forward pistol grip. Imperial War Museum, London.

aim to make the weapon as simple as possible, and of such a design that it could be stripped to its component parts using an absolute minimum of tools—preferably none at all. Maxim saw the value of this advice and simplified his design until he could claim that any component could be taken out and replaced within six seconds.

The movement of the barrel in Maxim's weapon was only ·75 of an inch, and by an ingenious device the rate of fire could be regulated from 1 to 600 rounds a minute. All that was required was to adjust a lever mounted at the side of the breech. Cartridges were supplied in belts seven yards long, each holding 333 cartridges, and at the end of each belt there was a neat little clip. While one belt was being fed through, another one could be clipped on the end so that the rate of fire could be maintained for as long as there was somebody to feed in the belts. Maxim also anticipated the later Lewis gun by devising a system using a flat drum magazine mounted on top of the weapon.

From 1883 to 1885 Maxim worked on automatic weapons and patented every system that he could think of that might be used. Many of the devices that he evolved at this early period are still in use today simply because nothing better has been devised.

Maxim's gun was demonstrated for the British government and in 1887 it outshot the Gatling, the Gardner and the Nordenfelt. It also performed remarkably well in Italy where, in addition, it was left for three days in the sea, taken out and fired without any cleaning being required. In 1888 it was demonstrated to an Austrian committee, firing over 13,500 rounds without a serious mishap. The mainspring, a striker and buffer broke but each was replaced within a few seconds and the firing continued.

With the Lebel cartridges, using the new smokeless powder, the the rate of fire was found to be anything between 1,100 and 1,200 rounds a minute. This big increase from around 600 a minute was due to the difference in the burning time of the new mixture. Black powder, which had previously been used in cartridges, literally explodes. Almost at once the pressure builds up very rapidly and decreases just as rapidly. With smokeless powder the pressure builds up to a maximum, which is maintained, even after the peak has been passed. This leaves a little extra energy available for operating any recoil mechanism.

German 08/15, 7·9-mm heavy machine-gun, water-cooled and fed by belts of ammunition. Pattern Room, Royal Small Arms Factory, Enfield.

Opposite, far right:
Browning automatic rifle designed by John Browning in 1917. It fires a ·30-inch calibre bullet at a cyclic rate of 550 rounds a minute. Pattern Room, Royal Small Arms Factory, Enfield.

Opposite, above left:
American Browning ·300-inch (7·6-mm) machine-gun of 1917, with the water-cooling tubing and reservoir attached. The box at the side holds the cartridge belts. Pattern Room, Royal Small Arms Factory, Enfield.

Opposite, bottom:
Lewis gun. This specimen is Russian (1916), but is fitted on a British mounting designed for this particular make of gun. Pattern Room, Royal Small Arms Factory, Enfield.

The Maxim machine-gun was officially taken into British service in 1891 and into the German army in 1899. By 1905, according to the German writer, Captain von Braun, nineteen armies and twenty-one fleets were using the Maxim, while nine armies and three fleets were using the Hotchkiss or any other system. The first use of the machine-gun in action seems to have been during the 1893–4 campaign against the Matabele of the Northern Transvaal. Fifty infantrymen with Maxims defended themselves against 5,000 warriors and, although there was no lack of bravery on the part of the latter, they were unable to get closer than 100 paces before being cut down by the Maxim.

The gun saw service again in India on the Afghan frontier in 1895 and in 1898 during the Sudan campaign. The Maxims were mounted on wheeled carriages and, to keep out the ever-intrusive desert sand, they were fitted with a silk cover which was left in position until just before the weapon started firing. At the battle of Omdurman, of the 20,000 Dervishes killed, it is estimated that three-quarters of them were cut down by the Maxim machine-gunners. In fact the Dervishes never actually reached the British lines.

In 1898 a long-range version of the machine-gun was produced in the ·75-inch calibre which could fire a disintegrating bullet. This had a central steel core with a range of segments fitted round it, held together by rings of lead. At the muzzle was a cutting device which could sever the retaining rings. The gunner, by operating this, could either fire a solid armour-piercing bullet or spray the area with the segments. Next came a Maxim weapon known as the Pom Pom, a name apparently given to it by the African natives, which fired a 37-mm shell at a rate of 300 rounds a minute. Not originally adopted by the British, it fired an explosive shell weighing 1 lb and many were acquired by the Boers through a purchasing agency in France. They wrought havoc against the British artillery during the South African War. When smokeless powder was used, there was no indication of its position and it proved a deadly weapon.

The rate of fire and the cost of the ammunition were two rather prohibitive features about this weapon. It is reported that when the Chinese asked for a demonstration they were very impressed. They asked the price of the shells and, when told these were 6/6d (35p) each, they are reputed to have said 'This gun fires altogether too fast for China'. The king of Denmark is reported to have said that the gun would bankrupt his kingdom in two hours. However, the British government had learnt its lesson during the South African War and, expensive or not, adopted the Pom Pom as one of their official weapons.

For a short time Hiram Maxim was associated with Nordenfelt, the financier, but in 1888 he joined with Vickers, the British manufacturing firm, to form Vickers Sons and Maxim Ltd. A number of minor improvements were made and in 1904 the first model of the new Maxim, officially known as the Vickers, was produced. Steel and aluminium were substituted for the heavier metals and this new machine-gun weighed only $40\frac{1}{2}$ lb, compared with 60 lb for the earlier weapon.

Ironically, although the Maxim was the invention of an American, his country was one of the last major powers to adopt it. It was tested by the United States as early as 1888 but was not taken up. In 1913, belatedly realizing how far behind the rest of the world's military powers they were, the United States once again tested machine-guns and adopted the Vickers. It was, in fact, built by the Colt Patent Firearms Company and was officially designated as the 1915 Model Vickers.

Germany had 50,000 Maxim-type guns ordered or on hand by 1914 and, as always, once the practicability of the automatic gun had been demonstrated, many other designers began to experiment and numerous models were produced. One of their problems was that Maxim had drawn up such tight patent specifications that almost every variation of the system was covered. One of the more successful was that produced by the Hotchkiss company in France from an original invention by an Austrian, Captain Adolph von Odkolek. His design was taken over by the firm, adapted and modified to produce a weapon known as the Hotchkiss. It was characterized by the large, cooling doughnut-shaped projection on the barrel. It differed from Maxim's design in that the movement was activated, not by the recoil, but by a small amount of expanding gas which was led off from the barrel by means of a small vent near the muzzle. The gas was fed back along a cylinder, where it pushed back a piston which was returned by a spring, again giving the reciprocating motion needed to work the breech block. The original Hotchkiss used metal strips about fifteen inches long, holding thirty cartridges. Later models used the belt system favoured by Maxim.

Another French gun was the Chauchat, which was based on an idea by a Hungarian designer, Rudolf Frommer. The unusual

Tommy guns.
Above. The model 1928A with the horizontal front grip and the small, round drum magazine which held fifty rounds of ·45-inch (11·4-mm) cartridges.
Below. The Model 1921 with front pistol grip and the large C 100 magazine. The butt can be removed as indicated. Note that the number has been chiselled off at some time, presumably in order to prevent the weapon being traced. Pattern Room, Royal Small Arms Factory, Enfield.

Right:
One of the finest light machine-guns was the British Bren – reliable and very accurate. It saw much service during World War II as an infantry weapon as well as being mounted on many vehicles.

Bottom right, above
German MP38 9-mm calibre submachine-gun with thirty-two round magazine and fold-away stock. This particular model has a special device fitted at the muzzle which enabled it to work when blank ammunition was used. Pattern Room, Royal Small Arms Factory, Enfield.

Bottom right, below:
The Moschetto Automatic Beretta 9-mm submachine-gun. The long, straight box magazine was clipped into the receiver at the front of the wooden stock. The cuts at the front are a form of muzzle brake intended to keep the barrel from rising as the gun was fired. Pattern Room, Royal Small Arms Factory, Enfield.

Below:
Villar Perosa twin-barrel machine-gun chambered for ·45-inch cartridges, a rather unusual calibre for this weapon. This Italian weapon was the forerunner of the submachine-gun.

feature of this weapon was the magazine which was a semicircular, rather clumsy design and held twenty 8-mm Lebel cartridges. It was, however, cheap, very easy to construct and very light, weighing only 19 lb, including a folding bipod. Large numbers of these were supplied to the American soldiers when America joined the war in 1917. It was not a popular weapon and the rate of issue was twice what it should have been, largely because the soldiers threw it away.

On June 7, 1912, a machine-gun was fired from a moving aircraft for the first time. The target was a piece of cheesecloth six feet by seven feet on the ground. Lieutenant Milling flew one of Wright's planes while Captain Chandler acted as the observer and machine-gunner. The gun was found to function well and the target was hit from an altitude of 250 feet. Further tests were made and one important discovery was that the firing of the machine-gun did not affect the balance or trim of the aircraft. The gun used for these vital early experiments was a machine-gun designed by Isaac Newton Lewis of Pennsylvania. He had served at West Point military academy and was approached in 1910 for some ideas on an air-cooled machine gun. In 1911 he showed his prototype to the army chiefs of staff but, despite the obvious capability of this weapon, the U.S. Board of Ordnance was remarkably reluctant to come to any decision.

In 1913 Lewis went to Liège, taking the four specially made guns with him. Eventually the manufacture of the weapon finished up in the hands of the British Small Arms Company (B.S.A.) of Birmingham. The new gun was soon in such heavy demand that the Savage Arms Company of Utica, New York, was contracted to produce them in addition to those being made by B.S.A. It had several unusual features including the use of a coiled spring situated

Israeli 9-mm UZI submachine-gun—compact, reliable and used in a number of countries, especially by security forces. Later models had a folding metal stock in place of the wooden butt. Imperial War Museum, London.

just in front of the pistol grip and trigger mechanism. The spring was easily accessible for repair and, being totally enclosed, was shielded against dirt and dust. The cartridges were supplied in a flat rotating drum which was made in two sizes, one holding forty-seven cartridges for use on the ground and the other ninety-six for use in aircraft.

Aircraft were to play an important part in World War I from the very beginning. German observers often armed themselves with a normal bolt-action Mauser or a self-loading rifle known as the Mondragon. This weapon, patented in 1904, was made in Switzerland and all models were actually diverted to Germany on the outbreak of war. On August 22, 1914, two British pilots (quite unofficially) fitted their aircraft with a Lewis gun and engaged in aerial combat with a German Albatross plane. Although they emptied the magazine at the German aircraft there was no effect. The British high command forbad the use of machine-guns in aircraft, for it was argued that the possession of such an offensive weapon would encourage pilots to seek combat rather than carry out what was then their prime duty of spotting troop movements and directing artillery fire. The prohibition did not last for long and soon aircraft were being fitted with Lewis guns. They were not the only machine-guns in aircraft. Maxims and others were also used. Although the Lewis gun saw much service with the British army, the United States never officially adopted it, a fact which caused a great deal of domestic controversy.

One other very important development was also taking place at the same time as Maxim was developing his machine-gun. Nearly all machine-guns, even the lightest, had to be mounted on some form of tripod or fixed mounting or on a wheeled mount. Few were capable, except perhaps the Lewis, of being fired when held by hand. One man whose name ranks with the greatest in modern firearm developments, Browning, was turning his mind to this problem.

Mention has already been made of Browning's work with the firm of Winchester, but he also designed weapons for Remington, Colt and other firearms companies. In 1889 he first consciously observed the effects of the blast of air and gas from the barrel of his rifle. According to tradition he was hunting at the time and noticed the bullrushes being parted by the blast. In the same way that Maxim had realized the potential use of the recoil so Browning

Top. U.S. ·30-inch (7·62-mm)
M.3 carbine with an infra-red
sight. The muzzle is fitted with a
flash eliminator. Such a weapon
would be suitable for night-time
sniping. Overall length 16 inches
(40·6 cm).
Above. One of the Armalite series,
A.R.18, firing a 5·56-mm bullet.
Produced according to the most
modern manufacturing methods,
these are very light, self-loading
rifles. Pattern Room, Royal Small
Arms Factory, Enfield.

saw the possibilities of this excess gas under pressure. A few
experiments soon convinced him of the great source of power
available here, and he now set about fixing a device at the end of the
the muzzle which would channel back some of this energy. Soon
he had a crude but nevertheless effective gas-operated machine-
gun.

In 1890 he offered the production of his new machine-gun to
the Colt Manufacturing Company. They took it up and in 1893
it was tested by the U.S. navy. The gas-activated arm swung to
and fro in a half circle beneath the gun. This movement reminded
its users of some simple farming machinery and henceforth it was
known as the 'potato digger'. Colt's machine-gun was neat
(except for this swinging arm) and was simple in construction,
although it needed a hundred separate parts and had a maximum
weight of 40 lb. The recoil was very slight indeed and, although
the gun was normally fitted to a tripod, the official report said that
it could be fired from the shoulder.

The U.S. navy acquired a number of these Colt machine-guns
but, despite the success of the model, Browning was convinced
that the short recoil was more efficient. In 1901 he succeeded in
producing an automatic weapon using this system.

Browning was also working on another important project, an
automatic rifle, which was intended to be fired hand-held, either
single or fully automatic, with a capacity of 400 shots a minute.
It was gas-activated, air-cooled and loaded with a thirty-shot
magazine, and was designed to be fired from the hip with a sling
over the shoulder. It was publicly demonstrated in February 1917
and the obvious value of this weapon impressed all those who saw
it. The U.S. government adopted it at once. Browning also produced the heavy, water-cooled machine-gun which again was
adopted by the American army.

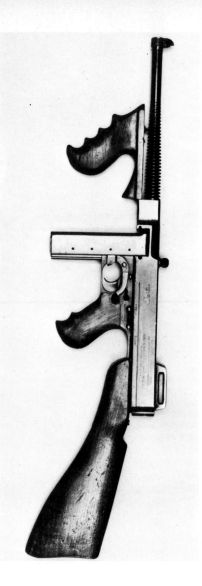

The heavy machine-gun established itself at the beginning of the twentieth century as one of the most potent weapons of modern warfare. During World War I there developed a new form of weapon which could be described as a machine-gun in miniature. The Browning automatic rifle was one of the outstanding examples of weapons of this kind, but it was not the first in the field. This was almost certainly the Revelli, invented by Bethel Abiel Revelli, also known as the Villar Perosa, the name of the factory in which it was produced. The big difference between the Villar Perosa and other machine-guns was mainly in the size of the cartridge used. Every machine-gun up to this period had been designed to fire rifle ammunition or cartridges even larger than those of the rifle. The Villar Perosa was designed to fire a pistol cartridge, in this case the 9-mm Parabellum.

The gun was granted an American patent in December 1915. It was fitted in aircraft and armoured cars but it also worked well as a hand-held machine-gun. It was often equipped with a folding bipod and carried into battle mounted on a flat board, suspended by straps around the soldier's neck, rather in the way that a cigarette girl carries her wares.

The distinctive feature about this weapon was that it consisted of two separate guns united to make one. Each could be fired separately or both together, when the weapon offered a cyclic rate of 300 rounds a minute. It had a blow-back mechanism and the two magazines held only twenty-five rounds each. Since these would very soon be emptied, the weapon was supplied with over forty spare magazines. Even when loaded the gun weighed only 16·3 lb.

The basic single weapon was developed and modified, and after World War I was fitted with a more conventional stock. Eventually developments led to the introduction of the Italian-made Beretta model 1918, which had the appearance of a carbine, with a very prominent, curved magazine holding twenty-five rounds, projecting above the stock just ahead of the bolt. It was also fitted with a folding bayonet. These smaller automatic weapons are now described as submachine-guns, a term first used in the late 1920s.

Beretta developed a number of very efficient submachine-guns, nearly all of them designed for use with the 9-mm Parabellum. The position of the magazines varied. Some were on top but in general it was found more convenient to place them beneath the breech or on the left-hand side. Beretta has continued in this field and are still producing some very fine weapons. The model 1953, with a magazine capacity of either twenty or forty rounds, has a cyclic rate of 550, and is a beautifully compact weapon, measuring only fifteen inches overall.

Right:
Above. Romanian AKM 7·62-mm assault rifle, fitted with a front wooden pistol grip.
Below. Hungarian AK47 7·62-mm assault rifle. The Kalashnikov is one of the most widely used automatic weapons and is produced in a variety of models differing in details. Pattern Room, Royal Small Arms Factory, Enfield.

The traditional image of the Tommy gun, in the hands of John Dillinger, a notorious American gangster of the 1930s. He is also holding a ·38 Colt automatic.

Another submachine-gun which only just saw service in World War I was that designed by Hugo Schmeisser—the German M.P.18. Development had begun some two years before but the first test weapon only appeared in 1918. By the summer of that year it was planned that all officers, N.C.O.s, and one in ten of the ordinary infantrymen should be trained in its use. Each company was to have a squad with six machine-gunners and six ammunition carriers. Arrangements were to be made for special supply ammunition carts to be available, one to every two guns.

Their adoption was too late to effect the outcome of the war and, in fact, by the Treaty of Versailles the German army was forbidden to use them, although permission was given for the police to carry them. The design was rather chunky, with an air-cooled cylinder around the barrel. It was again a blow-back type with a cyclic rate of around 400 rounds a minute. The gun was fitted with a snail drum magazine exactly the same as that intended for use on the Luger and it also fired the 9-mm Parabellum ammunition. Later models were designed to use other ammunition and varying sizes of magazines were produced. At least one model was made to be fitted with a bayonet.

In 1936 the newly created German armoured forces asked for a submachine-gun, but there was little support for it until 1938 when the German high command approached the director of the Erma Arms factory at Erfurt and asked him to produce one as quickly as possible. This was the weapon which saw a great deal of service during World War II and was always described as the Schmeisser, although it was not, in fact, designed by him but by Berthold Geipel. Designated the M.P.38, it introduced a novel feature in that the stock could be folded underneath the weapon if, for any reason, it had to be used in confined quarters. The long, straight magazine holding thirty-two rounds, protruded below the breech. The whole weapon was made of steel and plastic, without any wood at all—the first one to use this technique. Modifications were later made, one of the most important being an improved

Above:
Sten submachine-gun Mark II with the box magazine in position. The skeleton butt was later modified even further. Imperial War Museum, London.

Right:
Above. German-made copy of the British Mark II Sten, known as the Gerat Potsdam. The magazine held thirty-two rounds of 9-mm cartridges.
Below. British Sten Gun Mk V with a front hand grip—a feature later abandoned. Pattern Room, Royal Small Arms Factory, Enfield.

Below:
British Sterling submachine-gun L2A2. The skeleton stock can fold away. A slightly curved magazine holds thirty-four 9-mm cartridges. Pattern Room, Royal Small Arms Factory, Enfield

safety catch, for it was found that with the bolt in the retracted position, the M.P.38 had an unfortunate tendency to go off if it received a sudden knock. Various models, such as the M.P.40 and the M.P.41, were produced and all were very satisfactory weapons. Great use was made of stampings for cheap production. Since the war Mauser have entered this particular field as have several other German manufacturers including Walther.

In 1921 the most instantly recognizable of all submachine-guns appeared – the so-called Tommy gun or Thompson submachine-gun. It had been in process of development at the end of the war and the design for it is usually taken to be that of General John T. Thompson, although some writers have suggested that he was merely the head of the team. He was a man of vast experience in arms production. Having left the U.S. army in 1914, in 1916 he, with some other supporters, set up the Auto-Ordnance Corporation to exploit a design by Commander John Blish of the U.S. navy. When America entered the war in 1917 Thompson rejoined the army but research continued. It was found that the device they were using to lock the breech would only function with a ·45-inch cartridge. Instead of an automatic rifle – the original idea – it was decided to make the new weapon a hand-held machine-gun. A circular magazine was developed, which used a clock spring to drive the cartridges round and up to the breech. The type-C magazine held 100 rounds and the type-L 50.

Eventually a satisfactory weapon was produced, which was tested by the Ordnance in 1920. Colt was asked to manufacture it and in 1921 the Thompson submachine-gun appeared on the market. It could be fired either single-shot – or automatic. It was sighted up to 600 yards and could fire at a rate of 800 rounds a minute. The barrel was 10½ inches long and the weapon without a stock measured only some 25 inches overall.

Unfortunately for the company it was appearing at a time so soon after World War I that there was little real interest in weapons. Most countries had a surplus of them and some adverse publicity was received when some of the new guns fell into the hands of gangsters. John Dillinger, one of the most notorious, used a modified Thompson single-handed as a machine-pistol – inaccurate even if intimidating. It was officially adopted in 1938 by the U.S. army as the model 1928A1.

On the outbreak of World War II consignments were ordered by both France and Britain. The Tommy gun was produced in various styles: probably the best-known version has a pistol grip behind the magazine and another one in front. The front pistol grip was later discarded and a horizontal forward grip substituted. The weapon saw much service during World War II in the hands of soldiers of many countries.

Top:
The modern British service rifle, L1A1, 7·62 mm, with the carrying handle in the raised position. National Army Museum, London.

Centre:
British general-purpose machine-gun MGL7A2 which used the NATO 7·62-mm cartridge at a cyclic rate of 700–1,000 rounds a minute. It was adopted in 1961.

Above:
German assault rifle MK6 42(W) made by the firm of Walther from 1942. Only about 200 were produced, and this is No. 84. Pattern Room, Royal Small Arms Factory, Enfield.

Much time and effort were to be devoted to these new automatic weapons when it was realized how important they were. The ordinary soldier now had in his hands the equivalent in firepower of a whole platoon of riflemen in World War I. The British army, however, was particularly reluctant to consider the adoption of submachine-guns. In fact, it was felt to be a somewhat ungentlemanly weapon! A number were tested, including the Thompson, but none was adopted and it was not until World War II had started that any steps were taken to adopt or develop this particular form of weapon.

Then in 1940, when Britain was threatened with invasion, under pressure from the three services, the authorities decided that some form of machine-carbine or submachine-gun should be developed. The Air Ministry wanted 10,000 weapons based on the German M.P.38 and the Sterling Armament Company were approached to make copies. The new weapons were tested, but were not very satisfactory. However, after some modification the Lanchester, named after its designer, went into production for the services, the first consignment being supplied to the navy.

It was rather a complex weapon. What was required was a submachine-gun which could be mass-produced with a minimum of effort. A very simplified Lanchester, with a rate of some 520 rounds per minute, was demonstrated at Enfield in January 1941. Called the Sten, a name made up of the initials of Shepherd and Turpin, the designers, and the first two letters of the word 'Enfield', it was a very simple weapon indeed. The Mark I Sten had a wooden stock and a wooden front handgrip, but these were soon abandoned. Various improvements and sundry other designs were produced, including a Mark VI version, and the Sten proved itself, despite its rather 'tinny' appearance, to be a very satisfactory

The German MP 44, a fine assault rifle, known later as the Sturmgewehr, one of the earliest of a long line of successful sub-machine-guns. Pattern Room, Royal Small Arms Factory, Enfield.

weapon. It was produced in quantity at a unit cost of only about £5. It was distributed on a large scale to resistance groups in German-occupied Europe as well as to regular forces. So successful was it that the Germans manufactured a weapon which was virtually an exact copy of the Mark II Sten. The Mauser plant started work on these in 1944.

When World War II ended in 1945 military designers were convinced of the new and important role that submachine-guns could play in wars. Development of new models went ahead in almost every country. The trend, too, was towards smaller, more compact weapons, and the distinction between submachine-guns, machine pistols and other automatic weapons became far less sharp.

In Britain a much refined Sten-like weapon was designed and became eventually the Sterling or L2A3 submachine-gun. Germany produced a whole range of weapons by Walther, Mauser, Erma and other makers. One model much favoured by security men from many countries is the UZI, designed in Israel in 1949 by Major Uziel Gal. It is a compact, efficient weapon capable of automatic fire of about 130 rounds a minute. The UZI and the American Ingram M.10 and M.11 models, like many others in this group, have stocks which are retractable and can be pushed home to make the weapon little bigger than a large automatic pistol.

Another postwar development was the almost general adoption of the self-loading rifles (SLR for short) by most armies. They differed from submachine-guns mainly in the size of cartridge used – theirs was larger and more powerful, being intended for longer ranges than the smaller submachine-gun. During World War II

The Russian army of World War II made more use of the submachine-gun than other Allied armies. Its standard weapon was the simple, but effective PPSh 41, here being assembled at an arms factory.

the Germans had developed the concept of the assault rifle, a weapon capable of delivering a heavy barrage of fire during an attack, but also usable in a more conventional manner. The German light machine-gun, the M.P.43, had proved its efficiency, and in 1944 it was decided that the newer version, the M.P.44, should be renamed. In a blaze of publicity it was called the Sturmgewehr, Stg44, or assault rifle. It operated on a blow-back principle, with some gas being tapped off to drive back the mechanism. A thirty-shot, slightly curved, magazine was held below the breech. It was designed for ease of manufacture and proved very effective.

One interesting development which the Germans attempted was the 'round the corner' rifle. The Stg44 was fitted with a curved fitting, carefully designed to deflect the bullet through thirty or ninety degrees. The first, Versatz J, was intended for infantry engaged in street or trench warfare, whilst the ninety-degree Versatz P was to be fitted in tanks so that the crew might have a chance or clearing infantry from the 'dead' spot on the tank body. This could not otherwise be covered except by crewmen emerging from their vehicle.

The Soviet Union and the West have both developed weapons which are improvements on the Stg44. Before World War II the Soviet Union used a number of automatic rifles such as the Tokarev and the Simonov. Many Soviet troops fought the war with the PPd40, a submachine-gun with a large drum magazine holding either 25 or 71 rounds and giving a rate of fire of about 100 rounds a minute. After the war a Russian designer, Mikhail Kalashnikov, produced what is undoubtedly one of the finest assault rifles, the AK47, later modified to the AKM. It uses a 7·62-mm round, is gas-operated and has a thirty-round magazine. The muzzle velocity is high, well over 2,300 feet per second, and is capable of automatic fire at 100 rounds a minute. AK weapons are still used by most Eastern European countries and have been supplied in bulk to many other national forces.

In Britain postwar research and development led eventually to the adoption of the FN FAL rifle–Fabrique Nationale, Fusil Automatique Légère. Over twenty other countries also use this model which fires a 7·62-mm cartridge carried in a twenty-shot box magazine and is capable of a rate of fire of 120 rounds a minute. The maximum effective range is about 650 yards or 600 metres. Some modifications have been made and the present version is known as the L1A1 rifle.

Above:
Chinese AK47, Type 56/1, 7·62-mm calibre with an 11-inch (27·9-cm) folding bayonet. Pattern Room, Royal Small Arms Factory, Enfield.

Right:
American M62 general-purpose machine-gun mounted on a tripod. It can be operated with just the folding bipod fitted at the front of the barrel. It uses a 7·62-mm cartridge and is fed with a linked belt. Pattern Room, Royal Small Arms Factory, Enfield.

The United States had made use of self-loading rifles during World War II. The Garand M1 ·30-inch rifle was loaded with clips of eight cartridges and could maintain a rate of fire of about thirty rounds a minute. A carbine version was also produced from 1941 with a fifteen-round magazine and a rate of fire of about seventy-five rounds a minute. In 1954 a branch of Fairchild Engine and Airplane Corporation, called the Armalite Division, was set up under the direction of Eugene Stoner. From this group came many weapons ranging from the AR1, a sporting rifle, to the AR10 an assault rifle using a 7·62-mm and the AR15, using a 5·56-mm cartridge, to obtain a muzzle velocity of over 3,000 feet per second.

Another area of weapon design which has been greatly developed is that of sighting devices using infra-red or light intensifiers. The infra-red types are often rather bulky, particularly if they use a special projector, while the other type magnifies the natural light available.

Developments in weapons continue and new ones are being tested all the time. Bullets are becoming smaller and smaller – the latest British one is 4·85 mm in diameter. Muzzle velocities continue to increase and sights have become more complex. New ideas from other branches of science – lasers for example – are pressed into service and new materials are used for weapons manufacture. In a fast-changing world, however, no-one can safely predict what the next generation of firearms will be like.

Above:
Danish Madsen 8-mm Mod ·22 light machine-gun, mounted on a DISA tripod. This version used a box magazine but some models were fitted with belt feeds. Pattern Room, Royal Small Arms Factory, Enfield.

Top left:
U.S. M73 7·62-mm machine-gun, designed specifically for use in a tank, although here it is mounted on a tripod. Pattern Room, Royal Small Arms Factory, Enfield.

Bibliography

John Atkinson, *Duelling Pistols* (London, 1964)

Donald Bady, *Colt Automatic Pistols*, rev. ed. (Alhambra, 1973)

Frank Barnes, *Cartridges of the World* (Chicago, 1965)

James Belford and Jack Dunlap, *The Mauser Self-Loading Pistol* (Alhambra, 1969)

H. L. Blackmore, *British Military Firearms* (London, 1961)

H. L. Blackmore, *Guns and Rifles of the World* (London, 1965)

Claude Blair, *Pistols of the World* (London, 1968)

Hans Busk, *The Rifle* (London, 1859)

Roy Chandler, *Kentucky Rifle Patchboxes* (Duncannon, 1972)

George M. Chinn, *The Machine Gun* (Washington, 1951)

Fred Datig, *The Luger Pistol* (Alhambra, 1962)

William Dowell, *The Webley Story* (Leeds, 1962)

Robert Elman, *Fired in Anger* (New York, 1968)

Ron Graham, J. Kopec and C. K. Moore, *A Study of the Colt Single-Action Army Revolver* (Dallas, 1976)

Arcadi Gluckman, *U.S. Martial Pistols and Revolvers* (Harrisburg, 1956)

Arcadi Gluckman, *Identifying old U.S. Muskets, Rifles and Carbines* (Harrisburg, 1964)

W. W. Greener, *The Gun and its Development*, 9th ed. (London, 1910)

Charles Hanson, *The Plains Rifle* (Harrisburg, 1960)

F. W. Hobart, *Jane's Infantry Weapons, 1974–75* (London, 1974)

F. W. Hobart, *Pictorial History of the Sub-Machine Gun* (London, 1973)

Ian Hogg, *German Pistols and Revolvers, 1871–1945* (London, 1971)

B. P. Hughes, *Fire Power* (London, 1974)

Henry Kauffman, *Early American Gunsmiths, 1650–1850* (New York, 1952)

Henry Kauffman, *The Pennsylvania-Kentucky Rifle* (Harrisburg, 1960)

Charles Kenyon, *Lugers at Random* (Chicago, 1969)

Frederick Leithe, *Japanese Hand Pistols* (Alhambra, 1968)

Herschel Logan, *Cartridges* (Harrisburg, 1959)

F. W. Longstaff and A. H. Atteridge, *The Book of the Machine Gun* (London, 1917)

Jaroslav Lugs, *A History of Shooting* (London, 1968)

George Madis, *The Winchester Book*, 3rd ed. (Lancaster, 1971)

Daniel Musgrave and Oliver Smith, *German Machine Guns* (Washington, 1971)

Daniel Musgrave and T. B. Nelson, *The World's Great Assault Rifles* (Alexandria, 1967)

Robert Neal and Roy Jinks, *Smith & Wesson 1857–1945* (London, 1967)

W. K. Neal and D. H. L. Back, *Forsyth & Co: Patent Gunmakers* (London, 1969)

Thomas B. Nelson, *The World's Sub-Machine Guns* (Cologne, 1963)

J. I. Owen (ed.), *Brassey's Infantry Weapons of The World* (London, 1975)

J. R. Partington, *A History of Greek Fire and Gunpowder* (Cambridge, 1960)

H. L. Peterson, *The Encyclopedia of Firearms* (London, 1964)

H. L. Peterson, *The Book of the Continental Soldier* (Harrisburg, 1968)

E. G. B. Reynolds, *The Lee-Enfield Rifle* (London, 1960)

C. H. Roads, *The British Soldiers' Firearm, 1850–1864* (London, 1964)

Joseph G. Rosa, *Colonel Colt, London* (London, 1976)

Lois Schwoerer, *No Standing Armies!* (Baltimore, 1974)

Sibbald Scott, *The British Army* (London, 1868)

W. H. B. Smith, *Book of Pistols and Revolvers* (Harrisburg, 1968)

W. H. B. Smith, *Mauser, Walther and Mannlicher Firearms* (Harrisburg, 1971)

R. Q. Sutherland and R. L. Wilson, *The Book of Colt Firearms* (Kansas City, 1971)

A. W. F. Taylerson, *Revolving Arms* (London, 1967)

A. W. F. Taylerson, *The Revolver, 1818–1865* (London, 1968)

A. W. F. Taylerson, *The Revolver, 1865–1888* (London, 1966)

A. W. F. Taylerson, *The Revolver, 1889–1914* (London, 1970)

George Watrous, *The History of Winchester Firearms, 1866–1975*, 4th ed. (New York, 1975)

Henry White and B. Munhall, *Centrefire Pistol and Revolver Cartridges* (London, 1967)

Harold Williamson, *Winchester: The Gun that won the West* (London, 1963)

R. K. Wilson and I. Hogg, *Textbook of Automatic Pistols* (London, 1975)

Index

Numbers in italics refer to illustrations

Adams revolver 148, 150
Adams, Robert 150
Ager repeater 235
Albright, Henry 85
Allen, Ethan 138
American Civil War 148, 171, 172, 174, 183, 202, 233, 235, 236
American Revolutionary War 66
Armalite A. R. 18 *250*
arquebus 24, 51, 52
arquebusiers 32, *54*
Articles of War 120
Art of Duelling, The 106
assault rifles *230*, 249, 251, 253
Astra (Mauser-type automatic) 224
Austrian Pattern musket 79
automatic rifle 207

Baby Russian revolver 210
Bacon, Roger 8, *8*
Baker, Ezekiel 94
Baker rifle 94, *94*, 96, *97*
Ballita rifle *205*
Baltic lock 60
bar-hammer pepperbox revolver *140*
bayonets *62*, 64, 65, 90, 96, 99, 193, 202, 205
Beaumont-Adams percussion revolver *137*, *145*, 150, 214
Beretta pistol 226
Beretta submachine-gun 246
Bergman pistol 222
Berners, Captain 96
Bicocca, Battle of 33
Billinghurst Requa battery gun 234
Black Berthold 8, 9, 35
Blenheim, Battle of *73*
blunderbuss 60, *64*, 65
Board of Ordnance 63, 74, *74*
bolt-action needle-fire cartridge rifle 162, 163
Borchardt, Hugo 220, 221
Borchardt/Luger pistol 225
Borchardt pistol *215*, 221, 225
Boxer, Colonel Edward, 164, 165
box-lock flintlock pistol *70*
Brandywine Hill, Battle of 94
breech-loading weapons 154, *156*, *160*, 161, *163*
Breitenfeld, Battle of *22*
Bren machine-gun 205
British Bulldog revolver 216
British Code of Duel 106, 114
Brown Bess 58, 60, 62, 64, 66, 68, 69, 74, 78, *78*, 79, 84, 89, 90, 93, 96, 138, 181, 232
Brown Bess, firing sequence of 66
Browning, John M. *225*, 228, 244, 245
Browning 32 ACP pistol *14*
Browning automatic rifle *241*, 245, 246
Browning Baby automatic pistol *225*

Browning/Colt automatic pistol 228
Browning Hi Power 9 mm *221*, *229*
Browning machine-gun *241*
Brunswick, Duke of 96
Brunswick rifle 96, 99, 138
Buffalo Bill carbine 178
buffalo head (anvil) 85
bullet bag *25*, *31*
bullet moulds *182*
Burr, Aaron 123
Busk, Hans 156

caliver 24
Canadian target rifle *90*
carbine 24
cartridges 66, 94, 153; rim-fire 168, 172
cavalry 54
charger 27, 28
Charles II, king of England 56, *56*, 57
Charleville musket 181
Charola-Anitu automatic pistol 222
Chauchat gun 242
Chaumette, Isaac de la 157
Chassepot, Antoine 164, 165
Chassepot rifle *101*
Churchill, Winston 225
Cleff, Jean Paul *68*
Codes of Duel 106
Codex Atlanticus 39
Cody, William *177*
'Coffee-mill gun' *235*
Coldstream Guards *57*
Collier, Elisha 128
Collier percussion carbine *126*
Colt, Samuel 6, 140, *140*, 142, 143, 144, 146, 147, 148, 150, 154, 155, 190, 208, 213
Colt Army Model percussion revolvers *142*, *143*
Colt automatic pistols *220*, 228, 230, 231
Colt carbine *148*
Colt derringer *15*
Colt machine-gun 245
Colt Navy revolver 148
Colt Paterson Belt pistol *141*, 142
Colt percussion rifle *138*
Colt Pocket Police revolver 148
Colt pocket revolver 147
Colt revolvers 214, *214*
Colt rifled muskets 148
Colt single-action revolver *212*, 213
Cominazzo, Lazarino *73*
copper percussion cap 135, 136
cordite 198, 200
Corps of Riflemen 94
Cromwell, Oliver 53, 56, 57

dags 51
Danish flintlock magazine rifle *156*, 162
Davies, Edward 28
Daw, George 164
Deane Adams percussion revolver *137*, *147*
Dean Harding percussion revolver *153*
Derringer, Henry 91
Declaration of Rights 57
Delvigne, Captain Gustave 99
De Secretis Operibus Artis et Naturae et de Nullitate Magiae 8

Devilliers, Dr 123
Dickinson, Charles 123
dog-catch 61
dog's head 36, 37, 38, 39, 49, 60, 61
Dragoon revolver *146*, 147, 148
Dreyse, Johann Nikolaus von 162
Dreyse needle-fire rifle *89*, 164, 165
'duck's foot' 126
Dutch-style snaphaunce 61

East India Company 72, 73, *76*, 95
Eley, William 155
Elgin, cutlass pistol *180*
Enfield-Martini rifles *196*
Enfield Model I (E.M.I.) 207
Enfield Model II (E.M.II.) *200*, 207
Enfield percussion rifle *185*
Enfield revolvers *197*
Enfield rifle 10, 138, 156, 165
Enfield rifle 1853 207, 232
English flintlock musket *58*, 61
English flintlock pistol *74*
English flintlock rifle *92*
English Military Discipline, The 31
Exercise of Arms 19

Ferguson, Patrick 93, 94
Ferguson breech-loading rifle 93, *95*, 157
Fifth Monarchy Men 56, 57
firelocks 62
firing in three ranks *75*
flint knapping 121
flintlock 15, 16, 60, 61, *68*, *78*, 133, 136
flintlock carbine *57*
flintlock duelling pistols *106*, *110*
flintlock fowling piece *82*
flintlock holster pistols *66*, *73*
flintlock lock *93*
flintlock musket 63, *76*
flintlock percussion pistol *74*
flintlock pistol *73*, *96*, *108*, 115, 117, *125*, 153
flintlock revolvers *128*, 129
flintlock revolving rifle *95*
flintlock rifle *93*, *100*
flints *63*
Forsyth, Alexander John 16, 129, 131, 154
Fosbery, George 216
French duelling code 114
French duelling pistols *123*
French flintlock *66*
French flintlock pistol *104*
French lock 60, 62
frizzen 61, 119, 126, 127, 136
Fruhwith magazine rifle 196
fuzees 62

Galy-Cazalat, Professor 162
Gardner machine-gun 235
Garfield, President James 216
Gasser revolver 214
Gatling gun 233, 234
Gerat Potsdam gun *248*
German duelling code 114
German M.G.42 (heavy machine-gun) *246*
German M.P.18 (submachine-gun) *247*
German revolvers.*210*
Gonzalo de Córdoba 32

Greene, Lt-Col. J. D. 156
Greene carbine *182*
Greener, William 162
gunpowder 7, 8
gun tools *186*

hackbut *8*
hackbushes (hagbuts) 24
half-cock position 62
'half-hawks' 24
Hall, John R. 157
Hamilton, Alexander 123
handguns 25
Hawken, Jake and Sam 92, 93
Heckler and Koch pistol *226*
Henry, J. J. 91
Henry rifle *167*, 168, 171, 172, 174
holster pistols *105*
Hotchkiss gun 242
Humberger, Henry 138
Hungarian AK47 assault rifle *247*
Hunt, Walter 166, 167
hunting rifles 47, 84
huo ch'iang 7

ignition, types of *36*
Indian Mutiny 146
India Pattern Musket 72, 73, 74, *74*
Isandhlwana, Battle of 193, *194*

Jackson, General Andrew 123
Jaeger rifle 80, 82, 83, 84, *89*, 94
Jaeger riflemen 91
jag 117
Japanese automatic pistols *226*
Jennings, Lewis 167, 168
jezail (flintlock) *32*
Juarez, Benito 175
'Jungle carbine' 207

Kalashnikov AK47 (AKM) 252
Kalthoff, Wilhelm 166
Kentucky rifles 89
Kerr patent percussion revolver 150, *150*
King's Mountain, Battle of 94
Krag-Jorgensen magazine rifle 184, 199

Lahti 9-mm pistol *221*
Lanchester submachine-gun 250
Landsknechts *12*, 19
Lebel rifle 198
Le Bourgeoys, Martin 60, 62
Lee-Enfield carbine *195*
Lee-Enfield rifle 200, *200*, 201, 202, 204, 205, *206*, 207, 232
Lee magazine rifle 185
Lee Metford rifle *195*, 198, 200
Lee rifle *188*, 196
Lefaucheux, Casimir 162
Lefaucheux breech-loading gun *159*
Lefaucheux revolver *214*
Leonardo da Vinci 39
Le Page of Paris 52
Lewis, Isaac Newton 243
Lewis machine-gun *240*, 243, 244
Lexington, Battle of *92*
L.I.A1 rifle 207, 252
Liberator pistol 231

Løbnitz breech-loading pistol 157
lock 25, *27*, 55
Loffelholz, Martin 39
London Armoury Company 150
Long Land Musket 58, 69, *69*
Lorenzoni, Michele *128*, 166
Luger, George 225
Luger carbine *215*
Luger cartridge 227
Luger Parabellum pistol *222*
Luger pistol 6, *215*, 225, 227, 228

machine-guns *243*, *249*
mandrel 86
Mannlicker automatic pistol *221*, *222*, 228
Manton, Joseph 109, *109*, 116
Mariette (Belgian gunmaker) 138
Markham, Francis 29
Mars automatic pistol 228
Marston, W.P. *90*
Martini, Frederick von 193
Martini-Henry rifle *187*, *190*, 193, 194, *194*, *195*, 196, 232
Massachusetts Arms Company 150
match-holder *27*
matchlock 15, *19*, 26, 33, *33*, 34, 35, 36, 38, 40, *58*, 60, 62, 66, 232
matchlock mechanism 25
matchlock muskets *20*, *24*, 27, 28, *33*, *36*, 54, 57, 58, 66
Mauser, Paul *216*, 222, 224
Mauser automatic pistols *217*, 222, *223*, 224, 225, *226*
Mauser rifle 196, 244
Maxim, Sir Hiram Stevens 234, 236, 237, 238, 239, 241, 244
Maxim machine-gun 239–244
Maynard, Dr Edward 156
metal cartridge 164, 192, 219
miquelet lock 60, *71*
Milemete Manuscript 7, 9
Milemete, Walter de 9
Military Discipline 21
military flintlock *72*
Minden, Battle of 91
Minié, Captain Claude-Étienne 99
Minié rifle 99
mitrailleuse 234, 235
Monck, General George 54, 57
Monk's Gun 35
Mondragon automatic pistol *235*, 244
Mortimer, Henry *12*, *65*, 116
M.P.38 submachine-gun *247*, 248
musket drill 30, *31*
musketeers *22*, 24, *25*, 26–29, 31, *31*, 53, 54
muskets 24, 29, 32, *36*, 42, 43, *68*, 69, 71, *76*, *77*, 79, *79*
Mutiny Act 57

Napoleon Bonaparte 94, 161, 180
Nato cartridge 207
Navy Colt, 1851 *144*, *145*, 147
New Haven Arms Company 167, 171, 172, 174
New Land Pattern musket 74, 78, 79
New Model Army 53, 56

Nock, Henry *95*, 126
Nordenfelt gun 235, 236
North, Simeon 123

Office of Indian Trade 91
Orbea automatic 220
Ordnance Office 64, 69, 71, 72, 78, 131
Owen Jones rifle 196

Palmcrantz, Heldge 235
paper cartridge 28, 153, 154, 159
patch-box 46, 82, 88, 89, 94, 99
Patent Arms Manufacturing Company 140, 142, 143
Patent Firearms Company 177
Paterson revolver 146, 147
Pauly, Samuel Johannes 159, 160, 161, 162
Pavia, Battle of 33
Peninsular War *75*
Pennsylvanian Long Rifle 84, *84*, 87, 89, 90, *90*, 91, 92, 93, *93*, 94, 96, 181
pepperboxes *134*, 148
pepperbox pistols 138
Percussion Colt revolver 1851 *183*
percussion duelling pistols *113*
percussion lock 93, 108, 133, *133*, 134, 136, 138
percussion musket *100*
percussion Pennsylvanian Long Rifles *85*
percussion pepperbox revolver *153*
percussion pistols 115, *116*, *121*, 123, *134*, *135*, *138*
percussion revolver 63, *136*, 153
percussion rifled pistol *113*
petronel 20, 24, 33
pikemen 31, *31*, 32, 53
pin-fire cartridges 162
Pistole Parabellum 227
Plains rifle 92, 93, *93*
plug bayonet *58*, *61*, 65
pocket police revolver 148
pocket revolver 147
Pom Pom machine-gun 240, 241
'potato digger' (machine-gun) 245
Pottet, Clement 162, 164
powder flasks 25, 28, *36*, *50*, 120
powder horn *24*
Prince, Frederick 156
Puckle gun 233
'puffer' (pistol) 52

Quebec, Battle of 68
Queen Anne pistols *106*

ramrods 27, 58, 117
Remington percussion army revolver *148*
repeating flintlock *155*
repeating flintlock carbine *157*
repeating flintlocks 166
Revelli machine-gun 246
Rifle and how to use it, The 156
Rifle Brigade 94
rifled flintlock pistol *96*
rifled percussion pistol *74*
rifles, manufacture of 85–89
rifling 44
rim-fire cartridges 168, 172
Ripley, Brigadier-General James W. 171, 172

'rocket ball' bullet 166
'Roman candle' gun 125
Romanian AKM assault rifle *247*
Roosevelt, Theodore 177, 178
Root's side-hammer revolver 147
Royal Irish Constabulary revolver 216
Royal Small Arms Factory, Enfield 201, 204, 207
Russian submachine-gun *250*

Savage automatic pistol 231
Schmeisser submachine-gun *247*
Schnellfeuer Mauser automatic pistol 224
Schneider, François Eugène 164
Schonberger, Anton 220
Schutzen rifle 175, 177, 178
'screw-barrel' pistols 156
self-cocking pepperbox 138
Self-Denying Ordinance 53, 56
serpentine 24, 25, *27*
Serignola, Battle of 32
service rifle, British *249*
Sharp's carbine *148*, *168*
Short Land Pattern Musket 69, 71, 72, 74
Short Magazine Lee-Enfield *195*, 200, 201, *203*
skelp 85, 86
SLR LIAI, British self-loading rifle 201
Small Gun Office 64
Smith and Wesson revolvers 210, 216
Smith, Horace 167, 168, 208
Smythe, John 31
snaphaunce musket *55*
snaphaunce revolver *125*, *126*
snaphaunces 15, 16, 60, 61, 62, *66*
snap-lock 24, 33
Snider, Jacob 165
socket bayonets 65, *76*
Spanish flintlock pistol *71*
Spencer, Christopher 172
Spencer breech-loading rifle *169*
Spencer carbine *171*, 172
Spenser repeating rifle *138*
sporting rifle *80*
Springfield flintlock musket 181, 182
Springfield rifle 184, *188*, *199*
Starr carbine *182*
Sten Gun *248*, 250, 251
Sterling submachine-gun *248*, 251
Sturmgewehr assault rifle 252
Swedish Brigade (military formation) 31
swing-out revolver cylinder 210

tap-action flintlock pistol *130*
tap-action pocket pistol 126
target pistols *118*, *119*
Thompson, General John T. 248
Thompson submachine-gun *239*, *242*, *246*, *247*, 248 249
Thornton, William 157
Thuer, F. Alexander 213
toradors 33, *33*
touch-hole 25, 26, 124, 127, 136
Tower of London 64

Tranter double trigger revolver 153, *153*
Treeby chain gun 210
triggers 25, 26, 33, 37, 38, 47
Tschinkes 47, *47*, *48*, *49*
Turkish flintlock pistol 104
'Twelve Apostles' 28, 31, *31*

U.S. Magazine Rifle Model 1903 185
U.S. Model 1917 rifle 186
UZI submachine-gun *17*, *244*, 251

Vandenberg volley gun 235
Vauban lock *58*
Veneer, Thomas 56
Vetterli bolt-action rifle 174, 196
Vickers machine-gun *236*, 237 241, 242
Vickers Sons and Maxim Ltd 241
Victoria, Queen 120
Vieille, Paul 198
Villar-Perosa machine-gun 246
Volcanic carbine *164*
Volcanic pistol *166*
Volcanic Repeating Arms Company 167
Volitional Repeater 167
volley fire 68, 96
volley gun 126

Walker, Captain Samuel H. 143
Walker pistol 147
Walther pistols 6, *226*, 231
Waterloo, Battle of 79
Webley and Scott automatic pistols *225*, 228
Webley Company 153
Webley-Fosbery revolver 216, 220
Webley revolvers *199*, 213, 214, 216
Wesson, Daniel 167, 168, 208
wheel-lock, Austrian *42*
wheel-lock carbine *44*, 52
wheel-lock musket *36*
wheel-lock hunting rifle *50*
wheel-lock pistols *28*, *35*, *36*, 38, 41, *42*, *43*, *44*, 51, 52
wheel-lock rifles *42*, *46*, 47, *48*, 52, 80, 83
wheel-locks *10*, 15, 36, 37, 38, 39, 40, 41, *41*, 45, 46, 49, *49*, 51, 52, 58, 61, 124, 126, 129, 155, 180
wheel-lock tinder lighter 39
White, Rollin 208, 210, 213
Whitney, Eli 143, 144
Wild Bill Hickok 15
Wilson, James 126
Winchester, Oliver F. 167, 174, 175, 177
Winchester carbine *166*, *172*, 237
Winchester Repeating Arms Company 174, 175, 176
Winchester rifles *100*, *171*, *172*, *173*, 174, *174*, *175*, *176*, 178, 237
Wogden Robert 115, 123, *123*
World War I 201, 224, 228, 231, 244, 246
World War II 204, 205, 214, 231, 249, 250, 251

Zig Zag revolvers *202*